DATE DUE

NOV 1 5 1989	
NOV 1 5 1989	
DEC 1 2 1989	
MAY 1 2 1994	
MAY 2 2 1995	

ML
419
B298
A3
1986

Bernhardt, Clyde E. B.

I remember

$17.95

I Remember

Clyde Bernhardt, taken on his eightieth birthday, July 11, 1985.
(Photo by Dennis Chalkin Studios, New York City.)

I Remember

Eighty Years of Black Entertainment, Big Bands, and the Blues

An autobiography by
jazz trombonist and blues singer
Clyde E. B. Bernhardt as
told to Sheldon Harris

uPP

University of Pennsylvania Press
Philadelphia   1986

Library of Congress Cataloging in Publication Data

Bernhardt, Clyde E. B.
   I remember.

   Bibliography: p.
   Includes index.
   1. Bernhardt, Clyde E. B. 2. Jazz musicians—
United States—Biography.   I. Harris, Sheldon.
II. Title.
ML419.B298A3   1985   788'.2'0924 [B]   85-26355
ISBN 0-8122-8018-0 (alk. paper)
ISBN 0-8122-1223-1 (pbk. : alk. paper)

Printed in the United States of America

Contents

Illustrations

Foreword

The autobiographies of jazz musicians are few in number, and where they exist, often hard to find. A true fugitive literature. But their scarcity is surely not an indicator of their lack of interest or merit, for some (such as Sidney Bechet's *Treat It Gentle,* Charles Mingus's *Beneath the Underdog,* and Mezz Mezzrow's *Really the Blues*) were warmly received in literary circles when they first appeared. And the European and American publics have always been fascinated by the role of artist-outsider, especially where they perceive the underworld to be involved. Books and films like Dorothy Baker's *Young Man With a Horn* have something of the status of contemporary folk epics, and turn up in new manifestations with every generation—most recently in Josef Skvorecky's novels of wartime Czech jazz life, *The Bass Saxophone* and *The Cowards.* Their fugitiveness is better explained by the fact that jazz musicians, especially black jazz musicians (like black athletes), normally choose to speak through their own strengths: their arts. But when they do get coaxed into writing the result is almost always quite remarkable, and the basis for concerns much larger than those they describe.

In the West the idea of the universality of the black experience is a subtext of the work of Twain, Melville, Mailer, and a surprising number of writers in American literature. In part, this was one of many escape routes for late nineteenth and twentieth century artists from industrialization and the rise of the middle class. But there was also a special attraction in the life and manner of the black jazz musician, the double alienation of artist and color. Whatever it might be as an occupation, it was perhaps the first truly nonmechanical metaphor for the twentieth century. Not since the English Gentleman, with his modality of poise and authority, has such an image so dominated the world. Some abstraction or other of the lives of jazz musicians and their followers now gives shape to the mores of street punks and media executives; it informs the muscles of professional dancers as well as the timing of stand-up comics; and it feeds the languages and moves of fashion designers, basketball players, soldiers, and teenagers. Now, whether one has heard of Charlie Parker or not, one inherits a notion of cool, an idea of well-etched individuality, a certain angle of descent.

Given the lack of documentation of the music, jazz autobiographies might justify their existence by being merely lists of names and places, as evocations of artistic periods; but fortunately they are also characteral accounts, sprinkled with underplayed tragedies and lightly articulated triumphs. Survival stories is what they are, and if they are often written in a peculiarly cool middle distance from the richness of the events they witness, that too is part of the story. As one critic said of bassist Red Callender's autobiography, *Unfinished Dream*, in jazz, the survivor's secret is to remain incurious.

Other writers are often drawn to jazz writing, for there is a unique aesthetic strength to the musicians' autobiographies. Jason Berry makes a case for the existence of a genre which he calls jazz literature, a body of prose grounded in the music of Afro-American speech, a writing as heavily speech-inflected as black music itself, rooted as it is ultimately in West African tonal languages. The prose cadences of Jelly Roll Morton's autobiography (published as Alan Lomax, *Mister Jelly Roll*) were revealed to be more than rhetorically musical when the world finally heard the recorded Library of Congress interviews on which Lomax had based the book: Morton had quite literally played his autobiography, seated at a piano, foot tapping, his speech measured by accompanying chords. Similarly, Bunk Johnson's brief but eloquent life history came out in antiphonal structure, his statements repeated, call-and-response fashion, signaling the music itself by analogy. And the great Sidney Bechet overlapped his phrases in subtle waves of text which evoked the improvised polyphony of New Orleans jazz. In all jazz autobiographies it is possible to hear independent voices, for in the rules of Afro-American aesthetic discourse, every person's sound should be distinctive, whether on a horn or on paper; every tub should rest, one might say, on its own bottom.

From such roots, jazz literature grows outward to tangle in other orally structured writing of the twentieth century: Jean Toomer's *Cane*, Ralph Ellison's *Invisible Man*, LeRoi Jones, and, by extension, Faulkner and Kerouac.

Clyde Bernhardt's voice is in this root tradition, and mimes the clarity and precision he brought to his playing. But what he gives us most of all is a memory uniquely unclouded by fashion and change. Bernhardt, like many other musicians of his generation, was a sort of interior immigrant, with experiences that resonate with those who came from Europe and elsewhere. Stalking the landscape in search of a vocation, scuffling on the band trails, he managed to find a way to make a career in jazz stretch over virtually its entire history. From this he offers up a vision of music that is almost epic in scope, reaching from turn-of-the-century small town musicianship and regional styles to global influences; from the warm networks of kin and friends to the exigencies of racial etiquette in Nazi Germany. He describes rural dances in the South; house rent parties in New York City, and the early days of recording and broadcasting; life in the pit bands, Harlem fashion, in the 1920's, prohibition and the mob. He conjures up long forgotton bands like that of Edgar Hayes, and presents fresh, pre-bebop sketches of the young Dizzy Gillespie and Charlie Parker.

Among his most affecting portraits are those of King Oliver and Ma Rainey. Oliver the band leader is chiefly known to us through the eyes of his young protege, Louis Armstrong, and so we have come to think of him as an avuncular burgher. But from Bernhardt we get a glimpse of the gritty side of the man, and a sense of what it took to lead a successful black band in America during the early 1900's. With Ma Rainey we see a detailed account of the texture of travelling tent shows, with their exotic dancers, chorus lines and flash performances. Throughout, there is an odd sense of reverse deja vu, what with singers wearing glowing white gloves and country comics sporting too-short trousers with exposed white sox, a la Michael Jackson of the 1980's; and the stop-and-go dance instruction songs of Ma Rainey echo down to today in the Go-Go bands of the District of Columbia.

Clyde Bernhardt is writing of the past, but almost never indulges himself in exercises in crypto-memory: if he raises the dead, it's only to serve the living, not to pontificate nostalgically. He knows where things belong historically, and he tells us without odious distinctions. This, plus the fineness of detail, the fullness of description, and the pleasure in drawing connections in Afro-American traditions—we're not likely to ever see the equal of this for jazz again.

John Szwed
Yale University

Preface

Without a doubt, Clyde Bernhardt is an exceptional man.

During the preparation of my earlier book, *Blues Who's Who: A Biographical Dictionary of Blues Singers*, I interviewed many singers, musicians, and other performers. Some were fine talkers, some raconteurs. There were those who generally had good recall and those who chose their words carefully and cautiously, while a few played fast and loose with the facts or were simply outright fabricators.

Of all those I spoke with over the years, no one matched Clyde Bernhardt for meticulous attention to detail and an overriding concern for accuracy.

I Remember is a document that was long in coming. Clyde spent years laboriously writing his eighty-year life story in longhand before typing it himself. It was at this point he sought my help to develop his memoirs into a finished work. For almost two more years I probed, prodded, and pried out further experiences: long, detailed taped interviews at my home; countless telephone calls at all hours to delve further; questions on the way to the airport as he was flying off to another gig. Then I organized it all into a clear and concise story that might appeal to the nonmusical reader as well as the aficionado.

Clyde is a unique storyteller, and so I have tried to retain the language and the flavor and spirit of his remembrances. No one who has heard him speak at length would ever consider adapting his words to a more conventional style. His story is told just as he recalled it, expressing himself in his own way.

I was constantly impressed by his consuming interest in his fellow man. To me, it is an indication of high respect for his associates and friends and the many others whom at some time in his colorful life he had the good fortune to meet.

But most striking is the extent of his recall. During the many years of preparation of this work, not once did Clyde refer to any notes, scrapbooks, or other source material. This book is a tribute to the power of the human mind: it is entirely from his remarkable memory. Asked a question, he would relate names, places, and conversations just as if the event had taken place that very morning. Pressed for a specific year, he would casually mention a date perhaps more than half a century ago, often adding the month and day of the week. On the rare occasion when he could not supply a complete answer or simply did not know, he apologized for his apparent lack of perfection.

As a skeptical writer in oral history, I occasionally repeated a question of some months previous—one requiring detailed facts. I would ask it out of sequence, assuming the abruptness might elicit a different response, or at least a conflicting fact. But no, the answer was always as before, often embellished with added stories of even further interest. There seems to be no bottom to the well called Clyde Bernhardt.

While much of what this man has experienced has never been reported, some of his notable performances have been. Diligent research, sometimes digging back fifty or more years into public records, always confirmed his information.

This is by no means an analytical book, for that is not who or what Clyde is. While he candidly recalls the times, the famous, infamous, and obscure, he leaves the deeper meanings of art and influence to the historians.

Clyde Bernhardt holds an enviable reputation as a solid, reliable, hard-working New York musician and singer who can be depended upon to do the job he is asked to do. And do it well.

I also know him to be a sensitive and honorable person who meets his days with the resolve of a God-fearing man who is constantly being tested. His determination and drive to make something of himself, growing up in rural America and developing through the many flowering eras of jazz and blues, is the essence of this story. It is also about success and failure, fears and insecurities, dreams and ambitions. And faith. Lots of faith. The result is a fascinating tale—sometimes humorous, sometimes tragic. Even startling.

The portrait of Clyde Bernhardt that emerges from these pages is one of a black man struggling within the socioeconomic frailties of an American musical culture. This work is a contribution to us all.

Sheldon Harris

Introduction and Acknowledgments

Hello. My name is Clyde Edric Barron Bernhardt. I been part of music
long before my first professional job on Halloween Night, 1923, in
Elwood City, Pennsylvania. Now I am past eighty, still playing my horn
and singing my blues. And enjoying every single minute of it.

I remember so clearly the funny blackface minstrel shows I watched
in 1909 and 1910, the brass bands, the blues singers, ragtime bands, the
early black (and white, too) stage shows, circuses, and carnivals. Some
had black entertainers and musicians I recall as being very, very good.

My memory goes back to the famous singers I knew or saw: Ma Rainey,
Bessie Smith, Ethel Waters, Princess White, Mamie Smith, and a few the
history books don't remember. I heard Bessie, whose husband was a
first cousin to the wife of my uncle, sing in North Carolina in 1918.

I worked with Bill Robinson, the famous Whitman Sisters, Pigmeat
Markham, Lil Green, Pearl Bailey, Charlie Parker, and Dizzy Gillespie,
among others. I been in many orchestras, both black and white—jazz,
swing, dance, and society bands such as Marion Hardy's Alabamians,
King Oliver's Creole Jazz Band, Jay McShann, Vernon Andrade, Edgar
Hayes, Fats Waller, Luis Russell, Claude Hopkins, and so many others.
I also had my own groups, made recordings, been on radio and tele-
vision, sang and played on international tours, shows, and concerts.

But it's all here on these pages.

This is a story of a boy that decided on his own to make his life in
music and entertainment. I tell about events and conversations that is
important to me, not only because I experienced them, but because
somehow it all seems to fit in a kind of bigger picture. Perhaps a picture
of America. Or of the Negro in America. I don't know, that's too deep
for me. But I like to think in some way I was part of it.

They tell me I was born with a unusual memory. My grandfather on
my Papa's side was terrific and my mother had a good memory too. My
uncle Jonse Mauney, born in slavery and not able to read or write, was a
local "mathematician" with a computer mind. So nothing seems very far
off to me.

Many people interviewed me over the years, but only parts of my story been written in books and magazines. And not always right, either. I also read things my fellow musicians said I know damn well is wrong and it upsets me—some musicians' memories are not a inch long.

I believe strongly in telling the true facts, for if a person talks the truth, he can face the world. I want to tell blacks that keep saying the "man" is holding them back: read my story. I want to tell whites that may not know what it is to be turned away because of their color: read my story. I'm not putting anybody down. This is my life just the way it happened and I want everyone to know what I went through.

I wouldn't be telling the whole truth if I didn't use the very words that was said. If any part of my story or the words I use offends anyone, please skip over that part. I'm sorry, but the truth cannot be changed. If it is, it no longer is the truth.

There are events here I never told anyone before, because I'm a private person. Things very close to me still hurt to this day. And strange things that happened I can't explain but I'm telling them now. And while there was many good times in my life, if things got bad or people be bad, I'm telling that too. I don't hate. I'm not militant. If I hate, then damn it, somebody going to hate me back.

I heard it said that black is beautiful—hell, every color is beautiful. If we to live in this world in peace, then we got to try to get along with everybody. We all need one another. Anybody ever see a piano with all black keys?

I believe in people. Honest, sincere people, regardless of race, creed, or color. I never did get along with the notoriety kind. I was shy as a youngster and still back off from people that get out of line with me.

I also believe in the Bible. I believe in the hereafter. I believe in doing right. Treat others as I wish to be treated and I know He will favor us all.

Through the help of God, He made a way for me from when I was ten years of age. As a child, important people gave me their hand. Took me in. Taught and advised me. Because of this, I believe I was a success long before my music career began. After I was grown, others offered me encouragement when I needed it badly. Got me jobs and made it possible for this musician to play in top clubs, hotels, and theaters in America and over twenty-five foreign countries. Invited to stop at people's homes and treated like family. Some were preachers, some lawyers and doctors. Some were musicians, singers, entertainers, and writers. Others just old friends and relatives. All good people I respect and still correspond with around the world.

But I'm just a old country boy from North Carolina that appreciates everything he received. Many helped me to help myself. Any success I had in my life, I owe to the following people:

Gus Aiken
Napoleon Allen
Joe Allston
John Alston
Vernon Andrade
Harvey Andrews
John A. Andrews
Victoria Andrews
Avon City Jazz Band, *England*
Paul Barnes
Russell Barnes and wife,
  England
Elizabeth Barnhardt
Herman Barnhardt
Indie Barnhardt
Leonard Barnhardt
Paul Barnhardt
Sarah Barnhardt
Washington Michael Barnhardt
Will Barnhardt and wife
Tommy Benford
Dave Bennett and wife, *England*
Lou Blackmon and wife
Peter Boizot, *England*
Boston Broadcasters, Inc.
Jack Bradley
Herbert Branch
Mort Browne
Beulah Bryant
Charles Buchanan
Charles Burke and wife
Dan Burley
Clay Burt
Ray Bush, *England*
Jacques Butler
James Butts

Albert Caldwell
Leslie Carr
Peter Carr, *England*
Dennis Chalkin
John Chilton, *England*
Julius Christian and wife
Ernest Clarke
Ira Coffey and wife
Cozy Cole and wife
Jay Cole and wife
The Connecticut Traditional
  Jazz Club
Rev. Arthur R. Corwell
Herbert Cowens
Odie Cromwell and wife
Charlie Crowell, Sr.
Floyd O. Culp
Henry W. Culp, Jr.
Rev. F. A. Cullen
Stanley Dance
Walton H. De Hart
Bertrand Demeusy, *France*
Harry Dial
Dr. Morris Diener
Wilma Dobie
Bob Douglas
Rev. John F. Douglas
Frank Driggs
Frankie Dunlop
Laura Dunlop
James W. Durden
The Eady Family
John Eady and wife
Linwood Eady
William Eady and wife
Pete Endres and wife

Helen J. Ennico
Leonard G. Feather
Billy Fowler, Sr.
The Friendly Fifty Club
Leslie Frye
Theodore Frye
Joe Garland
Moses Garland and wife
Gilbert Gaster, *England*
Meredith G. Germer
Karl Gert zur Heide, *Germany*
Frank Gibbs
Russell Gibbs and wife
Charles Grear
David Griffiths, *Wales*
Luther Griffiths and wife, *Wales*
Dr. Thomas P. Grissom, Jr.
Dr. David L. Grossman
Charles W. Hadley
Michael Hansen, *Denmark*
Marion Hardy
James Harewood
Aaron Harris
Alfred Harris
Bea Harris
Sheldon Harris and wife
Willie Mae Harris
Wynonie Harris
Jack Harvey and wife, *England*
Edgar Hayes
Alex Hill
Teddy Hill
Chris Hillman, *England*
George and Christopher Hillman
Charles Holmes
Claude Hopkins
Mel Howard
Harmey S. Hyatt, Jr.
J. Wallace Ivey
Howard W. Johnson
Jeryl Johnson

Pete Johnson
Albert Jones and wife
C. W. Kaufman
Jack and Marian Kearns
Luvenia Kendall
Rufus G. Kluttz and wife
Earl Knight
Barbara Kukla
Wyn Lodwick and wife, *Wales*
Fred Longshaw
William Macklin and wife
Henry McClane
Jay McShann
John Marrero
Simon Marrero
Barbara Martyn
Barry Martyn
Helen Merrill
Peter Meyer, *West Germany*
John P. Miller and wife
H. Minton
Carrie Misenheimer
Clayton Misenheimer
Tim Moore
Fred T. Morgan
Dan Morgenstern
Mel Morris
John H. Mullen
Peter Muller, *West Germany*
Arthur Newman and wife
Jack O'Brien
King Joe Oliver
Harold Oxley
Ray Parker
Pasquele Pastin
Birdell Prince
Bob Queen
Madame Gertrude Rainey
Ed Rauch
Ellsworth Reynolds
Billy Roe

Mrs. Izzy Roe
Edwin Ross, Sr.
Phil Schaap
Walter Schaap and wife
Sammy J. Scott
Rev. Floyd Shadd and wife
Minnie Shadd
O'Neal Shadd and wife
Rev. R. E. Sharpe
Simons Sim, *Belgium*
John Simmen and wife,
 Switzerland
Ed Smalls
Bessie Smith
Pearl Smothers
Glenn Spears and wife
Bo Stenhammar, *Sweden*
Derrick Stewart-Baxter and wife,
 England
Eugeen Suykerbuyk, *Belgium*
Luther Thomas
Eric Townley, *England*
Larry Treloar, *England*

Rev. W. J. W. Turner and wife
Peter Vacher, *England*
Alajos Van Peteghem and wife,
 Belgium
Joe Vennie
Tillie Vennie
Dr. Albert A. Vollmer and wife
Hans Vollmer and wife, *England*
Sammy Waters and wife
George B. Weaver
Viola Wells (Miss Rhapsody)
Princess White
Alberta Whitman
Alice Whitman
Essie Whitman
Mabel Whitman
J. A. Williams and wife
Adam Wilson and wife
Brooks Wilson
Laurie Wright and wife, *England*
Steve Wright
Genevieve Zuhlcke
Theo Zwicky, *Switzerland*

1. The Beginning

Saturday, September 25, 1982, was the most exciting day of my life.

I was resting in my hotel room that evening down in Washington, D.C., trying to gather up my thoughts. My heart was still pounding. First, the Legends of Jazz, of which I'm a member, played the old Ford's Theater only hours before. It was a command performance for President Ronald Reagan, and he was sitting right there down front applauding, along with Mrs. Reagan and a whole gang of government officials. The cameras were rolling because this was to be a special television show.

And every time I glanced up at Abraham Lincoln's blue and black flag-draped box where he got shot in 1865, I got a chill. They say his ghost is still there some place. And I believe it.

But all that was nothing compared to being invited earlier in the day to lunch at the White House. I wish I could describe how it felt walking up that long staircase, past all the paintings of presidents, and into this beautiful reception room. And then the President of the United States coming over and shaking my hand.

This old trombone player from Gold Hill, North Carolina, shaking hands with the top man of the country. Maybe the world. I'm not political, but to me he represents all America—the Number One Man.

I couldn't sleep that night. I kept thinking about all the other people I met in my life. And the times I had. Where I came from and how they now call me a legend. Sure, I played in many name bands, and plenty without names. Been everywhere. But a legend?

I kept wondering what life is all about. No one plans to do everything he does in his life, but it happens. Why is that?

For a moment I thought I heard a voice whispering to me in the shadows of my quiet room.

My life was spilling through my mind. Good times. Some laughs. A lot of hurts. So much buried inside me.

I was sure I heard this voice calling. From long ago.

"Come on, Clyde, come out on the porch and make pee-pee."

It was old Mrs. Rose Parker calling me out one cool North Carolina night back in 1907. I was but two years old. They told me Mama was sick, so Mrs. Rose was watching over me.

"Hurry," she was calling, "pull your little night shirt up and come make pee-pee."

And man, I remember I watered those cornstalks out back of that country house in one big spray. It is my first memory and I can call it today just as bright as the Carolina moon shining through those dark trees.

The next morning, Papa came after me in his little black buggy. "Clyde," he shouted from the dirt road, "you got a new brother now."

I remember I got excited. With only two older sisters, I sure did want a brother to play with bad. I was clapping and jumping all the way home, but when I saw this tiny brown bundle laying on the bed I was very disappointed. I thought a real brother be my size and this was nothing but a little old baby. I pouted for days after that.

Papa was Washington Michael Barnhardt. That's Barnhardt with a double *a*. I changed the spelling to Bernhardt later when I was grown. Papa was born May 15, 1878, near Mt. Pleasant, North Carolina, and was one of about eight children. His mother was half Cherokee Indian and half Negro. His father Bush was three-quarter Cherokee. I leave it to you to figure out how much Indian blood I have in me.

In 1892, at the age of fourteen, Papa came to Gold Hill to work in the gold mines. It was a boom town then.

My mother was born Elizabeth Mauney, pronounced "Mooney." The date was December 27, 1872, and the place was a short distance out of New London, North Carolina. Mama's parents, Cad and Heddie Mauney, were slaves. The white master that owned them was named Vol Mauney, so Mauney became their name too. They got married when grandmother was only thirteen and lived in this old rough cabin on the Mauney Plantation up until Emancipation Day.

Cad Mauney was a dark brown Negro and grandmother was very light. They called her a mulatto. Don't know for sure if there's a white man in our family woodpile, but it wouldn't surprise me at all.

Mama had eight brothers and sisters. She went to Bennett College, a woman's school in Greensboro, North Carolina, where she studied to be a dietician, taking care of a family, and all that kind of stuff. Started college around the eighth grade and finished in the twelfth. Today they call it high school.

Mama was very smart, more then a lot of other colored people around there. But though Papa only went to fifth grade, I always thought he was smarter.

When Papa married Mama in 1898, she was teaching school and kept at it until I came along. I was born Clyde Edric Barnhardt on July 11, 1905, 2 A.M. to be exact. We was living in the Hannah Shaver place then, about a mile out of Gold Hill, in Rowan County.

Mama had eight children: Walton Hortense was the first, born April 6, 1899, but later she dropped the Walton and everybody called her Hortense; then two children that died as infants, Irene and Clifton; Agnes came on June 3, 1904; and after her was me. Then Paul, October 16, 1907; Leonard, June 9, 1910; and Herman on April 11, 1912. I remember Herman's birthday very well because a few days later we all heard about the great ship Titanic going down.

Mama always told me the Hannah Shaver place where I was born was haunted. A lot of white people moved in and moved out just as fast. Strange noises. Moaning. Scared the daylights out of them.

Papa knew what everyone said about the Hannah Shaver place. "No hants gonna get me outta here," he kept telling Mama. He meant the haunts, of course.

But they did. He bought some twelve acres of land in a all-white area of Richfield, about five miles below Gold Hill. Cost him a dollar a acre. Papa was then a foreman and timekeeper, the only black mine foreman there, and making $2.50 a day. That was high wages, so he could afford the property.

Mama ordered a wooden bungelow from the Sears, Roebuck Company catalogue, and when it came mail-order from Chicago, a local carpenter put it up in about a week. They spent most of their savings for it. Cost about five hundred dollars as I was told.

We moved in around September of 1905 when I was but two months old and stayed exactly eight years.

The big house stood off the ground and had six rooms, three on each side of a long hallway running right down the middle. Bedrooms in the back, a kitchen off on one side, then a dining room, living room, and the front parlor with the bay window was for company. The house had tall windows all around, a brick chimney, and a long porch out front. Even had a coal heater in there and a big fireplace. Shingles on the roof.

Mama put in the newest wood- and coal-burning kitchen range, which she also got from Sears, Roebuck. The stove was made of heavy black steel, and Mama said it took four big men to carry it in. Looked so pretty with fancy white metal trim all over the fire box and on the front and side doors. Had a big reservoir somewhere inside with a warming closet on top.

We was the only colored people around with such a good stove.

A family reunion in Allentown, Pa., May 1, 1948. Front row, left to right: *Clyde Bernhardt, Herman Barnhardt (brother), Leonard Barnhardt (brother);* back row, left to right: *Mrs. Leonard Barnhardt (sister-in-law), Agnes Barnhardt Thomas (sister), Maude Coble (cousin), Hortense Barnhardt De Hart (sister), Luther Thomas (brother-in-law), James Durden (uncle).*

Mama paid about twenty-five dollars for it, a top price in those days.

Off the back porch was a deep artesian well that Papa got somebody to dig. Had a big pump that brought up the freshest, coldest water I ever tasted. When other people's well went dry, they came and got water from us. Near the barn was our outhouse, and there was a yard out back for Mama's vegetables.

She kept a truck garden there just for us or anybody that needed food or was too lazy to grow their own. She had cantaloups, turnips, squash, onions, string beans, six-week white corn, greens of all kinds. Had peach trees. Apples and pears. Even a big old cow and chickens all running around picking and poking. Papa had this friendly horse he called Mary and a old gray mule, Kate, that wasn't very friendly.

Mama took in laundry after we moved to Richfield. Misenheimer's Springs health resort was three miles away and all the wealthy white people from the North came down there, so she got plenty work from them.

Mama bought this house from Sears, Roebuck and had it put up in Richfield, N.C., in 1905. (Photo courtesy of the late Mrs. Goodman.)

Most people didn't have what we had. The greatest ambition of working folks down there, black and white, was to own their own home, even if it didn't have but two or three rooms. And have their own horse and wagon. Maybe someday work up to a buggy. God-fearing, hardworking, get-along people that did section hand labor, worked in the textile factories or the mines. There was no shiftless kind around.

We never thought we was better then anybody else. Papa always tried to help, like when someone got laid off his job, he ask the whole family over for supper. Some of those men had four or five children, but Papa never wanted to see anybody go hungry. That's the way he was.

Working in those mines was hard for my daddy. He was only a kid when he started digging and breathing in all that bad mine dust and dirt. He was a powerful man, strong as a ox with bulging biceps. Stood sort of short at about five and a half feet or less and was on the stocky side. Never did shave as I remember but had a clean face, like tough leather.

He used to bring those old flint rocks home from the mine and we put them against the door to keep it from shutting. Some of those stones was as big as footballs and had sparkling gold dots the size of ten-penny nail heads all over. The mine people said they had no value so miners took them as souvenirs.

He told me about the time a dam broke on the creek above one of the mines. Water barreled in there like a flooding waterfall and a whole lot of men got drowned. It took about a week to pump that water out, and there was still bodies hanging from the ladders where they tried to climb out. Some of those mines hundreds of feet straight down.

Mama said he never talked about how dangerous it was working the mines, but he sure didn't want none of his children going down in there.

Papa seemed to favor me. And I favored him. Always bringing me toys like a little windup automobile that went around in circles. Once he got me this old red wagon for three dollars that all the kids in the neighborhood wanted to ride. Mama didn't like him spending more then a day's pay on me but he said he didn't care.

I can see now why all the local kids loved him also. When he brought home surprises, he tell me to share them with everybody. Didn't matter if they black or white. A box of peppermint candy. A big bag of red and blue gum balls.

"Mmmmmmm," my little friends say, jumping all around. "Mr. Wash sure is nice. I wish he was my papa."

When we be extra good, he took us down to the railroad station to watch the big trains go by, wave at the engineer man, and squeal when he let out the white puffs of steam. That was our *special* treat.

To me, he was not only my father, but a friend and a pal. All the people tease him—say he had a little shadow because I was always behind him. Then I sit for hours at his feet looking up at his smiling face. He tell me about his times and how it was. And how he wanted me to be.

"If you want respect, Clyde, you got to give it," he told me often.

There was no one better then my Papa.

I don't know why he liked to see those traveling shows that was always coming to town. He couldn't play nothing, had no kind of entertaining talent, but he sure did like those shows. Minstrels. Bands. Comedies. Things like that. Told me he was seeing them long before I was born and almost never missed a one. Mama and the other children couldn't care beans about them, so Papa usually went by himself.

It was Decoration Day, May 30, 1909. I was not even four years old yet, but I remember it clearly. In those days, just the colored people recognized that holiday. It was the day set aside to honor all the Yankee soldiers of the Civil War. They had, and still have, a big Yankee cemetery in Salisbury, which is the county seat of Rowan County, and blacks from all over the state and many from South Carolina all coming in for the celebration.

Papa was smiling down at me sitting there in front of him like always.

"Clyde," he said, patting me on the shoulder, "wanna come with me to Salisbury and see the street parade?"

I didn't know what a street parade was, but knew if Papa liked it, I wanted to see it also. The two of us rode to town in the buggy, which he tied to a hitching post, and we walked over to the main street.

Tall men in white hats and very long white jackets were selling good things to eat. Had on big signs sticking out of their hats with words on them. Papa bought me a big, steaming chili dog, which is a frankfurter covered with lots of hot sauce and onions. It cost two pennies.

Colored people were all lined up along the curb holding small American flags pasted on sticks. I stood beside Papa, holding on to his stubby finger.

Suddenly, from around the corner marched these colored men. Oh, they walked so tall and stiff. Bright buttons down the front of their uniforms, red caps on their heads with a round button right in the front. As they came closer I saw them playing flashy, shiny instruments that bounced the bright sunshine right in my eyes. Horns all raised up high, blasting so very loud. Some long ones, sliding in and out. Big fat ones going Umph, Umph. Banjos played fast, drums rat-a-tatting, and a huge round drum that boomed-boomed as it went by.

Everything was so new and frightening, had to cover my little ears. People all cheering and shouting.

Then the big flags came by, carried high and waving long. Men in Yankee uniforms standing up in red-and-white-draped horse-drawn wagons all posing like statues with rifles in their hands. Then another band came marching behind them. Even bigger and louder.

I never seen anything like this. The excitement was so great—the shining instruments, the music, real soldiers—I almost pulled my father's finger off asking fool questions. Questions only a wide-eyed child ask. I kept on and on and Papa just laugh. It was a unforgettable experience.

That night at home, I looked through the Sears, Roebuck catalogue for the musical-instrument section. Especially the page with the baritone horns, they now call them French horns. I tore out that catalogue page and wrapped it around a old comb so the picture was on the outside and blew on it like a kazoo. Did that for hours.

"Someday," said Papa, "maybe Clyde take up a real instrument. That boy got music in him." And he laugh some more as I paraded through the house, blowing and marching.

When I heard about the John Sparks three-ring circus coming to Albemarle a few months later, I begged Papa to take me again. He was working double shifts at the mine, so Mama kind of agreed to take me.

It was heaven all over again, only better. The street parade was bigger, longer, and flashier. This time, decorated wagons came rolling by with a band of white men in bright-color uniforms sitting in them playing peppy numbers like *Red Wing* and *Wait 'til the Sun Shines, Nellie*. The prancing white horses pulling the wagons had these high feathers all sticking out of their heads and heavy red blankets laying smooth over their backs. They were stepping so pretty.

Every wagon that passed had something new to see. Painted ladies in tights with big flappy capes. Men doing back somersaults. Growly animals in cages. Tigers. Lions. Big-toothed, bushy bears with spiked collars around their necks. That scared me.

In the last wagon I saw blackface comedians in huge spotted bow-ties and collars, wearing long coats and laughing like chickens. Playing banjos, buckdancing. Making funny faces, just at me I thought.

"Oh Mama," I shouted over the loud music, "looka there at them black ugly men. Ohhhh."

"Hush up, boy," she said, "they got stuff on their face to make them look like that."

We followed the parade to the circus grounds where all these sideshow fellows with long sticks was standing out front of small tents, calling everybody in. I saw bumpy ladies dancing up on little platforms. Next to them was a fat woman with three snakes crawling and twisting around her neck. One platform had this seal band—real seals all tooting horns, some playing drums and other instruments.

"Mama! Mama!" I hollered, pulling at her skirts as the seals took their bow. "Looka them funny-looking dogs up there."

"Shut up, Clyde," she said in a low voice. "People think you stupid. Those are seals."

Now, Mama had illustrated Bible books at home with pictures of Daniel sitting in the lion's den, elephants walking into Noah's ark, stuff like that. But no seals. This was new to me.

One tent in particular had this colored ragtag band playing slow and loud. Never heard that kind of music, not even on the cylinder records our white neighbors let me hear. This fat, black woman was out front, all painted with bright red on her cheeks and thick black eyelashes sticking out. Had on a wide hat with long, pretty feathers coming out the top. Glittering spots all over her tight dress, all jiggling, and her waist was pulled in very, very tight by a big belt.

When she started to sing slow, people came around.

I'm Alabama bound,
I'm Alabama bound,
If the train don't wreck on the road,
I'm Alabama bound.

I stood there listening to the blues until Mama pulled me back. "Come 'way from there, Clyde. That's not for you."

Finally we went inside the big top, which cost Mama fifty cents but was free for me. The man said I was too small to pay anything. We sat over in the colored section where I could see all the fantastic things happening around me.

My head was going in all directions at once. Animals running and jumping over there. Horses doing tricks. Elephants standing up high, with small hats on their heads. White girls swinging on ropes over long nets. Clowns falling down. Dogs wearing big glasses. Long, tall men walking on fenceposts. Little people no bigger then me rolling on the sawdust floor. Band music playing. Streamers flying. I just couldn't keep still. Was laughing and clapping for hours.

"Mama! Mama!" I shouted, "can I stay here with the circus? Can I, huh?"

"Boy, what you goin' to do here?"

"Wanna carry water to the big elephants."

"Come home now, Clyde," she said dragging me out, "or you get a good whipping tonight."

I knew she wasn't fooling so I went right along.

Mama liked to whip her children. The only time I ever saw my daddy get mad at Mama was when she beat us. Grandmother Mauney believed it was necessary to beat children—thought it was sinful if she didn't do it often and I'm sure Mama thought so too.

I remember one time Mama couldn't find a kitchen knife and accused us kids of taking it. Said we had to find the knife or she punish us all. When we couldn't, we all got a good whipping. Later, she found it on a chair under her apron where she left it. But we still couldn't sit down.

When I was about seven, some lady in the neighborhood everyone knew didn't half feed her children stopped me as I passed by. "Come on in Clyde and get something to eat."

"Don't want none of your 'something to eat,'" I sassed her. "You ain't got enough for your own boys."

She went and told my mother what I said. Mama got a old peach tree switch from out back, pulled my little pants down, and near about tore my hide apart.

"Sass grown people will you?" she hollered. "Next thing you know you liable to back talk me." Then she whipped me some more.

That's when Papa came in. "All right Liz, you done enough whipping." He didn't like that kind of treatment to kids. "You act like you don't love your children, puttin' those bloody marks all over their behinds like that. Confound it woman, what's wrong with you?"

Oh man, they had it out hot that night.

Mama had a standing floor-mirror that some white lady gave her. After every whipping I turn my bare behind around and see what was happening back there. When I see all those zebra stripes on my butt, I cry some more.

But Mama never stopped whipping her children. The boys *and* girls. Sometimes for practically nothing. Like maybe we didn't move fast enough when she said move. I once saw Hortense get horsewhipped so bad she left home when she was fifteen and worked for white people. Man, Mama was brutal and strongminded. Papa would scold us sometime, but never hit nobody.

They never cussed and never, never used the Lord's name in vain. Never heard either of them say "damn." Once in a while Papa would say "doggone" when he got mad, but not very often.

The Gold Hill mines closed in 1910. Not because they didn't have no more gold, but because people came from all over to work and they couldn't handle the crowds. Everybody hollering for jobs that wasn't there. Families living in little tents, drinking out of the lake they made. And the sanitation was a bad problem, too. So the mines closed and are closed to this very day.

I know there's still gold in those deep shafts. Some of them go down almost eight hundred feet, but they are permanently flooded and nobody can get in there.

So Papa went to work in the Candor mines, about thirty-five miles from Gold Hill. Went by train and lived over there in a little miners' shantytown. Came home every other Saturday and stayed the weekend. I sure missed my Papa when he was away in Candor.

I started school in November of the next year. Mama fix up a nice lunch pail for me and 7:30 every morning I walk the road some four miles to school. It used to be a old grainery but they cleaned it out, put little tables and chairs inside.

My teacher was Miss Louvenia Parker, a mean old lady. Treated the kids very strict, and every day one of us got bent over for a good paddling or rapped on the knuckles with a ruler. Maybe go stand in the corner on one foot. Yes sir, I got my share and didn't like it at all.

But colored school was barely three months long. Some children needed for spring work, and schooling was just not the most important thing.

Papa kept taking me to all the weekend shows that came around. Silas Green Minstrels was in often. So was the Rabbit Foot Minstrels. And the Florida Blossom Minstrels. We didn't miss many. I once saw a minstrel trombone player take off his shoes and work the slide with his bare feet. It was the funniest thing I ever saw. And every time I heard a ragtime band with a blues singer, I went around the house the next day trying to act and sing like them.

"Now Clyde," Mama would say, "stop singing those nigger reels."

She didn't take kindly to that kind of music around the house. Sometimes I went outside to imitate the funny dance steps I saw the black minstrels do, and some of the cranky old colored people around town tell Mama it was sinful. She stopped me from doing that, too.

Besides Papa, I was the only one in the family that liked the minstrel and ragtime band shows.

It was spring that Papa came down with his heart attack. March of 1912 it was.

"Pray hard for your daddy to get well," Mama told me.

I was so upset seeing him laying down all day. Wasn't like him at all. I was old enough to realize it was the mines. Living in drafty shanties, eating bad food, working in all that dirty, thick dust.

People came from all over to see Papa. He was head trustee of the Morning Star Methodist Church and had many friends. They bring food. Leave a piece of money. That's the way people was in those days.

When he started getting better, the doctor told him to stay away from the mines. So he went out with his wagon, buying up loads of farm foods, and peddled it around. Sometimes on Sunday he open the front yard for a big country picnic. Put out a gang of wooden chairs and tables he made, all painted nice in green and white with yellow trim. And right in the middle set a wood-burning heater with four grates. Papa was a good cook and when he got the heater to flaming, put a big pile of lard in the four pans and fried up the best chicken and fish you ever put your teeth into. Could smell the tasty, flavoring food blowing in the breeze for miles.

Mama cooked a whole table full of cornbread, chocolate cakes, and apple pies and sold slices for a nickel. She also had five-cent bottles of soft drinks all sitting in big ice tubs.

Papa made some handbills and passed them around as far as Salisbury. Colored and white folks buggied over from ten miles away to buy fish fries and chicken sandwiches, sit and enjoy themselves.

One time Papa hired out the eight-piece Mt. Pleasant Brass Band to entertain the crowds. Some people stayed all day. Others until the next day. Papa put them up on a cot or in our rooms and made a pallet on the floor for us. Others slept in blankets out in the yard.

I was always helping Papa because of his sickness. Sometimes we ride the Saturday train some two hundred miles over to Morehead City to get him his fresh fish. We leave on the 7 A.M. train and travel all day. Stay overnight, come back the next day. I do anything for my Papa.

One time I brought home a empty wooden milk crate, the kind that held twelve bottles. Got up at 4:30, stood on that box, and hitched our old horse, Mary, to the wagon. When Papa woke up, it was waiting for him.

"Who did that for me?" he asked. "Must have been one of the Patton or Owen boys."

"I did it, Papa. I wanna help you 'cause you ain't feelin' good."

"Well, doggone, if you ain't a little rascal. Seven years old and doin' a man's work." And he patted me on the shoulder.

Papa brought me home a pet squirrel when I was about eight. Cost twenty cents with the cage. One day I was playing and it bit my finger right down to the bone. Wouldn't let go. Papa heard my screams and choked the animal until it fell off dead. I never liked squirrels after that.

Just before we moved from Richfield, a medicine show came to town and stayed a few weeks working under a canvas tent. People came from thirty miles away to see that show. Had four musicians playing ragtime music and four dancers—two ladies and two men. Only the boss was white and he sold the bottled medicine. Said it was good for everything: spells, whooping cough, pimples, toothaches, the vapors, even big bunions. The show was free if you bought the medicine for fifty cents. People buying medicine so fast, they run out of the stuff before the show was over. But they always had more for the next performance.

By September 1913, Papa decided his luck be better in New Hope, which was down the road from Richfield. Got a house there for two and a half dollars a month and rented out our Sears, Roebuck place for three, which gave Papa a fifty-cent profit. Our new house wasn't as modern as before, but it had five rooms.

New Hope was near Palmerville, Millertown, and Ebenezer. Eventually, they made those four towns into Badin. At that time, New Hope only had a grocery store and livery stable.

Mama got four girls to help her with the laundry. Sometimes she got as much as a dollar for a big load after scrubbing and ironing all day.

Papa and I would go around with the horse and wagon and pick up those white people's clothes for Mama. Then deliver them back later.

On the days we wouldn't be delivering, we go out for a wagonload of
vegetables, muskmelons, and corn to sell in the levee camps all around
Palmerville. They were building a power dam, and all the French people
from Pennsylvania, New York, and Connecticut came there looking for
work. Just pitched their tents any place and some even put up old one-
room shacks. The owners also brought in a lot of Italian immigrants for
the real heavy work. Couldn't even speak English.

Those levee camps was everywhere. So was money. Pretty soon
the gamblers came in. Then the fast women. It was such a rough area,
people started getting killed. Especially in the Hardaway Levee Camp
that was building the big power dam across the Yadkin River.

That camp was run by a tough giant called Kid Heavy. Without a
doubt, he was the meanest, roughest man in the whole state of North
Carolina. Stood almost seven feet tall, weighed at least three hundred
pounds, wore a big western hat, and always had a .44 pistol in a belt
holster and a .38 in his waistband. But the worst was his long, leather
bullwhip. Anybody make trouble or try to leave the camp without paying his debts got that whip across his back. Men *and* women. Black *and*
white. Beat them right to the ground. Maybe stomp them a few times
because he felt like it. Back talk him and the guy liable to shoot you
dead. No questions asked. I once saw a well-known white man cuss Kid
Heavy's horse in the presence of Heavy's wife. That white man needed
doctoring for three weeks after that.

I met Kid Heavy many times when I delivered his laundry, and he
usually gave me double what Mama charged. He was good to us, but
I always kept my eye on that whip.

When the First World War broke out in 1914, everybody started
going back north, and by the following year the boom was over. Nothing
left but empty tents. Cook stoves all tossed about. Beds, tables, chairs,
everything just laying out in the sun for anybody that wanted them. It
was like a ghost town.

I took my first automobile ride in 1914. A red-front, T-model Ford
owned by a local white man. I was thrilled even though the ride was
only around the corner. But it sure impressed my friends.

We moved to Grandpaps' place in New London in May of 1915. That's
a few miles back toward Richfield. Grandpaps Cad Mauney had this big
old six-room house which was built for him after slavery. Had three
great oak trees around it and fruit trees in the back. His oldest son,
Jonse, had died, and then Grandmother Mauney died after taking fever.

It was hard for Mama, taking care of old Grandpaps, her own family,
and keeping up with the day work. Papa was feeling poorly too and

couldn't go out very often. Some of Mama's sisters and brothers sent money, and the white people Mama worked for was sympathetic and helped out also.

Then Grandpaps died in August. Three deaths within six months in the same house. It was a sad time for everybody.

But it didn't stop Mama from whipping me when she felt like it. She found I been playing with a local white boy, Wallace Ivey, and took a strap to my behind.

"You got enough toys here to play with, Clyde. You don't have to go looking for more."

Papa started having real bad trouble by summertime. The doctor called it dropsy—all I knew was he couldn't catch his breath and had to keep sitting straight up in a chair, even when he slept. Mama tried to take care of him, but I'm not lying if I say I was scared. Never saw him look so bad.

I helped Mama take the bags of wash over to the white people's places by train, a fifteen-cent fare for her, a dime for me. Along with the rent we got for our house in Richfield, we struggled along.

One time I had a white neighbor, Mr. Crowell, make me a little shoe-shine box, and I walked seven miles into Albemarle, bought some polish, a old brush, and a rag and made myself over two dollars. When I got back I handed the money to Papa.

"Where you get this money, boy?" he breathed heavily.

"Made it shining shoes in Albemarle, Papa."

"What?"

"Yeah, Papa. I wanna help you out."

"Clyde, you sure a special boy. Got this job all on your own just for your old sick Papa. You my little man."

"I love you, Papa."

He was resting late one October night when Mama and me returned from Albemarle after delivering. When we walked in the house, I heard this old hoot owl screeching in the big oak tree next to the back kitchen window. Screeeeech! Screeeeech! Screeeeech! Never heard any there before.

Now, everybody know that a screech owl hollering outside your window at night is a bad omen. Yes sir.

"Papa," I cried, running over to him. "You gonna die?"

"Now Clyde, don't pay that owl no mind. I'm not gonna die." He sat me down at his feet. "You a good boy, Clyde, always have been. I'll never leave you. You may not see me, but my spirit will be near. I might be in the body of a old colored man. Or Indian. Maybe even a white

I used to shine shoes on the streets of Albemarle, N.C., 1915. (Photo courtesy of Fred T. Morgan, Stanly News and Press.)

man. I'm gonna see they treat you good. You listen to your mother and the good Lord will bless you all your life. And your Papa always be watching over you, Clyde—don't you worry none."

I wasn't sure what he meant but felt comforted.

Sometimes I went out in the woods and found him some dittany leaves everybody used for healing. Or I walk to town and get Papa the red peach soda he liked so much. Buy it with the pennies I saved from shining shoes every weekend.

Papa took to sitting under the big oak tree out front in a old rocking chair. Day and night. Then he started talking to people, only there was no people there. I heard him talking to Grandpaps. And Jonse. Said he saw his brother, saw his father. But they all dead, we knew that.

"Mama," I would ask, looking out the window at him, "you think he sees all those people he talking to?"

"Hush up, boy," was her reply. And I cry quietly.

I woke the morning of October 27, 1915, to the tolling of a faraway church bell. Way back in the woods.

Bong . . . . Bong . . . . Bong . . . .

It was very slow.

I knew what that meant. I jumped out of bed and ran over to the front window. People all standing about. I dashed out in the cold morning air and ran as fast as I could up to Papa. He was still sitting in his rocking chair under the big oak tree, but a blanket was pulled over his head.

"Papa! Papa!" I cried. A neighbor man came over and held me back, but I tore away. "I ain't got no Papa no more," I screamed. "My Papa's gone. My Papa's gone."

I ran back in the house and broke down completely. It was the end of the world for me.

This is the tree that my Papa died under while sitting in a rocking chair, New London, N.C., Oct. 27, 1915. (Photo courtesy of Henry W. Culp.)

2. Troubled Times

For many months after Papa died, I suffered terribly. The days were without joy and the nights so very dark and frightening. Stayed in my room and had no feeling to come out. Stopped talking, cried to myself almost all the time, and when Mama would holler, I cry some more, only quieter. Even her beatings didn't stop me.

At night I lay in my dark room and be afraid to sleep. Perhaps I dreamed all this, I thought, maybe Papa was still out there sitting under the oak tree and it was only a bad mistake.

When I did fall asleep, I seen him standing in my room, open arms, calling me. "Come on, Clyde, come with me." Then I wake up screaming for Papa, but he wasn't there. Many times Mama come in to see if I was fevering. But I couldn't tell her what I saw.

When her friends came over I hear them talking.

"Liz, I always knew that boy was in for trouble."

"What kind of trouble?"

"Being born in the old Hannah Shaver place, that's what. About the worst house around here for hants."

She meant the mysterious, unexplained happenings. Nobody lived in that old house for long, black or white. Strange noises got everybody out.

"You got some of that Hannah Shaver place in you, Clyde," Mama often said.

And she could have been right. Always telling of how she was scared while carrying me. Chairs falling over and loud groaning under that house, and when somebody looked, nothing was there. At least nothing nobody could see. Even the Bible in the house didn't help.

Told me one time she was sitting out on the porch talking to her friend and started to hearing all the dishes, pots, and pans crashing to the floor. Thought one of the local goats or donkeys got in and rushing inside, found everything in place. That's when the neighbor lady picked up her long skirts and scooted all the way home. Mama sometimes heard voices moaning and crying at night. Still didn't see nothing.

I kept thinking of all the other strange things she used to tell me. Once when Mama was twelve, she and her sisters toted a big burlap bag out to collect pine knots for firewood. Up around New London, near Stokes Ferry. On the way back they heard this herd of horses come running down the road. They knew there was no herds of horses around those parts, especially running down this old dirt road. But as hard as they looked, they see nothing. As the beating hoofs got louder and

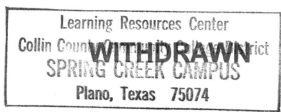

louder, everybody ran and jumped in the drainage ditch by the side of the road.

As the sounds passed by, Mama peeked out. Wasn't a thing to be seen, not one horse, not a mule, nothing. Not even a cloud of dust.

Grandmother didn't whip them for lying when they got home but said hundreds of years ago there was Indian tribal wars in that area and maybe that was what they heard.

Mama might of been strict and hard, but she never lied to me.

I couldn't get out of my mind the story of this nice Christian lady everybody liked and how two bad men came to beat and rob her and then threw her down in the well where she drowned. At her funeral, people all crying, fainting, and moaning, and everybody swore they still heard her screams coming from deep within the well. I thought I heard her screaming through my dark window every night, but it all happened miles away. And long ago.

My dreams started getting worse. Nightmares. Hants talking. Papa was in them almost all the time.

I kept thinking of this medium-sized American Indian man I started seeing in my dreams when Papa had his heart attack in 1912. Came many times in the middle of the night and talked to me, told me of his life and how he came from far away. He was brown, kind of mahogany color, had a high bridge nose, and his beady eyes kept looking and looking at me. Sometimes he took me out the window and we flew all around the countryside. Told me not to be afraid. It seemed so real.

One dark night my Indian friend said he was going away. I remember his very words. "I'll see you again when you a grown man." And then he left, but I kept thinking of him long after he was gone.

Uncle Jonse Mauney kept coming to mind, too. A gold-colored, yellow man, he died some months before Papa. Born in slavery and unable to read or write, he was the smartest man I ever knew. They called him the "Mystery Man"—could figure out any mathematical question right in his head. Anything. Everybody said his mind was as good as twenty college professors, and twice as fast.

I once saw him watch a slow freight train go by that had these long serial numbers on the side of each car. After the train passed he give me the total of all the numbers.

People ask him how many railroad crossties there was between Salisbury and Norwood, some thirty-five miles apart. He knew. Someone wanted to know his age in days, hours, and minutes. Told him right off.

If a man was building a house of a certain size, he ask Uncle Jonse the number of bricks, shingles, and planks needed. Then he order the exact amount he said. Storekeepers called him down at inventory time and did all their figuring through him. And the man couldn't read a single word on a page.

School teachers tried to trick him with hard questions. Like how many ticks a clock would make in three days, seven hours, and fourteen minutes of ticking. Knew that too.

One time some New London men put together a almost impossible question. How many chickens would there be, they wanted to know, if one chicken hatched twelve chicks, each chick then laid and hatched twelve more eggs, and so on for a certain number of cycles. The answer was up in the billions, I think, but Uncle Jonse gave the answer immediately.

Nobody knew how he did it and neither did he, but everybody said it was a God-given gift. All the circuses wanted him but he never went—didn't want to be called a freak.

How could Uncle Jonse do what he did without knowing how to do it? I was frightened just thinking about that answer.

After he died, we started hearing noises in the house. Two months later, when Grandmother's five-gallon stone crock exploded in little pieces, we knew something bad was going to happen. Grandmother died early the next morning. I knew it was Uncle Jonse that give us the token.

I kept remembering the time a few years back when I went with Papa to get a wagonload of vegetables. Well, this particular night we riding home after dark. The moon was moving in and out of the clouds. The woods all quiet. We were along on the road when we got up to this old Baptist churchyard where all the white slave-masters are buried.

Suddenly, our horse stopped and Papa couldn't make him go. Something was holding old Jim back—was prancing about crazy-like, snorting, ears twitching, eyes big and white. He never done that before, so I started crying and Papa looked kind of shaken. Just then, the old horse got turned loose. Now, this horse was sort of lazy and slow, but when he got turned loose, he just took off, running wild from one side of the road to the other, off almost in the ditch, then up against the meadow fence and back down again. The wagon was bumping and jumping, melons rolling out the back. It was more then a mile before Papa got him to stop.

Papa never went back that way again at night, and it took weeks for me to get over that scary ride.

Uncle Fred once told of seeing a twelve-foot giant black man when he was a kid, with big red eyes like fire coals, a white beard that touched the ground, bright painted red lips, wearing a long black robe, and carrying a staff as he came slowly out of the woods. That made me tremble just to hear tell of it.

More and more such thoughts kept running through my troubled ten-year-old head. Each one worse then the next. Didn't know what it all meant. Strange, frightening dreams. Hants all around, some standing back there in the shadows waiting to get me. Papa not there. I was alone, confused, and very afraid.

It was the most fearful time in my life.

3. *The Influential Years, 1916–1923*

"Lizzy, something has to be done to help that boy."

It was Mr. Rufus G. Kluttz talking to Mama. His wife's family, the Pecks, knew my father's father very well, and Papa was raised as their own from the time he was ten. These were good white people, yes sir.

"We all know how close Clyde was to Wash," continued Mr. Kluttz. "He's grievin' almost six months, and if we don't help him he's going to have big trouble." He pointed to his head.

They talked a long time about me. I heard him tell Mama he wanted me for the summer and he pay for my food and clothes. Said he take me to shows in Concord and Salisbury, be like a real father. Mama wasn't sure and kept hesitating.

"He can come back any time he wants," he said.

"Mama, please let me go," I cried. It was the first time I spoke up in months.

"See Liz, he's feeling better already." And Mr. Kluttz patted me on the shoulder, just like Papa used to do.

I went to live with him around the middle of March 1916. He and his wife lived in a new house just two miles outside of Gold Hill, about eight miles from New London.

The first thing Mr. Kluttz did was buy me a piggy bank.

"I'm going to give you twenty-five cents a week, Clyde," he told me. "When you go to church, you put a nickel in the collection box. If you want some penny candy, you buy it whenever you want. And if you save the rest, maybe you can get your own bicycle."

That excited me because I saw a sixteen-inch-frame bicycle with

Mr. and Mrs. Rufus G. Kluttz, the wonderful white people that took me in after my father died, standing in front of their new house in Gold Hill, N.C., 1914. (Photo courtesy of Mrs. Carrie Misenheimer.)

solid tires in the Sears, Roebuck catalogue that cost $5.98. It sure looked pretty.

"I want my boy to have his own," Mr. Kluttz said.

After about a week, he took me to the dry-goods store in Concord and bought me a seven-dollar knickers suit that only wealthy white kids wore. It was salt-and-pepper color with a stylish Norfolk jacket, the kind with a belt in the back. He got me a pair of full-length patterned stockings and tan, hand-buttoned shoes. Paid $2.50 for them. Then a small straw hat with a bright-colored band. Could wear the soft brim either up or down all around. Mrs. Carrie Kluttz was a good seamstress and made me a matching short-sleeved shirt with two breast pockets. Got me a little brown bow tie to go with it.

Man, I sure looked great. And felt so neat. This was a time when most colored boys wouldn't dream of buying even a two-dollar suit for Sunday wear. Some of them boys went raggety as buzzards, walking around in patchy clothes with their little behinds coming through the worn pants.

"Your new clothes are not only for Sunday," Mr. Kluttz said, "you wear them whenever you want. I want you to be *somebody* all the time."

"Why's that, Mr. Kluttz?"

"Because appearance is half the battle in life, Clyde."

That advice impressed me very much. I never forgot it.

The next Sunday I went with Mama to church. It was the M.E. Methodist Church, but they call it the United Methodist now. When I walked in so straight and stiff wearing my new clothes with the hat brim down all around, everybody's eyes was on me.

Some old flappy-mouthed women just sitting there, buzzing. Noses going up. "No wonder old Clyde look so good," they grumbled. "He raised by *white folks*."

Mama only smiled.

"You be careful, Liz," somebody sneered, "after a while he won't have nothin' to do with colored people."

After church my little friends started teasing me.

"Clyde got a white papa! Clyde got a white papa!"

"That's right," I teased back.

"You white now too, huh Clyde?"

"Yeah, I'm white."

"What?"

"Yeah, I'm a dark-skinned white boy!"

And we broke up laughing. It was a lot of fun being white.

I started smiling more often during those months with the Kluttz family, and my bad dreams gradually stopped. I felt like there was sunshine again all around. Someone had taken interest in me.

When school started eight months later, I got ready to return to Mama in New London. Schooling in North Carolina was usually sixteen weeks, but for black schools it was always less. Depended on how much money the county had to spend that year for local schools.

It was just before Thanksgiving, and Mr. Kluttz opened my piggy bank and counted out the change. More then enough for my bicycle. I ran all the way home holding my money very tight and gave it to Mama, telling her to order my bike right away so I have it for Christmas.

When she hadn't ordered it by the following week, I started pestering her about it.

"Hush up, boy," she said. "I have taxes to pay and need that money. You can't have a bicycle."

When I started to cry, she grabbed a hickory switch and like to beat me to death. Knocked me down and put her foot on my neck. Kept striking me. Wham! Wham! I was screaming. Big bumps came out all over my head, my face swelled up, and my eyes were puffy slits.

Opened a big gash that ran from the bridge of my nose down under my eye and half way back to my ear. Blood was all over.

"And I don't want to hear no more about it," she said.

Mama was having a hard time then, even though she got a sixty-dollar death benefit off Papa's insurance.

I started getting sick after that beating. Got weak, started coughing. Came down with a high fever. The doctor said it was the "flu" going around, and by Christmas Uncle Will Barnhardt was dead from it. Two of his six children was next, and his wife, Maggie, was gone by February. That's when they closed the schools and we all stayed inside for a few months.

By the first of April I was feeling better and back with the Kluttz family again. Couldn't wait to get back, because Mrs. Kluttz was better then my own mother.

I run errands for her, go to the store for maybe a bag of coffee, or sugar, carry it home in a big basket. In the morning I was expected to make up my bed and carry out my chamber pot. Then work in the garden if I wanted or help around the house just like I did for Papa. Feed the hogs. Cows. Mrs. Kluttz had no other children at that time so she gave me her full attention.

I was feeling so good at being loved I gave myself another middle name. I remembered Grandmother Mauney telling of being loaned to the Barron family during slavery and how nice they be to her. I liked the name and adopted it. Clyde Edric Barron Barnhardt. Had a nice ring to it.

Living in this white people's house and wearing expensive clothes, I felt big enough to buy myself a chaw of apple tobacco one day and sneak a bit on the way home from the store. It made me so sick and dizzy I had to lay by the side of the road for a hour. Never did that again.

Mr. Kluttz took me to many circuses and shows. One was the Brown and Dyers Carnival. Didn't have to be grown-up to know those carnival bands had trained musicians. One of them was all Italian and nobody spoke much English, but they played hell out of the latest popular music.

Once I saw this little old minstrel show coming through town. They hired two horse-drawn wagons, and all the musicians sat up there blowing and wailing. The trombone player had the flap down in the back of the wagon and was playing songs like *Slidus Trombonus*, shooting out his horn, slipping, and growling. Laughing. Sure looked like a lot of fun.

Living with the Kluttz family was like being on a summer vacation. Gradually I began to understand what Papa meant when he said he would work through other people. And watch over me.

Mr. Kluttz was just like my Papa.

Mama had moved to a six-room bungalow in Harristown by 1917. They called that area Codytown then, and now is part of Badin. I joined her there about mid-year with a cow Mr. Kluttz gave me and started looking for odd jobs.

I wasn't but all of twelve years old yet but got work washing dishes in a Greek restaurant. Then I stacked pies and cakes in Pete Endres' Bakery. Took a job as water boy at a construction site for a dollar a day. Shined shoes and brushed coats in a white barber shop.

And ran a lot of errands for people. That's how I met the great black singer Madame Gertrude Rainey, that everybody called Ma. It was June 1917 when her own all-colored minstrel show, "The Georgia Smart Set," came to Badin for a few weeks. They set up their big canvas tent right behind the cemetery, on Falls Road.

I was always hanging around her tent in case she got thirsty, then run to the store for some Coca-Cola. She loved Coca-Cola. Cost five cents a bottle, but I knew where to get three bottles for a dime. And she tip me a dime. During the day the whole company be outside cooking or exercising. Or just talking about show business. And I was running around, keeping busy, getting a nickel here and a dime there. Sometimes I made almost a dollar a day that way. But I was so thrilled being around those show folks I would of done it for nothing.

The people were all so nice, especially Ma Rainey. She was then rated to be the greatest blues singer in the world. Ma was very dark, had a wide nose, big lips, and a mouth full of gold capped teeth. She wasn't pretty—her natural complexion was black, but on the show she looked much lighter, almost high-yella.

"Honey," she say, "it's hard work to be light like me. Takes a hour to put that makeup on and another to get the damn stuff off."

She spoke with a little lisp-tongue, but you couldn't hear it when she sang. I liked Ma Rainey. She was a happy-go-lucky person, a religious-hearted person. You could see it in her. Always helping the underdog.

Everybody talked about her famous gold necklace. I never seen such a necklace before—one-hundred-dollar gold coins all strung together with some fifty-dollar, twenty-dollar, and ten-dollar ones stuck in between. The smallest was five-dollar pieces. It was like a trademark for her. One day I found her scrubbing her necklace with Old Dutch Cleanser in her washbasin.

At night I was right down front in the colored section to watch the show. The tent was big and square, almost two hundred feet long. Men selling popcorn and roasted peanuts in the shell.

I remember she had a string band in front of the stage. A bass fiddle, violin, viola, piano, and drums, and it was the first time I seen the big bass played while straddled. Couldn't stop from laughing.

After the band overture, the curtain opened and out danced eight long-legged gals in short costumes. They weren't the prettiest I seen, in fact they were downright ugly. With light makeup they were passable, but they could sure dance up a streak. Then the chorus boys came out and danced in the same line. The audience just loved the old gals and boys.

As they danced off, the backdrop came down showing a large illustration of a cotton field. Two blackface rubes came out dressed in stovepipe pants that ended just below the knee to show white socks going down in their big, extra-long shoes. When they started telling those old, funny stories, everybody broke up.

Bertha Forbes was one of the ballad singers on the show, and John Miles was another that sang *Sweet Adeline* dressed in a long tailcoat

The great blues singer, Madame Gertrude Rainey, who I ran errands for in 1917. (Photo courtesy of Frank Driggs collection.)

with walking trousers and a top hat. They also had a terrific dancer doing buck and wing steps and some tap. Another comedy act was hip-bumping Roxy Caldwell and her lady partner. These were two funny women.

It was a straight two-hour show, no intermission. One time this funny juggler, his name was Joe Fraser, put two oil lamps on his head and both were lit. He turned his body up, down, around, back flipped, and never dropped a lamp. Didn't even blow out. Later, a man riding a bicycle came on dressed as a Japanese and holding a umbrella. Rode that thing every which way, sitting, standing, on his head, on his back, and finally one wheel fell off and he rode it as a unicycle. He was good.

Ma Rainey closed the show. When she was ready to go on, the great lady start singing in the wings and as the curtains opened, strutted out flashing those gold-plated teeth and her expensive gold necklace. She wore a long, gold silk gown that swept along the floor, gold slippers, and carried a sparkling rhinestone walking cane. Her hat was high and wide with large feathers stuck in it, had gold earrings dangling and diamond rings on all her fingers. When she got to center stage under those amber spotlights, the audience just went wild. She was all of what show business was suppose to be. She *was* show business.

Her first song was *St. Louis Blues* in a slow-drag tempo. Then maybe *Yellow Dog Blues* with a spoken introduction about her "easy rider" and other problems. She close with her own *See, See Rider Blues* and for the big finale go into *Walkin' the Dog*, which was also called *Get Over Sal, Don't You Linger*. Then the whole chorus line come stepping out behind her and she dance along, kicking up her heels. The song had dance instructions in the lyrics, and as she call a step, everybody would do it. Soon the whole cast was out on stage, jugglers, riders, singers, comedians, all dancing wild with Ma Rainey shouting and stomping. She call "WALK!" and everybody walked together before breaking out fast. She call "STOP!" and everybody froze. After many calls she finally holler "SQUAT!" and the whole group squatted down with a roar. Including Ma Rainey.

It was a exciting show and the audience kept cheering and whistling. The whites in the audience usually applauded the longest.

I was there every night to see the show. It was better then Silas Green or the Florida Blossoms Minstrels, except those shows had brass instruments and could play louder music. And have street parades, too. But Ma Rainey put on a hell of a act. I liked her music better in person then on her later records. Much better.

I saw the show again the following year and it was just as good. At that time the famous singing comedienne Carrie Adams was with her.

She sang *Tree and a Possum* with all that hound dog mocking that the people liked. She was good, too.

School let out in March of 1918 and I got a job working for the big Tallahassee Power Company, which later was the Alcoa Aluminum Company plant. Paid twenty-five cents a hour for a ten-hour day just for soaking rusty bolts in kerosene.

When I told Mama how I saw these big cranes in there, a couple hundred feet up lifting big buckets of hot, liquid metal, how men was cutting things all over with big rains of sparks falling down, how hot and sweaty it was all the time, maybe 125 degrees, she didn't like it at all.

"A twelve-year-old boy don't belong in a heavy plant like that. It's dangerous."

But after me working two weeks at the plant, Mama got work there too, at thirty cents a hour. With her and me working full time and my sisters cooking in domestic work, we got along.

The Community Theater in Badin was on the black circuit and held about seven hundred·people. It showed moving pictures as well as stage shows.

After work I run over and see if I could do errands for the entertainers like I did for Ma Rainey. That's where, in April, I first saw the one and only Princess White. That was her real name—she was part Indian. A slender, streamlined older woman with pretty dark hair that rested low on her brown shoulders.

I liked to watch her handle the audience while she performed. She sing the *Hesitating Blues* or *Drafting Blues* in her low contralto voice, and people throw money up on the stage, they scream and shout, wouldn't let her off.

Some people liked her better then Ma Rainey because she sing other songs besides blues. And was so much prettier. People drive in forty miles from Charlotte to see her. She was a real headliner. A top name.

One time I took a train to Winston-Salem to visit relatives. While I was there I stopped in at the Lafayette and Lincoln theaters. I remember once this slender, dark gal was headlining—her name was Bessie Smith. She was singing *Memphis Blues, St. Louis Blues*, and other W. C. Handy numbers. Clarence Adams played clarinet and sax in the pit band. Willie Wilkins was on piano, and there was a drummer and a woman trombone player.

Bessie was moaning those blues and dancing up a storm, but I'll tell you something—I thought Ma Rainey and Princess White was much better. Yes sir. Bessie didn't have the magnetism then as the others had. She was just another black woman singing the blues.

I remember November 11, 1918, when all the factory whistles began blowing. Automobiles honking. People jumping up and down. Some crying. Everybody embracing each other. Blacks and whites. Young and old.

"Thank you, Jesus," they were saying. "The war is over."

But as soon as the men started coming home, Mama got let go from the plant. So I got a extra job working for a independent contractor. His name was Andy Fabian. When I went to get my $5.25 pay after the first week, the rascal done slipped out of town.

Mama got hot at me for being cheated and just whipped the daylights out of me again. That's when a lot of colored neighbors started talking about her.

"Why you treat that boy so mean?" they ask. "He's a good boy." When Mama tell them to mind their business, they warn: "When they take the boy away from you we'll see whose business needs mindin'."

Mama always been strict. Deep down I loved her but I wasn't sure she loved me. At least she never showed it. Everybody always told me how proud she was that I got jobs and tried hard. But she never told *me*. Just wasn't in her to show her true feelings.

I worked at that power plant for almost fourteen months and went to school at night so I could keep my day job. By 1919 I was plant messenger boy, taking papers around and running letters to the post office in a special mail pouch.

"It's time I got you children up north," Mama said one day. "That's where you can get a good education and not have to pay if you want to go higher. Besides, we'll get better jobs there."

But my boss, Mr. C. W. Kaufman, told me it wasn't that good up north for jobs. Said all the colored jobs went to white boys.

"He's lying," Mama said. "Just trying to keep you down here."

By July we all on the way to Roanoke, Virginia. Mama gave away most of the big furniture, sold the Sears, Roebuck house in Richfield, packed the trunks, and off we went. She really wanted to go to Harrisburg, Pennsylvania, but said it be better if we went there in two steps—afraid some of her cousins might think she was loaded with money going direct. That's the way women were back then.

I wasn't of a mind to leave Badin. Liked my job at Alcoa and thought I was doing good. After about a month in Roanoke, we moved on to Harrisburg. Mama had some second-hand furniture and sold it back to the store when she moved on.

Harrisburg was a big jump, hundreds of miles from Badin, and I didn't know where we were heading. We were not alone. Everybody was moving at that time, especially to industrial cities like Pittsburgh, Cleveland, and Detroit. Lots of good jobs to be had in the North, they all said.

I found living in our new working-class neighborhood strange. All the houses stuck together in a row. People coming in and going out all day, and night too. Whites. Blacks. Polish. Italians. Romanians.

Mama got a job in a beer factory, but when the smell got bad, took another as a domestic for a rich white lady. I tried hard, but jobs were scarce for little black boys.

School started in September and I wasn't going but a week, before this Hungarian bully-boy started getting on me.

"I don't like Southern niggers," he said, giving me a push. Nobody ever called me a nigger before. I was always a sensitive, shy boy, sort of bashful around new people. And Mama's whippings never did help my confidence. So I was scared and ran away.

The only one I could tell what happened was my white teacher. He said to always stand up for what I believed to be right. Otherwise I lose before I start.

The next time I saw the boy he was coming down the street, pointing his finger at me, and singing a song.

Nigger, nigger, never die,
Black face, shiny eye.
Nigger, nigger, never die,
Black face, shiny eye.

Kept repeating it over and over. Laughing. I was carrying my books tied around with a long belt, and before I knew it, I swung those books around my head and knocked him down. Then I jumped on him like white on rice, punched his face, and knocked a tooth out. Grabbed his hair and pounded his head on the street. Again and again.

Never had no trouble from that boy after that. And I thought a little bit more of myself. Yes sir.

By late October we moved three miles down to Steelton, Pennsylvania. This was a worse job-town for me then Harrisburg. Bethlehem had one of their biggest steel mills there, but I was too young to be hired. Mama was pushing me to find a job. I tried hard, I really did. Got up before daybreak and was at the food stores by 5:30, hoping to find something.

"What you doin' out here?" the man say.

"Looking for a job, sir. Need a good boy to help around?"

"Yeah, I do, but don't want no coloreds. Be on your way."

Mama said I wasn't trying hard enough. "You gettin' lazy like the rest of these Northern boys," she mumbled.

I been secretly writing to Mr. Kaufman in Badin, and he kept answering, saying my Alcoa job was still open.

So, on November 1, 1919, at the age of fourteen, I packed my suit-case, left home, and went back to Badin. I was on my own. Papa would watch over me, I was sure. Everybody said I was independent like him. And kind of hard-headed and stubborn like Mama. They were right.

The day I returned to Badin, Mr. Kaufman put me up in his house and started me again at the Alcoa plant. A few weeks later, I met Mr. Charlie Crowell, the same Mr. Crowell that made my shoeshine box when I was helping out my sick Papa. Now he was the railroad station agent of the Western Union telegraph office in Badin and was looking for a new messenger boy. Offered me the job.

Everybody knew they never had no colored Western Union mes-senger in that town before. Or any town in North Carolina that I heard of. When he explained the twenty-five-dollar monthly pay I get, plus the daily tips, special fees for far deliveries, free telegrams to Mama, free train fare all over the United States, one week paid vacation, and four weeks paid sick or emergency time off, I grabbed it. It was the best job I ever had. But I told Mr. Kaufman to hold my Alcoa job open, just in case.

I worked from 9 to 6:30 P.M. and went to school five nights a week. They gave me a little cap with the words "Western Union" printed on it, a special blue jacket, blank telegram pads, and a indelible pencil. Taught

This is how Badin, N.C., looked in 1919 when I used to deliver telegrams. I was the only colored Western Union boy in the whole state of North Carolina. (Photo courtesy of Fred T. Morgan, Stanly News and Press.)

me to bow correctly and explained good front-door manners: Yes Sir. No Sir. Thank You. Good Day.

I was expected to walk all over with my telegrams because they didn't supply bicycles, but I didn't mind. Some homes more then three miles out in the country and I got a seventy-five-cent delivery charge for those trips. Telegram rates was fifty cents to New York, sixty cents to Chicago. North Carolina was only thirty-five cents.

I sent Mama twenty dollars a month and put everything else I made in a good U.S. Postal Savings account. That was the safest bank in the country.

They never saw a readier boy then me. I hustled, yes I did. If a message come in, I always seemed to be standing next to Mr. Crowell ready to go. If it was past 6:30, after everybody left, they knew I still was there to take it out. No extra pay, but I was ready to go. Many of the older customers couldn't read or write, so I help with that too, compose their messages, told them how to save money by keeping within ten words. Always talked polite to everyone, especially when they start crying when I knock on their door, because many telegrams were death notices.

By the end of the month I was delivering more then all the white boys and making double their tips.

Wasn't long before I bought my own bicycle, the only messenger boy to have his own wheel, as we called it. Then I was able to take telegrams some five miles up the highway, and way off in the woods. The only thing I didn't like was them slippery snakes, all wiggling and skittering across the road. Then I get off my wheel, find a big stick, and beat them old snakes to a low gravy. I hated them.

Shows such as "Oh Baby" and "Oh Daddy" with pretty white chorus girls and singers barnstormed through town at the Badin Theater. I was always backstage taking it all in.

I saw Princess White again at the Brooks Dreamland Theater that just opened. She usually tipped me one dollar for the telegram, especially if the news was good. The comedy team of Butterbeans and Susie came in all the time. So did Bessie Smith, Clara Smith, Ida Cox, Jennie and Doc Straine, Edna Hicks, Josie Miles, Hattie V. Snow, Al Wells and Company—so many, many black acts.

I thought Gertrude Williams, who sang *Bo Weevil Blues*, was a great entertainer. A pumpkin-colored woman with long black hair, she had a top spot with the Roy White stock company and upset every house she played in Badin. I put her up there with Princess White and Ma Rainey. Oh yes.

I never did go back to the Alcoa job. Worked for Western Union
till April 1, 1921, when I got homesick for my family and returned to
Steelton.

Mama wrote me to come back, and from that time on, she treated me
as a adult. Gave me the understanding a son should get. No more whippings, no more meanness. I guess I earned her respect.

We all moved to Sibletown around June, which is outside Harrisburg.
I tried to get another Western Union job there. Even had a long letter of
recommendation that said I was the best messenger Badin ever had.

The manager only laughed. "We don't hire no colored boys for that.
That's ridiculous."

That's when I started to realize how lucky I been coming up in North
Carolina.

After I turned sixteen in 1921, I wasn't required to complete my
schooling. Moving around so much caught me in the middle of the
eighth grade when I stopped.

So it was back to odd jobs again. One was carrying sandwich boards
on my front and back, advertising the Russ Brothers frozen ice cream
Eskimo Pies. They were just coming out then. I also split kindling for
widow women and washed their windows. At night, I go over to the
Majestic Theater on Walnut Street and run errands as I did in Badin. Go
out for cigarettes, cigars, sandwiches, dinner plates, anything to make a
ten-cent tip. In the winter, I joined a work train shoveling heavy snow
drifts from the railroad tracks.

My friends all laughed at me because they wouldn't take those kind of
jobs. But they had fathers and mothers to get money from—and I
didn't. I also worked as a plumber's helper for fifteen dollars a week,
which was considered good for Harrisburg. I gave Mama eight dollars
and kept the rest.

I remember it was the first part of October 1921. The great Ethel
Waters was making a personal appearance with her Black Swan Trou-
badours at the Chestnut Street Auditorium. Fletcher Henderson was directing a seven-piece band and Joe Smith was on trumpet. When I got
there the man wouldn't let me in, said I had to be sixteen. But I *was*
sixteen, only didn't look it.

As I was standing on the curb, this man came over, told me if I helped
him sell soda pop at the show, we both get in free. Even gave me fifty
cents. Yes sir, Papa was watching over me that night.

It was a great show, and when Joe Smith started playing the first solo
chorus of *Bugle Blues* from the top balcony, every nerve in my body
started jumping. Ethel Waters sang her *At the New Jump Steady Ball*
and *Down Home Blues*.

After they got to know me at the door, I was there regular. I saw the famous Gibson Family musical comedy show featuring five-year-old Baby Corrine Gibson. Irvin C. Miller's "Broadway Rastus" show played there, so did the "Ebony Nights" show. All of them had good orchestras playing hot jazz and blues along with the latest music of that time. I went to every show that came to town.

It was March 2, 1922, that I saw the dancingest show of all: "Shuffle Along" at the Orpheum Theater. The Number Two company featured Lucille Hegamin. Charles "Luckey" Roberts was leading the band, but I kept watching the trombone player—can't call his name. That was a *real* New York show.

Mamie Smith with her Jazz Hounds, a package show with five vaudeville acts, came in two weeks later. She was a sensation singing *Daddy, Your Mama Is Lonesome for You* and *Crazy Blues*. When she did *It's Right Here for You, If You Don't Get It, 'Tain't No Fault of Mine*, she broke up the house. Coleman Hawkins was in the band, slap-tonguing his tenor sax while laying on his back with his feet stuck up in the air. A riot. The comedian Boots Hope was also on the show, telling all those funny lies.

The Princess Theater started bringing in TOBA shows, that's the Theater Owners' Booking Association, around April. They opened with Sara Martin singing the *Money Blues*. When she later recorded that number on OKeh records, it was changed to *Sugar Blues*. Female impersonator Andrew Tribble was also on the bill.

One of my bad memories was watching the Al G. Barnes Circus parade one June day in 1922. Just as the parade started, their jumbo elephant Tusko got scared or something, picked up his trainer and smashed the screaming man to death against a circus wagon. That frightened me and I always been a little worried about elephants ever since.

I seen every show that came to town and then run home and try to imitate the music on my kazoo. We called them "cazoots" then. Sometimes I get to fooling around with my friends, make believe we all hot jazz musicians. One fellow had a cazoot saxophone, another had one in the shape of a trumpet, someone else had a toy accordion with keys painted on—only made one note if he opened and closed it. I tied a comb wrapped in paper on a old broomstick and made believe I had a slide trombone.

We called ourselves the Sibletown Jazz Hounds after Mamie Smith's Jazz Hounds and went out on the street at night to play and sing a little. Maybe get out there in my ten-cent tennis shoes and cut some fancy old dance steps. We do *Crazy Blues* and *Royal Garden Blues*. Mary Stafford recorded those songs, and we tried to sound like her. Sometimes there was five or six guys in the band, but nobody was a regular. Never expected any money, never passed the hat or anything—it was only for fun and we were happy to get a hand from the crowd. But we did have fun.

One day I was passing Nathan's Pawnshop in Blackberry Alley and spotted this pretty silver-plated trombone hanging in the window. It was well worn and beat up a little, but it sure looked nice to me. And the sign read "Only $25." When I brought it home, Mama asked what I was planning to do with it.

"Learn to play," I said firmly. Didn't even know how to put the damn thing together because there was no instructions, but I sat and looked at that slide horn for hours. Even patted it a couple times.

Everybody talked about Mr. Joe Vennie, the best black music teacher in Harrisburg. Said he was strict, didn't take anybody he couldn't teach or wasn't capable. But I knew his daughter Tillie was one of the best local piano players and worked dances around town with her own band.

It was 7 P.M., Monday night, May 8, 1922, when I showed up at his front door holding my horn just like a regular musician. A stern-looking old man answered my knock.

"My name is Clyde Barnhardt," I said faintly, standing there scared to death. "Can you teach me trombone?"

"Come in, son," he said and led me in the parlor.

"I got my own horn here, Mr. Vennie," I blurted out, "and I wanna learn to play it."

"Let me see what you got there, boy," and he opened the case, took out the parts, and looked them over like he was inspecting a new horse. Before I knew it, he put them all together and was moving the slide in and out.

"Very slow," he mumbled, "and it's a mightly old instrument. But we can try."

"How much you gonna charge me, Mr. Vennie?"

"*If* I decide to teach you, it will be fifty cents a lesson. And a lesson is exactly one-half hour. No more, no less."

"Can we start right now, Mr. Vennie?"

"You jumping on something hard, boy."

I knew that. I was sure I could learn if somebody only give me a chance. He started explaining all the parts to me, showed the seven positions, and blew a note in each.

Handing me the horn, he put my hands on correctly, then told me to blow just as he did. I took a deep breath and let out a mighty blow. My cheeks poked out and my eyes bugged. The wind rushed through the horn, and I felt proud I made such a big blow. Unfortunately, no sound came out. Tillie Vennie was back in the kitchen and let out a loud laugh. I was ashamed but had to laugh also.

During that first lesson he got me to blow all positions on C scale except the seventh—my arm wasn't long enough to reach out that far. I got excited to be doing something I couldn't do before. He kept on, and in two hours I learned other scales.

"Don't usually spend this much time," he finally said, "but you got good prospects."

"Do I?" I asked.

"Yes, you're ambitious, young, and very eager."

I leaped up. "Gee Mr. Vennie, how long before I play in Tillie's band?"

He smiled and sat me down. "Now Clyde, you starting at the bottom and got a long, long way to go. There's much for you to learn: Keys. Breathing. Reading. You got to know time. Then tone. Syncopation. Technique. If you learn all that, *perhaps* then you'll be a good amateur."

"But how long before I play in Tillie's band, Mr. Vennie?" I guess I looked discouraged.

"How old are you?"

"I'm gonna be seventeen."

"Well, I see you are above average in picking this up. Most boys would take at least six years to get with a band. If you study hard, practice every day, put your mind to it, and don't get discouraged, I would say when you are twenty or twenty-one you may be good enough to play in my daughter's band. Three or four years is not long, son, not if you really want to do it."

I went home that night and told Mama I was learning a whole lot and my teacher said I would soon be playing in Tillie Vennie's band. I couldn't believe my good luck and kept practicing all the rest of the night.

Every time I went back for a lesson, Mr. Vennie kept me for a hour or a hour and a half. He seemed to like me, especially when I didn't rush home like most of his other students.

Mama thought my studies was a good idea and had my brothers Leonard and Herman taking piano lessons. They all in the front room practicing together on the piano Mama bought for them and I was in my room blowing my horn.

Many times brother Paul laugh, say I was wasting my time. Eventually they all lost interest in their music even though Mama kept after them. Kept after me also, but it was to *slow down* my practicing. I never missed a day.

Annie Laurie was my first steady girl friend and lived in Steelton. She was happy I was starting to play some.

"When you learn to play better," she would smile, "maybe you get a job with Mamie Smith, we get married and see the world together."

Daydreams of course, but it sounded so good. I had to agree with her. Annie was one pretty sealskin brown gal. High cheek bones, a medium-high-bridge nose, real thin lips, and straight black hair. She liked music and I enjoyed being with her. She was always laughing and happy. Late in 1922 she got the flu and died a few months later.

That Annie Laurie was sure one pretty gal.

Mama got a letter from a cousin in Columbus, Ohio, that said there was plenty good jobs there for coloreds even though the town was Jim Crow. Mama packed up and by the end of 1922 we all in Columbus. I was sorry to leave Mr. Vennie. After more then a year studying with him, he said I was improving. And I felt that to be true.

In Columbus I got with the Buckeye Steel Casting Company doing small jobs. The factory noise was unbearable. Mama found a job in the Federal Glass Company at thirty dollars a week. That was better then she could get in Harrisburg.

Mama's cousin sent me to Mr. Albert Jones, a local music teacher. He had patience with his students and made them feel at ease. I liked that. He used the same beginner's instruction book as Mr. Vennie, but he did more.

"Son," he always called me that, "I want you going up to those week-end dances and see what the big colored bands playing. Get right up and watch. Listen carefully. If they play something you like, remember it."

He was good that way, because I heard many teachers warn their students to stay away from jazz bands. Said they ruin you so you never able to play "right."

Oh man, they had so many bands in Columbus. The Synco Septet was at the Garfield Hall, led by Bill McKinney on violin. He later changed the name to McKinney's Cotton Pickers. Claude Jones was playing fast passages on trombone and Dave Wilborn was the singer. I heard Sammy Stewart and his Deshler Hotel Society Orchestra at a public dance before he left to play the Sunset Cabaret in Chicago. The orchestra didn't swing, but was the only black band to play steady in that lily-white Columbus hotel.

There was Scott's Syncopators with Lloyd and Cecil X. Scott at the Dreamland, which was on Fourth and Long Street. Sylvester Briscoe was on trombone, and that black boy could play some horn.Yes sir. Stand next to him for set after set watching him shake his slide to get that pretty vibrato. I was surprised to see the whole band nothing but a bunch of teenagers, just like me. But they were some blowing band.

I always put my age up to eighteen to get in these places but usually had trouble because I looked young and was so short—I was nothing but a runt. When I did get in, I run right over to the bandstand and stand quietly next to the trombonist. Never went to dance, although I could dance pretty good. Never went to drink, which was illegal anyways. Just stood around and watched. Followed every move the musician made.

I remember hearing a hot new number, *My Honey's Lovin' Arms*, and there was solos in there I knew wasn't written on the music sheet— long slides that reminded me of those crazy old minstrels. And in every set it sounded different. I was fascinated. I knew I would never get to play as good as those musicians—not sure even if I could make Tillie Vennie's band in Harrisburg.

Those players doing things even my teacher didn't know about.

All the bands in those places looked so nice in their neat uniforms. They been all over the United States. Maybe the world. And when somebody from the band came over and talked to me, I get chills up my back. I sure admired them.

As long as I went to black theaters and halls, I could usually get in. But when Mamie Smith's Jazz Hounds came to the Grand Theater, no colored people allowed. Period. Other black shows came in there but they also closed to blacks. I didn't like that at all. In Harrisburg, colored come and go most anywhere.

The Lyceum Theater allowed segregated audiences, whites on the right side and blacks on the left. I saw the black show "Plantation Days" there with Sam Wooding's band in early 1923. R. H. Horton was on trombone—just hearing him play gave me so much inspiration. I especially liked his growls.

Maude DeForest was singing *Aggravatin' Papa*. Everyone knew this was a *top* New York show, because all the chorus girls had straight hair, neat and very short, and the men had the latest Rudolph Valentino hair style—slicked down flat.

The "7-11" show played there also with Garland Howard and his wife, Mae Brown. Cook and Brown were the comedians—Sam Cook and Troy Brown.

My job at the casting company was a bore. I got tired of taking the man's money and not doing a day's work for it, so I quit and went in the Winslow Glass Factory, moving lumber around now and then from outside to the inside. Not much better then before, so I still felt sort of guilty for not earning my pay.

Man, I never knew winter could be so cold as a winter in Columbus.

That's one cold town. And when all those big, black rats starting looking for warmth, coming in our house and eating Mama's chicken right off the table, I tell you I was scared. One night I awoke to find my forehead all covered with blood where some old rat bit me. Didn't want no part of that town after that. No sir.

It was May of 1923 that I left for Pittsburgh. Told Mama I would check out the jobs and let her know if it was worth coming out. I found a place to stay with Mr. Glenn Spears. He just started talking to me one day on Wylie Avenue. Reminded me of my late father, and I took a liking to him and his whole family. They welcomed me in as their own.

I got a job at the Jones & Laughlin Steel Mill, doing lazy things again. When I tried to do more then I was supposed to do, the other workers didn't take to that. I got hollered at many times for being too busy.

Bands were all over Pittsburgh. At the Royal Garden Dance Hall, Lois B. Deppe and his Symphonium Serenaders had the seventeen-year-old sensation Earl Hines on piano; Vance Dixon on clarinet; Thornton Brown, trumpet; Harry Williams, drums—sorry I can't call the rest of the players, but it was ten hot pieces in all, the best I ever heard. Sometimes they didn't let me in the hall, so I stood under the lamppost on the corner and listened hard.

Many times I be standing out there for hours and a crowd gather. Talking. Laughing. Coming and going. Everybody having a good time. I appreciated they was interested in the music as I was until Keg-o'-Nails, the big black cop, come slapping his billy club in his palm.

"Gimme this corner," he shout. "Gimme this corner! Get your old whore asses outta here 'fore I run ya all in."

See, I was a green, small-town boy that didn't know what was happening. The cop never bothered me, because I always wore my Jones & Laughlin badge so he knew I was a working boy. Loafing wasn't allowed in that town, at *any* hour. By anybody.

After hearing one of those hot bands I go back to Mr. Spears' place and practice my lessons. Felt I was getting rusty because I couldn't find any teacher, but I did what I could. Kept at it. At about eighteen years of age, my only interest was music—there wasn't much else on my mind.

I was in Pittsburgh about two months when I wrote Mama and told her not to come. So she went back to Harrisburg and said I should meet her there.

I thought it a good idea if I stopped off a while at my aunt and uncle's home in Ellwood City, Pennsylvania. Most of their children all played instruments and I wanted to be around young musicians for a while. I needed some encouragement.

On a chance stopover like that, my musical career began.

4. Bill Eady and his Ellwood Syncopators, 1923–1924

It was after Labor Day in September of 1923 that I arrived in Ellwood City. I stayed with my Uncle John Eady and his wife, Laura, who was the younger sister of my mother. They had five children. It was their son Bill's six-piece family band called the Ellwood Syncopators that played dances all around the area.

I insisted on paying for my keep, so I got a day job working in the steel mill over in Koppel, about three miles from Ellwood City—I had to cross the Beaver River in a trolley car to get there.

At night I practiced my trombone down in Uncle John's basement. Sometimes I would mute my horn so none of the good musicians upstairs could hear me. And I practiced and practiced.

Bill Eady wasn't much interested in me or my horn as I hoped. "You can't play nothin'," was all he would say.

But Uncle John came to the head of the stairs and listened real hard. "Clyde, you learning to play now. Keep practicing, keep at it, boy."

Many times he told me if I was going to depend on music alone, I should get a regular day job and save every penny I could rake and scrape for the bad times.

"Because," he said, "the music business is sometimes slow and you might not be doing nothin' for a while. If you have a steady pay day, you never have to worry about no money comin' in when you laying off music."

It was a little over a month later that he came down the cellar. "Clyde, you sound good enough to be playing in Bill's band."

I didn't believe him. I knew the Ellwood Syncopators was far advanced over me. Some of them guys been playing back in 1913 and I only started taking lessons in 1922.

On Halloween night in October, the band had a job coming up at the Ellwood City High School. Bill came to my room the night before. Didn't seem too enthusiastic.

"Papa says I should use you at the dance tomorrow," he mumbled. "Pay you three dollars *if* you wanna come."

I thought if he wanted me, I would try.

Bill played tenor banjo and mandolin and also sang in a nice tenor and baritone voice when he wanted. His brother Linwood, my twin first cousin, played violin; sister Geneva was on piano (sometimes her sister Dorothy filled in for her); Bill Davis was the drummer that later mar-

Right, *William "Bill" Eady, who gave me my first band job in 1923 with the Ellwood Syncopators. His son Johnny is on left, and a cousin, Geraldine Leftwick, is center. (Photo taken in New Brighton, Pa., 1968.)*

ried Dorothy; Jimmy Good, trumpet; and his brother Billy, alto and C-melody sax.

I walked in the high school that night and saw kids all running about, laughing, and talking to one another. Dressed so nice. I began to get excited but wasn't nervous.

"Which one of the Eady boys are you?" somebody asked.

I was beginning to feel like part of the band. When we started to play, the young kids seemed to enjoy our songs and applauded loud after each number. Nobody in the band read music too much but we all had good ears, made up our harmony as we felt it. I been hearing the latest trombone players on records, musicians such as Herbert Flemming in Johnny Dunn's Original Jazz Hounds, Miff Mole with the famous Memphis Five, Dope Andrews with Mamie Smith's Jazz Hounds.

We did numbers like *Mister Gallagher and Mister Shean*; *Yes, We Have No Bananas*; *Barney Google*; *It Ain't Gonna Rain No Mo'*; and other popular syncopated tunes.

The thrill of playing in public was so great, it seemed like a dream, more then reality. Of course I didn't have the tone I got later, but I knew how to fill in and find the key. After that night, Bill took me on three more jobs the next week at double my pay.

The excitement wore off quickly. I knew inside myself I was still a amateur and had to work harder if I wanted to play with the better musicians in Harrisburg. That Eady band was strictly country. None of the boys ever became known outside Pennsylvania, although they did get plenty jobs down in Newcastle, Beaver Falls, and Butler.

Bill once tried to get connected in New York, stayed about a month and had to come back. Couldn't make it.

When I got laid off my day job in March of 1924, I returned to Pittsburgh to stay with the Spears family again. I got my old job back at the Jones & Laughlin Steel Mill.

It was just like before—pick up a few bricks over here and put them down over there. I hustled and tried to do my best, but the foreman tease me, say I was doing too much for a damn runt.

I kept practicing my horn every night but was getting discouraged because I couldn't find another music teacher.

I was out listening to the dance bands and shows almost every night. I remember hearing A. J. Piron and his Creole Orchestra. He had a New Orleans style that was different from the others I been hearing, but still real hot.

Ma Rainey and her revue was at the Elmore Theater in May. She remembered when I ran errands for her back in Badin. Told me she was now making records.

"Honey," she said, "I thought they overlooked this old lady. But I had faith in the Lord."

I thought her show was good, but not as good as in 1917.

Bessie Smith was at the Lincoln Theater backed by Irving Johns, on piano, who sat right up on stage with her. She was very popular now behind her big-selling records but would only sing two songs and then wave off. Never did get to hear her sing *Down Hearted Blues*, and that's what everybody wanted.

In a few months I took a leave of absence and went to stay with my cousins Charles and Birdie Atkins in Duquesne, about twelve miles east of Pittsburgh. Never returned to Jones & Laughlin, but found another job in Duquesne at the Carnegie Steel Mill paying fifty cents a hour.

My cousins was older then me. Charles was nice, but Birdie (they called her Bird) was a big pain.

The moment I walked in, she started to giving me a hard time. "You think you gonna be a musician?"

"Yes I do."

"You ain't never gonna learn to play nothin'," she say.

But cousin Charles stood up for me. "Why'n hell don't you leave the boy alone, Bird?"

"'Cause he too dumb, that's why. He ain't gonna go no further then right now."

Whenever I practiced and ran my scales, she stick her fuzzy head in the door and imitate me: "Toot-toot, toot-toot, toot-toot." Whatever sound I made, she mug it. "Toooooooot-toooooooot!"

It was not funny and she was always getting on my nerves. Sometimes blood relatives ain't as good as your friends.

I finally went back to Harrisburg where my mother was doing domestic work for some rich old white lady. I wasn't home but five weeks when we all went up to Philadelphia to take care of the white lady's big house. I found a job in a second-class white barber shop sweeping hair off the floor and shining shoes again. Paid twelve dollars a week.

While I was there, I was lucky to find Professor Aaron Harris, a trombone teacher that had his own music studio on Broad Street, near Bainbridge. A smooth, dignified brownskin, he wore glasses and had black curly hair with just a edge of gray. Wore a little mustache and looked and talked like a distinguished college professor. I turned nineteen, and none of his students was any older then me.

I liked him because he took a interest in me. "When you get older," he told me, "you are going to play in fine bands and meet colored society. You are going to be popular because you talk properly and do not use profanity. And you always act like a little gentleman."

I wanted to be with respectable, God-fearing people, but I sure was not particular about going out in society. I knew a whole lot of them was nothing but phonies, putting up a front. I found that out myself when I saw a lot of boys, with mothers and fathers to pay their way, going to college and still not have a change of clothes. I was only a shoeshine boy but able to save enough money to buy four good suits. Many times I loaned my clothes to some of them flashy college guys that needed them.

"God has blessed us," my mother used to say. "We are getting along better then some of the school teachers around here."

Bessie Smith's sister, Viola, had a restaurant called Viola's Place across from the Standard Theater on South Street. Bessie put up the money for it. I used to go in there, but most of the time Viola had no food to serve. Not even a pot of beans. I would get up and go down the street to eat. One time I was standing in front of the Standard, and Bessie came riding up in a taxi. It was lunch time and Viola be sitting out front resting herself. Not a customer in sight. I tell you, there was cussing and hollering coming out of that place for at least a hour. Bessie closed it not long after.

This was also the time I saw the famous Whitman Sisters' show at the Standard. Mattie Dorsey was singing hard-core blues and the band sounded real good. Comedians, dancers, pretty girls, pretty dresses— the Whitmans had one of the top shows on the circuit.

I asked Professor Harris if I would ever be good enough to play on a sensational show like that. He said it took lots of study, lots of practice. Be able to read fast and play in different keys. And have good tone.

"Work hard, son," he said, "and if you want it, you can do it."

Later that year we were all back in Harrisburg because Mama's day work was getting hard to find. One day I walked in Grunden's Drug Store on Sixth and Boas Street, and Doctor Grunden saw my trombone and thought I was playing in Tillie Vennie's orchestra. Told him I didn't play good enough to work in her band but was looking for a music teacher. Sent me over to Mr. Meredith Germer, a German-American musician that was playing at the Majestic Theater, down on Walnut Street. He was not a jazz musician but a concert artist. Later he worked in John Philip Sousa's Brass Band.

He showed me how to get lip vibrato and that's a hard study. Puts beauty in there when you take a solo or add grace notes. Not the easiest thing to learn and one has to keep practicing until he gets it under control and then do it every day after he gets it, in order to keep it. Many professional jazz trombonists never learned that—they shake their slide to get vibrato—but he showed me how.

He also taught me proper breathing and playing techniques, so I would not tire myself out. Showed me how to play syncopation and syncopated notes in common and cut time. That all been in my head, but when I saw it on paper, I didn't know how to bring it out. Taught me to read faster, like they did in the good dance orchestras.

I bought some orchestrations of the latest dance music and practiced the trombone parts, then played it for Mr. Germer, very slow of course. Told me I was progressing better then his other students.

"I'm going to prepare you," he said, "that when you leave Harrisburg, you will not have to come back."

That was just what I wanted. Mr. Meredith Germer was the best teacher I ever had.

Once a week I went to the music store to buy the latest band records and listen carefully. Play them over and over, especially the trombone and other brass parts. Sometimes I even try to play along.

The biggest black politician in Harrisburg was Mr. Theodore Frye. He was a Republican and also the supervisor of black workers for the city street-cleaning gang. All blacks that worked for the city were considered to have good-paying jobs—and nobody ever had to worry about layoffs when they worked for Mr. Frye. I took a day job with him for nineteen dollars a week, gave Mama nine dollars, and kept the balance for myself.

I swept the streets every day with a big, stiff broom. Up this street, down the other. And not just the curb but everywhere. There was a whole mess of horses in that town and we was always busy. Behind our gang the boys followed in a hack—a old horse pulling a older wagon. I sweep the manure from all over to make little piles and the boys in back load it.

Bill Bentley, the only white in our gang because he said he got along better with coloreds, always smoked this corn-cob pipe. We tease him, say he worked with us because we got to pile the better quality manure that he sneaked for his pipe. We laughed a lot, but it was long, hard work.

So I kept cleaning streets by day and practicing my lessons at night. And listening to my records, of course.

5. *Tillie Vennie's Orchestra, 1925–1926*

By April of 1925, Mr. Germer told me I was playing stronger, with a fairly good tone. Said I could learn faster if I sat in with other musicians—maybe work with a local dance orchestra.

My first thought was Tillie Vennie. I kept remembering that her father, Joe Vennie, told me back in 1922 someday I might be good enough to play in his daughter's orchestra.

Tillie had the best band in Harrisburg. That woman could play some piano. The only one I knew to compete with her was Earl Hines—and I wouldn't put him over her. She had offers to go to New York time after time but never left. That's because she was born under the sign of Cancer, and when Cancer people get to doing what they like, they hard people to move. I should know, I'm one too.

Tillie and her family were living over at 1304 Wallace Street in Harrisburg. She was glad to hear I was improving in my music and I had worked in a band in Ellwood City.

When I reminded her what her late papa said, she agreed to let me sit in for rehearsals and offered to help me whenever she could.

Most of her men were older then me and considered professionals, so I knew I had much to learn. She used different musicians at different times: Jim Jackson, a young bass player that was near my age; Jack Potter on banjo; Joe Fisher, drums; Charles Lamb the saxophone player; and Tillie's two brothers, Paul and John, on trumpets. Allen Deamus was her regular trombonist.

If Paul Vennie hadn't let whiskey get the best of him, he might of been famous. Mamie Smith came through Harrisburg once in 1922. She was hot as a pistol, and if you got with her, you were on top. Coleman Hawkins was working with her along with George Bell on jazz violin.

She was looking to pick up some musicians and got Paul Vennie and Lonnie Poston. Lonnie was Tillie's trombone at that time. After rehearsal, the band thought these guys were better then the ones that left. So they went on the road with Mamie Smith—Paul was nineteen and Poston was a little older—but their parents said they was too young and had them come back after only two months. If they stayed on, they be in the history books today. Poston died in 1925 and Paul took to drink.

After I began sitting in at rehearsals with Tillie's established band, Mr. Germer started teaching me to double tongue—told me it would come in handy when I had to play fast numbers. I practiced that and sometimes triple tongue too but never had any real fast pieces at Tillie's rehearsals.

Sometimes I hung out at Marshall's Drug Store on the corner of Cowden and Boas. Budd Marshall used to tease me when I walked in carrying my big horn.

"How yawl getting along on that old *tram*bone?" he say mockingly, mispronouncing the word. "Your teacher telling you a damn lie. You ain't never gonna learn to play that old *tram*bone."

And everybody laugh. I didn't take kindly to that teasing, but I was shy and tried to laugh along.

Soon, everybody in town started to calling me Tram. That name hung on me for years, and I'm known by it in Harrisburg to this very day.

I remember I had another one of my strange dreams just about this time. It was so clear and real. I saw this distinguished white man sitting on our front room sofa. Told me his name was John Evergreen and kept saying how nice the house looked and was pleased. He got up and started looking around.

When I woke up, his name was still on my mind. I asked a old colored neighbor if he knew who lived in our house before us. After thinking for a time, he said many people been in there but only called the original owner, and that was a white man by the name of *John Evergreen!*

I didn't tell anybody I saw Mr. Evergreen the day before. They liable to say I was lying. Don't think I ever told Mama. All I could think of was how nice Mr. Evergreen looked and spoke, even though he been dead for over 25 years.

But I tell you, it worked my mind.

August 9, 1925, was the first day the great Fletcher Henderson band was to appear over at the Paxtang Park Pavilion. It was a big event because Louis Armstrong was in the band and I never heard him in person. He was playing cornet, actually, the third trumpet and solo parts. Henderson also had Joe Smith on second trumpet and solo, Elmer Chambers, first trumpet, and Big Charlie Green on trombone. Didn't know the others.

Louis turned up a storm that night. He was so exciting, playing things on his horn that seemed impossible. But he was doing it. The man was way ahead of his time, very advanced—at least for Harrisburg. Joe Smith wasn't as exciting, but whatever he played was so beautiful—had those curves in there and trills and triplets over a simple melody, it all sounded so soulful, so mournful. While Louis was playing more then anybody I ever heard before, Joe Smith was doing what the people understood. Even the musicians. I loved Joe Smith's work and knew this was the way I wanted to sound. Exactly.

In the later part of August, Tillie had a big job coming up at the Chestnut Street Auditorium. It was a invitational full-dress ball with all the dicty set attending, including doctors, school teachers, even the police.

I remember we finished a rehearsal and Tillie came over. "Tram, you did good today. All your parts were correct. You playing better then you think you are." She was always giving me encouragement like that. "My regular trombone player can't make the dance next week," she continued. "Would you do me a favor and take his place?"

Me sit in with one of the best bands in town? I had no answer.

"My Papa be proud of you," she insisted.

I ran right out to the Hart Schaffner and Marx clothing store and bought myself a fifty-dollar tuxedo suit from the money I saved cleaning streets. It was a beautiful suit, tailored special for me in the latest style. A one-button, single-breasted jet-black jacket with a satin lapel, and the black pants had a satin stripe down the side. Then I ran across the street to the Walk-Over store and bought myself a smooth pair of spit-shine black patent leather shoes that came to a point in front. This was my first formal band outfit and I wanted to look as good as anybody else in the band. And I did.

When I arrived at the auditorium in my new tuxedo with the shiny pointed shoes, all the other musicians had their eyes on me. Some people at the dance that seen me cleaning their streets in the morning wondered why I was there. Someone even asked Tillie what I was doing up on the bandstand.

After about a hour of playing stock orchestrations and popular tunes, Tillie announced the band would take some jazz numbers. She called *Sweet Georgia Brown* and we hit it hard. When my part came up, Tillie pointed to me and I stood and took a hot solo just as I heard trombonists Miff Mole and Abe Lincoln do on records. Put my horn right in the megaphone and blew my heart out.

Suddenly, the whole audience got in front of the bandstand and started to hollering and applauding. Tillie yelled for me to take another chorus. I didn't know what was happening.

After the hot set, Tillie put her arm around me. "Oh, I wish my Papa was living," she whispered, "and could of heard you play."

But I was thinking of *my* father. It seemed like he was standing right there listening to me. It was a funny feeling. I can't explain it, but I felt him there with me—only I couldn't see him. He was *there.* I knew it.

Budd Marshall from Marshall's Drug Store was at the dance. Kept

Tillie and her Toilers at the State Theater, Harrisburg, Pa., Jan. 1927.
Left to right: *Howard Brock (ts), Clyde Bernhardt (tb), Jack Potter (bj), Charles Lamb (as), John Vennie (tp), Tillie Vennie (p/ldr), Sammy Scott (d), Jim Jackson (tu), George Norris (t).*

shaking his head. "That Tram always so damn quiet, never knew he could play."

Other people came up and wanted to know where I came from. And some of those society people that knew me as a manure pusher, now knew me as a *musician*. It was a damn good feeling.

I could not forget that old Mr. Vennie told me by 1925 I would be with his daughter's band. He said it would happen. And it came true.

When my mother heard how people accepted and praised me, she seemed happy. "You are making a start now, Clyde. Playing for all those big colored people, doctors, and lawyers. Doing something that everybody can't do."

She was really talking friendly to me, not mean and hateful like she did when I was younger. Mama was a real mother now.

"You're coming into another part of your life," she continued, "so this should make you work harder. Study, learn, and listen. Be spic and span like you always are, and you will get more jobs."

I followed her good advice all through my career. I still do.

After that first night, Tillie let me play other dates she had—some three a week and others just two. I made five dollars, sometimes seven when the gig was really big.

But I knew I wasn't as good as people said I was and I could not stop here. I had to try to get better as a musician. There was a whole lot for me to learn. And things out there I wanted to do in the future.

6. *Odie Cromwell's Wolverine Syncopators, 1926*

Odie Cromwell was a alto sax player in Harrisburg and been looking for a couple fellows to take to a Michigan job. He asked me to come along.

People didn't understand Odie Cromwell because he was so outspoken. A lot of times he say things he did not mean in his heart, snap people up, get them angry, and then laugh about it. You just had to know his ways—that's the kind of person he was.

I quit my street-cleaning job and took the train that Monday night along with Odie and Sammy J. Scott on snare drums and George "Dusty" Norris on trumpet. The date was March 22, 1926.

Some of the passengers on the train noticed we were musicians, and before I knew it we were stomping off *Sugar Foot Stomp* and *Five Foot*

Odie Cromwell gave me my first steady job playing music, Mar. 22, 1926, in Battle Creek, Mich. (Photo courtesy of Frank Driggs collection.)

Two, Eyes of Blue. Everybody was dancing in the aisles, even the train conductor. One white passenger passed around his hat and collected twenty-five dollars for us.

We changed trains at Buffalo, New York, and arrived in Battle Creek, Michigan, the next day. The first thing we did was join up at musicians local 594. Gave us a reading test we passed easily. Paid our dues. Like all the other unions, it was lily-white, and we were quickly told nobody should try to attend any meetings, not even come to vote in elections. Just stick to our jobs they said and keep our noses out of their business.

Well, that was OK with us. In fact we all laughed up our sleeves because even if they wanted, we wouldn't of come. The union promised us no work, so we damn sure had no business with them. Our jobs all lined up by Odie Cromwell for more money then we ever expected.

Odie added three more pieces when we got to Battle Creek: Williard Walkup from Chicago on piano; George Torrence, a second sax and clarinet; and Ted Colin on trumpet. They were all good players.

He called the group The Wolverine Syncopators, as Michigan is the Wolverine state. Our jackets were light blue with black pants and shoes and a blue bow tie on a white shirt. Everybody liked us—we looked good, had a catchy name, and were *some hot stuff.*

We played at a local roadhouse from nine to midnight, Tuesday through Saturday. A private club for upper-middle-class white people where they served good food and sold real Canadian whiskey from under the table, as it was Prohibition time. Lawyers and judges came in there, doctors and school principals too. Very private and *very* restricted.

It was my first steady job playing music.

Cromwell always checked *Billboard* magazine for the latest popular songs, and that is what he used. Ordered his music direct from Feist & Feist, the big publisher in New York, that all the leading orchestras were playing all over the country.

One of our specialties was *Up and at 'Em*, a terrific number he must have taken off the California Ramblers' big-selling record. He kept us rehearsing that doggone piece until we got it down just like he wanted. *Milenberg Joys* was the New Orleans Rhythm Kings' hot number—we had a stock arrangement on that but always improvised, adding a lot more to it. When we did *Yes Sir, That's My Baby*, the whole band would sing in unison while clapping on the off-beat. We always sounded like a band higher then our class.

Colin and Torrence left after a couple pay days—got some money in their pocket and went back to Chicago. Cromwell had a hard time replacing them as most local guys couldn't play doodley-squat even though he paid pretty good. Sometimes we got nine dollars a night or played on percentage and made as much as fifteen dollars.

But I quietly got myself a little part-time day job in a Greek shoe-repair shop in downtown Battle Creek. I remembered my Uncle John's advice and wanted to have a ace in the hole. Just in case.

Once, on our night off, a couple of the boys decided to drive over to Chicago and have a good time. After doing the town, we ended up at the Plantation Club to hear King Joe Oliver and his famous orchestra. I been hearing King Oliver's records for years and greatly admired his cornet playing.

I remember that night the band had Darnell Howard, Barney Bigard, and Albert Nicholas in it, three top-rated reedmen.

I went up to the great musician at intermission. "Hello, Mr. King Oliver, sir." I took a big breath. "My name is Clyde Barnhardt and I play trombone with Odie Cromwell's Wolverine Syncopators." The big man turned around and faced me. Didn't look like he ever heard of our band.

"Hello, son," he said in his low voice.

"I'm glad to meet you," was all I could stutter. "I think you have a great band. I just hope I get good enough to play in your orchestra some day." I was twenty-one and very young.

"Well, that's possible," he said thoughtfully. "All you gotta do is keep practicing. Never can tell."

That made me feel good, but I knew it was unlikely.

So I played with the Syncopators all through the summer of 1926 at this roadhouse in Battle Creek. The band was well liked by the customers, but Cromwell knocked himself out of other jobs because he had this way of making people angry. I think he was that way because he been a only child and thought he never had to do nothing he didn't want to do. He was raised that way.

Although I was getting a lot of experience with Cromwell, I kept practicing hard and trying to make improvements. Whenever I could, I listened to those King Oliver records, especially the ones with New Orleans trombonist Honore Dutrey on them.

Winter was blowing across Michigan and I was feeling homesick. By the middle of November I gave Odie my notice and returned to Harrisburg.

I started taking offers to work with Tillie Vennie again. She was now calling her band Tillie and Her Toilers—might have gotten that name from the popular comic strip, I don't know.

There was also jobs coming in from Pearl Smothers' orchestra and Priscilla Richard's orchestra, two other big Harrisburg bands. Pearl was one hell of a piano player and just as popular in black clubs as Tillie, but didn't compare with her because she couldn't read music. Pearl depended on her good ear—after hearing something twice, she play it. Her trumpet player, Chalmers Harley, really led the band and went with Jelly Roll Morton in 1929. He play a beautiful melody but couldn't take a hot chorus or any solo get-offs.

All those women just leaders or fronts and the bands always men. Guys didn't mind working for women as long as they didn't walk all over them. If they get nasty or hateful for no reason, the guys would say something like, "Goodnight, Tillie" and walk out. That sure brought the old gals down to earth.

While I was doing this pickup work, I took a job with the Perseverence Brass Band of Harrisburg, run by James Jones. This was a well-known marching band with almost fifty members. We wore Army-type uniforms with a yellow stripe down the side of the pants, Army caps, and a shoulder strap with a filled water canteen attached. We played *Poet and Peasant Overture* and some popular Sousa marches at Elks conventions and parades over in Philadelphia, Baltimore, and Atlantic City.

I worked those kind of jobs for some months, but I was not satisfied. Wanted to travel and see places I never seen before. Maybe even New York City. The big time.

At almost twenty-two, I was ready.

7. Charles C. Grear's Original Midnite Ramblers, 1927

While I was working with Odie Cromwell in Battle Creek, I made friends with Charlie Grear, whose Midnite Ramblers was working on the lake. So when I got a telegram from him asking me to join the Ramblers, I accepted the offer.

He sent me a railroad ticket to meet the Ramblers in Huntington, West Virginia, where he lived. I caught a train out of Harrisburg and got in Huntington on a Sunday afternoon, April the 3d, 1927.

There were many bands then using the name Midnite Ramblers. Tim Moore, the famous black comedian, started all that Midnite Rambler business. I met Moore in 1920 when he and his stock company came in the Brooks Dreamland on the TOBA circuit. Badin was booming and the big Alcoa plant was working three shifts—the second shift got out at 11 P.M. and everybody had good money to spend but no place to spend it.

So Moore got the idea of putting on a extra show at twelve that he called the "Midnite Ramble." When it became a success he took that late show through the southern circuit and the name caught on. After a while, bands picked up the name, but Tim Moore started it all.

While Grear was getting his Original Midnite Ramblers together, I stayed with some of the other bandsmen at the home of Jimmy Cole that was also crowded with his mother and four children. I remember I had to sleep on the sofa in the front room. So I went out the next day and bought some beef, beans, pork sausage, and some eggs and gave it all to Mrs. Cole to cook. I did that because she didn't charge me anything for staying there.

As soon as the band was ready, we left by touring cars to play a dance in Fort Wayne, Indiana. There was ten men and a valet: Grear took first alto and Jimmy Cole was second and baritone; Hilary Price, piano; John F. Splawn and Joe Branch, trumpets; Montgomery Morrison, a good solo tuba player; Slim Johnny Jackson on tenor and baritone; Paul Easley, banjo; Shorty Johnson, drums; and me on trombone. I don't remember any of the valets' names, they changed so often.

Touring with Grear and his Midnite Ramblers was a experience I will never forget.

We were one hell of a ragtag outfit, riding in two beat-up, seven-passenger cars—a big black 1923 Buick and a ratty old Studebaker. Must of had hundreds of thousands of miles on them. They were open touring cars with isinglass flaps for windows that always let the heavy rain and choking dust blow in on me. Our patched suitcases, packages, drums, tuba, and all that stuff was piled high on top of the cars, some even packed on the front hood and down on the running boards. Everything was all tied around and under with long knotted ropes.

We all pack in the narrow front seats, tight back seats, and the two little folding chairs in between. Then we stuff the extra boxes and luggage all around us. I always held my horn case between my legs—nobody going to hide my new instrument where I couldn't see it.

Oh Lord! I was so cramped and uncomfortable—felt like a circus clown in one of them tiny midget cars. Then we take off down some back roads, with deep dirt ruts and mud holes that try to shake out my teeth. When the road was open, Grear have us coast down the hills fast so we could pick up speed to get up the other side. Sometimes the cars couldn't make those steep grades so we turn around and go up backwards. They went stronger that way for reasons I never found out.

Those damn cars always causing trouble. The tires were almost bare and blew out any time they felt like it. Then everybody get out to try and fix them or push the car to the next repair station—if there *was* a repair station up ahead. When it be raining and we all be pushing, my shoes got muddy and sticky. Then I slip and hurt myself. After it was fixed we ride a distance, hit a big puddle, and the wires shorted. Then the car stalled out.

Everybody fell out again and pushed some more, never knowing to where. If it was too dark, we stayed by the side of the country road and slept all night. Many times I woke up in the morning to see those dumb old chewing cows looking at me.

There was always gas, oil, and water to be put in, but everything leaked out just as fast. Whatever there was to be fixed, filled, or replaced, maybe like new second-hand tires, we each had to pay our share. Grear took the deduction out of our pay at the next dance.

So we ride as best we could from job to job—pass woods, open fields, big farms. Sometimes we travel twenty miles and never see a single person or even a house. The guys always be stopping and run off in the bushes, but I knew there was damn snakes in those woods so I stayed by the cars.

Sometimes the drivers be acting a fool trying to race each other. The back car have a blowout or something and the one in front keep on going, maybe five miles before they knew the other broke down. Then they come all the way back. Didn't always make every dance we suppose to play.

If we get hungry, we roll into the next town and look for colored people—they always had something for us to eat. If the town was all white, we knew not to stop. When we be starving, and that was frequently, we take a chance and pull up behind some white food store. Grear was a smooth talker and went in with his hat in hand to explain our situation. Ask if they feed us in the back or maybe allow us to take food out. Most of the time they wouldn't, so we move on.

Once, I remember, the man felt sorry so he squeezed a couple of tables in his old dirty storeroom and hid us in behind a big curtain. "Don't want any white people to see you," he whispered.

We traveled on and on playing mostly black one-nighters like the Black Club Resort near Gary, Indiana; The Wisconsin Roof Garden Ballroom in Kenosha, Wisconsin; The Oasis Ballroom in Michigan City, Indiana; and Augustus Holtzcamp's Dancehall near Terre Haute, Indiana. We also played the University of Indiana and stayed right there on campus. We continued through to Ohio, Illinois, Tennessee, and Kentucky. From nice ballrooms down to low dives. Right into the winter months when things got worse.

I guess I had no sense to mind all this—it was hard, but I was young and adventurous. The truth was, I didn't know any better. Everything was one big thrill, lots of laughs. When we drove up to the colored dancehall with our raggity luggage piled high, steam coming out the radiator, and all our black shadows packed tight behind those isinglass flaps, we all treated as heroes. We might of looked like a band of gypsies, but it was just like a trademark. We loved it.

The smiling, young women all come around and follow after us. Offer money. Food. Wanting dates. Some catch the train to the next town and meet us there with a boarding-house room reservation. I sure got lots of experience with that band.

Charlie Grear and his Ramblers was just a little, jumped-up band, a bunch of young black kids blowing and clowning, booting hell out of their instruments. Old Slim Jackson sit up there with his big, flappy feet going fast, just like a machine. Be blowing and stomping until the people got to laughing. Then lay on his back playing his horn and break up the house. Montgomery Morrison took very fast bass tuba solos, more then a lot of trumpet players could do. Between those two blowers, the band always tore things up. And those black customers out on the dance floor would just *shake* their butts.

We played everything that was popular then and featured *Ain't She Sweet* and *Someday Sweetheart*. Copied *Snag It* just like King Oliver played it on his record. Also did *Where Shall I Go When I Go Where I Go?*, a number Hattie Snow sang in clubs as *The Song of the Wanderer*.

Grear's Original Midnight Ramblers at the Oasis Ballroom, Michigan City, Ind., July 1927. Left to right: Clyde Bernhardt (tb), John F. Splawn (tp), Montgomery Morrison (tuba), Joe Branch (tp), Shorty Johnson (d), Paul Easley (bjo), Hilary Price (p), Charles C. Grear (as/cl/ldr), Johnny Jackson (ts/cl), Jimmy Cole (as/cl).

Most of the time fights always seemed to break out in the places we went. Lots of hell raising—never knew what would happen in those small out-of-the-way halls.

Once we worked some roadside joint out in Indiana. Just about closing time this heavy black gal appeared. She was as wide as she was tall. Had on a big cowboy hat, a old work shirt, and men's dirty overalls held up by a pair of red suspenders. Stood back there in the doorway stomping road mud off her boots, complaining like hell about paying the admission charge.

"Hope you boys as good as they say you are," she grumbled.

"We gonna play our closing number now," Grear said.

"Say what?"

"Aw mama, it's 2 in the morning and we been on since 8 last night. Give us a break."

"I don't give a sheet if you all playing since last Tuesday. I paid the man a dollar fifty to get in and I damn well better get my money's worth."

"We quiting out after this number."

"The hell you are."

Before we knew it, out comes this long, black revolver from somewhere down inside her overalls. BANG! BANG! BANG! and all the lights go out. Like a flash, the ten of us jump up and leap out the back window into the cornfield. Morrison still had his big tuba wrapped around himself and was first out. We all landed running and never did play that last number.

We laid off in Indianapolis because Grear was sick, so I went over to the Booker T. Washington Theater on Indiana Avenue to see the Bessie Smith "Harlem Frolics" show. Fred Longshaw was the pianist and leader of her six-piece jazz group.

Before the show I went backstage to see the band. Longshaw heard me with the Ramblers and said Bessie was looking for a new trombone player. Just then, Bessie came in and asked me to join the show. For a few minutes, I saw big things happening for me with her troupe: Clyde Barnhardt working for the greatest blues singer of the time.

Then I thought of Grear, who was sick, the dates we still had to make, and my promise to finish his tour. I turned Bessie Smith down.

I went out front, sat down, and watched the show. Even imagined seeing myself there in the pit, working in her band. But I told the famous singer no.

I regretted that decision to this very day.

Wasn't to see Bessie again for many years. That was up at Aunt Emma's house on 133d Street in New York. She was the first cousin to Bessie's husband, Jack Gee. Bessie was staying at the Olga, Harlem's leading black hotel, but was renting a room at my aunt's. Bessie called it her "quiet place."

I was there for a birthday party and saw her give Aunt Emma a thousand dollars to hold because she was going out to a hot poker game.

"Don't gimme it back," she said, "even if I holler."

It wasn't long before Bessie was back, hollering—she lost her playing money and needed more. Aunt Emma let her have a hundred, and I never did see her again that day.

But let me get back to Grear and the boys. Everything about him and his band was not all laughs. Many times I noticed things that bothered hell out of me. Some of his guys was smart alecks—thought they knew everything. Come out of the five and dime store with pockets filled with soap, shoe laces, and other stuff I knew damn well they didn't pay for. When I asked about it, they only laughed, called me dummy, said there was something wrong with *me*. I wasn't raised like that and didn't take to that dirty business, no how.

One time, we had a blowout near Louisville and pulled off near some white people's house. As we patched the tire, Jimmy Cole noticed a clothesline in the backyard.

"Man, looka that sharp tie hangin' on the line."

"Yeah," said Grear, "ain't but one light in the house."

"Wouldn't be much to sneak over and slip off with it."

I was scared. "Don't do it Jimmy, don't do it," I said.

"They ain't got no dog," he said, brushing me aside.

"They'll catch you," I pleaded. "We all be put on the gang. *Please* don't do it."

He laughed, ran over, grabbed the tie, and we all roared away. I knew then this band was going to come to no good. God punishes the bad. It was Jimmy Cole got burnt up in 1940 with Walter Barnes in that Natchez club fire, and was not surprised when I heard the news.

But this problem of Grear deducting for this and deducting for that was the worst. Never knew what some of the ducts were for, there was so many. Guys usually had no money left to buy food after his ducts came out, but Grear was always ready with a excuse, tears coming to his eyes while he explained. He was a smooth, sweet-talker.

We were supposed to work on a percentage of the door with a guarantee of twelve dollars per job if they had no cover. All over twelve dollars we promised 50 percent of gross. On every job we played, the place be packed but when it come time to pay us, there was not much to go around. And after Grear finished with his ducts, I got maybe two dollars.

If he was short-changing us, he did it very smooth.

When we worked a long stay at Bill Boswell's Paradise Club in South Bend, Indiana, Mr. Boswell let me work in his restaurant during the day for a few extra dollars.

That's when one of the strangest things that ever happened to me, happened.

One day this man comes in the restaurant and sits down. I kept looking at him, because I was sure I met him before. He was a brownskin American Indian, had black hair, a high-bridge nose, and beady eyes. Every time I look around, those beady eyes was staring at me.

"Where's the regular waiter?" he asked, staring at me again.

His voice even sounded familiar. I was positive I knew the man, but although my memory is good, just couldn't call his name.

After I quit work I was still wondering. It was beginning to work my mind when later that night, it struck me. And then a cold chill went up my back. It was the very same Indian I seen in my dreams back when my Papa was sick some fifteen years before! It was him exactly, no doubt about it.

"I will admit," he said the next day, "I think I met you someplace before also."

He didn't seem surprised about my story at all. Told me about what happened to *him* in 1915, about the very time my Papa died—how he been poisoned and declared dead, and the bad Galveston flood came up some twenty-five miles away that kept him from being buried. Then, after three days stretched out with mourners all about, he woke up with the memory of being in Galveston helping to rescue women and children.

"Life certainly is mysterious," was all he could say.

His name was John Sol and we got to be friends. I often helped him write letters to a lady in town he later married. And every time I returned to South Bend, I stopped in to visit him and his wife. We remained friends for years.

I never told anybody I met John Sol in my dreams back when I was a little boy, because they liable to think I was crazy or telling a lie. But it happened just that way. Yes it did.

Most of the boys in Grear's Midnite Ramblers came from Virginia, West Virginia, and other southern places. They thought Grear was just a yellow Jesus—anything he said was gospel. I never did believe his hard-luck stories, and John Splawn didn't neither. But we kept our mouths shut, just went along, and even after I quit the band, still didn't say nothing.

That happened when we returned to Huntington to play a double homecoming dance at the fancy Prichard Hotel on Christmas Day, 1927.

The place was sold out. Must have been at least a thousand people there. The dance promoter, Mr. Sylvester Massey, told us Fletcher Henderson worked that hotel and we out drew him.

We played the early dance from three in the afternoon till seven that night and were preparing for the late show. I was getting out my instrument when suddenly the place filled up with bulls. The police. And they looked mean. A few even had their pistols drawn and were coming up on the bandstand.

"Don't take nothin' out of here," the white officer shouted.

They were all over us, grabbing at our instruments.

"Wait a minute, wait a minute," somebody hollered.

"We not gonna have trouble with you boys, are we?" he said, raising his club.

They were pushing, talking loud and nasty. People all started coming around to see what was happening. I was getting embarrassed. This was the finest white ballroom in Huntington. Somebody put his hand on my horn.

"Hold it!" I said. I must have looked like I meant it.

"This your instrument, boy?"

"Yes sir."

"Where'd you buy it at?"

"It was at J. H. Troupe's Music Store on Market Street in Harrisburg." I spoke nice and calm. And plain. Then I opened my wallet and pulled out the receipt. Something always told me to carry my receipt.

The policeman took it and passed it around to the other officers. "Alright, boy, hold on to it." He handed it back and walked away.

I found out later what this was all about. Some of the boys got their instruments on credit in Huntington and hadn't been paying on them. And Grear was one of the boys.

So the man just came in and took them all back, right in the middle of the dance. Mr. Massey was doggone mad and promised to pay all the money owed the next day if the police let the dance go on. Everyone respected Mr. Massey. He was a light-skin colored man and was known all over town. Even the bulls called him *Mr.* Massey.

So he guaranteed payment and the late dance went on as scheduled, 9 to 2 A.M.

The next day Mr. Massey paid for everything, but it was with all our money for the dance. Nobody ever saw a penny for the nine-hour gig. The band broke up after that.

Grear was crooked as a barrel of snakes.

8. Henry P. McClane's Society Orchestra, 1928

The best dance orchestra in Huntington, West Virginia, was rated to be Henry McClane's Society Orchestra. He was a wealthy black man about forty years old, well respected, owned four homes, and was considered class. Had at least two or three years of college. His wife, Minnie, was a music teacher. Although McClane was a good concert violinist, he never played in his orchestra—just managed the business.

After I quit the Ramblers, I heard that McClane wanted me for some good New Year's jobs coming up. He was living in his nine-room house at 803 Seventh Avenue and nearly died laughing when I told him about Grear's ducts. Said I had nothing to worry about with him—he paid what he promised.

Also said if I stayed in Huntington and worked his jobs, I could live and eat at his home with some of the other guys, and wouldn't charge me nothing. That sounded good.

We rehearsed right there in his big front room overlooking a large porch where the wooden swing was. Sometimes we worked all day getting down a hard number, and he have to stop us, we worked so hard. But it paid off.

McClane's Society Orchestra played three or four nights a week, sometimes five, in and out of Huntington. I was getting eight dollars a night and got what he promised every time. Sometimes we went out working clubs in Ohio and Kentucky, but only in the best rooms, many of them private. Like that big millionaires' club that sat high on top of a mountain. That was *very* private. And *very* white.

Some weeks we came back and worked three nights at the Prichard Hotel, where I kept hoping Mr. Massey would not call the bad time I had with Grear.

McClane was one of the best band leaders I ever worked for. Treated me just like family, in fact often called me "son." Put me up in a large upstairs room with some of the other fellows, and I ate Minnie's good cooking right there with him every day. All I had to do was pay for my laundry, and the lady that did that lived a few doors away, charging me fifty cents regardless of how much I had.

The orchestra had McClane's younger brother Freddy—he looked like a Mexican—playing banjo and calling numbers; Montgomery Morrison played fast bass tuba; and Frank Fairfax, a college man, was second bass

Henry McClane was one of the best band leaders I ever worked for. (Photo courtesy of Frank Driggs collection.)

horn and trumpet. Ed Belton on first alto and Walter Minor—he was out of the TOBA—on tenor. Edwin Black was the other alto.

Thomas Grider took feature trumpet. Everybody called him Sleepy because he nodded off just about anyplace, sometimes during a number. But he was wide awake when it was time for his solo. There was also Lloyd Saunderland, a sensational drummer, and Jack Mayes, piano and musical director.

McClane handled the bookings, made all arrangements, and usually sat nearby while we played.

We worked a lot of social clubs, society affairs, and high class parties, both black and white. McClane's book had many heavy jazz numbers such as *Black Maria, Beau Koo Jack,* and *Brainstorm.* Whites loved to dance to real black music, and the class colored dancers wanted hot, lively music. Sometimes as a gag I would slip my shoe off and take a couple solos with my toe working the slide. I saw Claude Jones of the Synco Septet do that back in 1923 and all those funny minstrels, years before that. The people all laughed, crowded around, stopped dancing. It was quite a novelty but I quit bothering with it because my slide kept getting out of line.

Other times I would scat a chorus of *Mississippi Mud*—I liked that number—get up with this old megaphone and sing like Louis Armstrong when he was with Fletcher. Even bought a A-flat harmonica and learned

to play a jazz solo on *Tiger Rag*. McClane was good that way. Never
held his men back.

He ordered his music and stock arrangements from Feist & Feist of
New York City, the same as Odie Cromwell did. Sometimes we alternated with big-name bands from Detroit and New York, and that gave
me confidence because I noticed they be playing the same stock arrangements as McClane.

This was a good reading band. If you didn't read by 1927 or 1928,
you got left out. No place for you in a good-quality band. Even the stock
arrangements of 1928 was different then four years before, and the
pressure was starting to hit nonreaders hard.

When Jimmy Harrison went with Fletcher Henderson, he wasn't up
on his reading and Fletcher had to let him go. But Jimmy got wise, went
to the woodshed, came back reading, and got with Henderson again.

Even the advertisements in the *Chicago Defender* and the *Pittsburgh
Courier* warned you: Get wise and learn to read or by next year you
won't have your job. And that was the truth.

One time McClane alternated with the Lloyd and Cecil Scott band.
Cecil remembered me when I was a kid in '23 standing next to his
band with my mouth open. He was surprised to see me working with
McClane after only five years.

Trombonist Dicky Wells was now with Cecil. Bill Coleman was on
trumpet. They asked why I didn't come to New York.

"Kid, you gonna miss out on a whole lot of stuff," Coleman said.

"I don't think I can play good enough for New York," I said shyly.

"You kiddin'?" he laughed. "You not Dicky Wells but you read better'n
a whole lot of them cats working steady in New York."

I thought they telling me a whole bunch of lies. But I did know no
matter how much money a musician made working country towns,
New York City was where the big names were. You had to be *someone*
to get there.

Sometimes I wrote my uncle in New York and say I'm coming up. He
always said to wear my Sunday suit because it was not right to come
out on the streets of New York with old clothes on. Even musicians in
Harrisburg used to tell me I couldn't get a job up there unless I had a
new tuxedo.

When we went to Cincinnati on a job, I bought myself two new tuxedo suits: a black single-breasted and a midnight blue, double. These
were good suits. I paid twenty dollars apiece for them—the same kind
that was selling for thirty to thirty-five dollars in New York and maybe
fifty dollars in Harrisburg. I wore those tuxes often with McClane because the band always had to look *class*.

It was the second Saturday night in September 1928. We played a big formal dance at Huntington's Vanity Fair, the largest and finest ballroom in all of West Virginia. Didn't take a back seat to the Savoy, the Roseland, or the Arcadia in New York.

We finished up about three in the morning, but McClane wasn't there to pick up our pay. Freddy took the money over to the house and woke Minnie up so she could pay us. It was late and she started to hollering, talking real hateful. Said she was tired of cooking for all the free-loading musicians living in her house and the sooner we all moved out, the better she feel. That really surprised me because I worked with McClane almost a year and he said I always be welcome in his house. My feelings were hurt. I was on that first morning train out of town.

Went to Duquesne to visit my sister and her children and then on to Harrisburg—the first time I was back since I left to go with the Ramblers.

I was talking to Leslie Frye, a trumpet player with the Pearl Smothers' orchestra. When I said I might go to New York to check out some band work there, he started to laugh. No Harrisburg boy like me, he said, could get with any big New York band. That gave me some hesitation and doubt. I had to agree with him.

After a few days, I left for New Jersey, where most of my relatives now lived. Mama had moved to 4 Boyd Street in Newark. I also had five uncles and aunts and some cousins living in New York City.

While I was staying at my mother's apartment, a telegram came in from Henry McClane. Said he didn't know why I left and he would send money if I returned. Now, I never did like to come between a man and his wife. You can't win a deal like that.

I wired back I was going to try New York.

9. Herbert Cowens' Orchestra, 1928

It was in September of 1928 that I rode the Hudson tubes train right to New York City. Walked up the stairs and took the elevated express uptown to see my Uncle Arthur Mauney, my mother's youngest brother that ran a store in Harlem. When I got off at 125th Street and looked around, everybody seemed so neat and dressed up. People walking down Seventh Avenue and Lenox Avenue had on their best clothes and this wasn't even Sunday.

I just wandered about. The good looking gals, especially those tall chorus girls from the Cotton Club, Smalls Paradise, and Connie's Inn all strolling around in big furs with old snooty Chow dogs pulling on their long chains. Those kind of dogs was popular but I never trusted them: look so nice and sweet and all at once, *snap*, they got you. Some gals wore semiflapper dresses with the belt way down low in the back and small hats close on their heads.

The fellows standing on the corners all looking over the long-browns coming down Lenox. Guys wearing form-fitting suits—oxford gray with pinstripe pants, jackets very short, didn't hardly cover their butts. Vests and spats too. Shiny shoes in black patent leather. Some had real flowers in their buttonholes with a long, fancy handkerchief hanging out the breast pocket. That was *real class*.

Others wore smooth, camel hair topcoats, maybe four inches off the ground. Derbys and homburgs everywhere.

But I heard for a fact that many of them fancy, jive-ass niggers didn't have a nickel to buy a hot dog. Those corner dudes—they were all flash.

The famous Jelly Roll Morton was playing at the all-white Rose Danceland Ballroom on 125th. Walked inside and stood back where the band was because coloreds were not allowed in. Jelly was really fronting Bill Benford's band, his brother Tommy Benford was on drums and Billy Cato, trombone. Jelly would do a piano number and then go out to the corner bar across the street while the band played the rest of the set.

As I walked around Harlem, I sniffed all that great food cooking in those down-home places. Restaurants with big handmade signs pasted on the windows or slate boards out front with daily specials written all over them.

Some had meals for only twenty-five cents but the better places, with full courses and lots of extras, charged fifty cents a dinner. And the places all jam-packed with whites that seemed to be enjoying the good food they couldn't get downtown.

Man, this was my kind of town. I felt comfortable. Felt at home. As a matter of fact, I had the strange feeling I been here before. But I hadn't.

When I came to Uncle Arthur's place on 134th and Madison, I saw it was a combination meat market and grocery store. He told me the restaurant around on 135th, across from the Lincoln Theater, was his also and he did all the cooking.

We got to talking and when I told him I wanted to get with a New York band full time, he smiled wide.

"You think you big-time now, Clyde?"

"I been playing in some bands, Uncle Arthur."

He started to laugh. "They only hire the top professionals in this town, boy. You nothin' but a little old chickenshit, country horn blower with a big head." When I tried to object, tell him I was practicing four and five hours a day, he wouldn't hear. "Bill Eady better'n you," he went on, "studied longer, had to go back. You think you catch up with him? Take my advice, Clyde, work in my store. I'll give you twenty a week, steady. Only ten hours a day for six days—you can't do no better."

Now, he was saying all that and never heard me play a note. When I told him about the offer I had from Bessie Smith, he only laughed louder and said I was lying.

I came home that night very discouraged.

The next day found me at Major's Band Box, the famous musicians' club that name jazzmen all hung out at. It was on 131st, near Seventh Avenue, and was run by Addington Major, who been cornet with Mamie Smith's Jazz Hounds.

The Band Box been open for about five years and was doing good business. Had a gambling part there in the back and at night musicians like Louis Armstrong, Jabbo Smith, Jimmy Harrison, Coleman Hawkins, Miff Mole, Jimmy and Tommy Dorsey, and other top men that was in town would jam there.

It was terrific being around big names, talking music. I was there night after night.

One evening around eight, Herbert Cowens comes in. At that time he was rated to be one of the best show drummers in New York. His wife, Baby Cox, was one of the headliners up at the Cotton Club. I remember seeing her and her father, Jimmy Cox, working minstrel shows around 1912 when she was only four.

Sitting on the bench next to me was Dicky Wells. He was working with Lloyd Scott's Band right then at the Savoy. I liked to make friends with other trombone players. Knew they had connections and couldn't play but one job at a time.

So Cowens came over and asked him if he knew any trombone in town that could read and take a good jazz solo.

Wells turned and pointed to me. "Here's your man, Herb. Heard him work in the best band in Huntington—ain't no Wells, but he plays."

"How long you been in town?" Cowens asked me.

"About a week."

"You read?"

"Yes."

"Belong to 802?" That's the American Federation of Musicians' local.

"Yes."

"Have a black tuxedo suit?"

"Yes, sir."

"Black shoes? Black bow tie?"

"Yes, *sir.*"

"Be at the Audubon Ballroom tomorrow at nine. Wear a Arrow collar white shirt.

Luckily I had everything needed to be a real New York musician.

The next night I went to the Audubon on 166th and Broadway, walked upstairs and in the hall. It was one of the top-name ballrooms and New York's biggest. There was a private party starting and all the guests wearing formal dress.

Herb Cowens was at the drums; Ray Corn on first trumpet; Bill Lewis, second horn and get-off man; Castor McCord, tenor, and his brother Joe on alto were both from the Horace Henderson band; Eric Brown, a yellow guy that reminded me of Paul Whiteman, on alto; plus a pianist, bassist, and banjo player. A ten-piece band in all.

I met the McCord boys in Harrisburg when I first started out. They came over, shook my hand, told me not to be scared because they knew it was my first New York job. I also heard Ray Corn and Bill Lewis snickering, saying I looked too young to be playing anything. Kept complaining about having a schoolboy on a big-time job. Somebody asked somebody else who I was, and nobody knew. Other then the McCord boys, nobody spoke to me. This was the *big time.*

I kept thinking of my brother laughing at me. And Budd Marshall telling me I never would play my *tram*bone. Leslie Frye saying no Harrisburg boy could make it in New York. And Uncle Arthur trying to discourage me.

I was getting nervous, hoped I wouldn't be making a damn fool of myself.

Before the first set, Herb Cowens told me to lay out if I come to a hard part, not try any passage I couldn't play. There was no rehearsal.

We played two sets. The music seemed like average arrangements—I saw no hard parts. As we started the third set, Cowens called some of his best jazz arrangements and I heard Corn and Lewis whispering loud that everybody going to see some good fun now.

"This gonna be reeeeeeel good," they were saying. "The boy's goin' back where he come from, *fast.*"

So Cowens stomped off a set that included *Black Maria* and *Beau Koo Jack*, difficult pieces that asked for your butt. But I knew right away they were the exact stock arrangements Henry McClane used, the latest songs ordered from Feist & Feist direct from New York City.

When my solo part came, I stood up and easily played it note-for-note as written. And very loud so that everybody could hear. Before I sat down I put in a little extra stuff especially for Corn and Lewis.

After the set, Cowens came over. Said he knew I never seen those numbers because only New York bands played such hard arrangements, and here I read them all at first sight.

Bill Lewis jumped up when he heard where I learned to play. "Man, all them Harrisburg niggers read as fast as you?"

Ray Corn was slapping me on the back, said those numbers cut even the best sharks in town. I acted like I thought it was easy music—never told anyone I been playing those same arrangements for months and almost knew them by heart. Kept my mouth shut and nobody never found out.

I even remained polite when Corn wanted me on his own weekend gig. Said he hired somebody else but was going to cancel him out for me.

Cowens paid fifteen dollars for that night. The Corn job got me twenty dollars on Friday and twenty-five on Saturday—sixty dollars for three nights' work just because I could read the latest arrangements. Never made that much before for three jobs.

Corn's weekend job was under the Luckey Roberts name, downtown for some rich whites. It was a Roberts pickup group, one of about five bands he had going at the same time. Luckey was working up at Yale, and Ray Corn was in charge that night.

I told my mother all that happened and the money I was making. She felt proud. Said many musicians come to New York, can't find work, and go back to take a day job. And her boy, only 23, making it in the toughest town in America.

After word got around the Band Box about my fast reading, jobs started coming in. I could not understand that, because I saw other trombone players in town I knew was better then me. And they all starving.

That is why I believe, why I *know*, God has always helped open the doors of success for me.

And my Papa told me before he died he would look out for me. And I knew he was. He definitely was.

10. Richard Cheatham's Orchestra, 1928

Early in November, I went with the Richard Cheatham orchestra into the Club Alabam in Newark, on the corner of Arlington Street and Branford Place.

This was a high-class white cabaret with a black floor show—singers, dancers, chorus girls, comedians, a M.C., and all that. The few blacks that did come in there were the gambling type: big sports, big shots, big-time spenders, and fancy men.

The Alabam was the Cotton Club of Newark. Had a fast floor show with about ten chorus girls, all light skin with very, very short costumes spotted with pretty beads and shiny things. Had on little hats covered with colored feathers. The girls were beautiful and terrific dancers and singers. Put down hot leather, just as good as anything you could see in New York—precision steps that the Rockettes do today. These girls were so good, many of them went on to the Cotton Club or Connie's Inn.

The master of ceremonies, in tails of course, would introduce the comedians with a great flourish, and Little Bits Turner and her small humpbacked partner came out—he was a little on the gay side. They dressed in patches and tatters, supposed to be right off the farm. Little Bits' hair was black, nappy, and stood straight up like a porcupine.

They told those old down-home stories with so much mugging and slapping they make a monkey laugh.

I also remember a piece of funny business at the Alabam where a straight man came out arguing with this blackface fool.

"Never again will I take you to a swell party," he said.

"Whataya all mean, Wilbert?" drawled the blackface, sort of dumb-like.

"You acted terrible, that's why."

"Hold up there, cousin," said the comedian, bulging out his eyes.

"That's right," continued the straight. "You remember when the lady brought out them olives on a silver platter?"

"Yassah. The lady done brought them out."

"And you asked her how long she had to soak the green peas in vinegar 'fore they swelled up that big?"

"So . . . ?"

"Aw, man!"

Of course, in the end the blackface fool always caps the straight and then it be even funnier.

I couldn't take my eyes off the Creole girls from New Orleans, especially Jenny Lee Betts. She sang a number like *Ain't She Sweet* that everybody just loved—a knockout.

Lorraine McClane, who used to have a act with young Moms Mabley and looked like her sister, was on the bill too. Sang *Mississippi Mud* and then went into some fast dance steps with her feet moving like crazy. Something like Nina Mae McKinney would do. Nettie Perry also sang some ballads.

It wasn't possible for me to see the whole show because I had to watch my cues, be ready to hit it.

For the finale, the entire cast appeared, everybody doing a fast close with lots of loud singing, wild dancing, and the band up on stage roaring a hot number, maybe like *Diga Diga Doo*. It was great being part of a good show.

Pound for pound, Cheatham had a better band then McClane or Grear. Could play behind acts, chorus girls, and full shows. Play in different tempos, different styles, and segue from one to another.

Other bands were only dance bands—didn't have the experience to do shows like that. At least not as a whole.

I worked the club for a month, playing acts for a hour and then about a half hour of dancing—working right on with almost no rest. The job paid fifty dollars a week for seven nights, two shows a night.

I got along good with Little Jeff, the trumpet player. Never knew his full name. He set a riff, I took the thirds, and he took the tonic. We played those head arrangements and made them sound like something special. Never worked with a trumpet player as good as he was.

There was also two saxophones, a tuba, drummer, and a banjo player in the band. Cheatham played piano.

The famous Whitman sisters were working Newark's Orpheum Theater, and one cold, December night they came in the club. The owner acted as if royalty came in: special reserved table, free booze, lots of attention. And they *were* royalty. Between sets, a note came up they wanted to see me at their theater.

The Whitmans still had one of the most highly respected acts in all of black show business, maybe the highest of them all. They traveled back and forth across the country with their own troupe, working only the finest vaude theaters and were better known then even the popular Blackbirds show.

The next morning, bright and early, I was talking to sister Mae, who handled all the business. Told me her trombone, Alvis Travis, left and she needed a replacement. I was grateful that the Whitmans wanted me, but when Mae offered forty dollars a week, I hesitated. That was ten less then I was getting with Cheatham.

"Well," I said like a big-time New York musician, "I can't go out for that."

"Forty-five is as high as I'm goin'," she said.

"I'll take it."

I took it because the five-dollar cut was worth it. My ambition been to work in a show like the Whitmans' ever since Professor Aaron Harris, my old music teacher, told me in 1924 that someday I would be good enough to go with them. And now it was coming true.

A big show. All big names. Lots more experience. I gave Mae Whitman no argument. I gave Cheatham my notice.

11. The Whitman Sisters' Show, 1928–1929

Monday, December 10, 1928, I played my first show with the Whitman sisters. It was at the Lafayette Theater up on Seventh Avenue, between 131st and 132d in New York, where they presented the best black stage shows and revues in the country. And believe me, the shows *had* to be the very best. When you play for black people, your best is not too damn good for them. You either put out or get out.

The Lafayette held about two thousand people, and outside on the marquee the Whitman Sisters' name was up in bright lights. Toward Connie's Inn on the corner was the famous Tree of Hope where performers out of work go to wish for a job. Sometimes it get crowded under there with all kinds of wishing going on.

That night my family came to see the show. No one ever seen me work before. Uncle Arthur, who told me a few months back I was not good enough to work in New York, sat right down front—almost able to reach out and touch me. Kept staring and staring, trying to see if maybe it was someone else that looked just like me.

My mother was there. So was my brothers and some cousins. It was a good show, but Mama watched me all the time, and I kept looking over at her to see if she was looking over at me.

Later backstage, everyone seemed so proud of me. My family all crowded around, everybody talking at the same time. Uncle Arthur said he been following the Whitmans since 1910 and never dreamed he see his kin in their pit band. Mama cried and I embraced her. I think I cried a little, too. It was the most exciting time in my whole, young life.

The Whitman sisters were Bert, Alice, Essie, and Mae. Mae's real name was Mabel. She was the oldest and took care of business: bookings,

In the 1920s and thirties the Lafayette Theater in Harlem presented the best black stage shows and revues in the country. The Tree of Hope is seen to the right, in front of the Ubangi Club. (Photo courtesy of Frank Driggs collection.)

hirings, firings, props, transportation. Mae used to sing in the early days but was retired from that.

Alberta, or Bert as she was known, was a male impersonator and dancer, one of the best in the business. Was so realistic—dressed exactly like a good-looking young man.

Alice was the youngest. Blond, light, and looked like a white girl. She was a great comedienne and a sensational time dancer. Could do many of Bill Robinson's tap routines like dancing up and down stairs. I heard Robinson agree she was the greatest woman tap dancer. Nobody knew, but Alice was not a Whitman sister at all. They billed as sisters, but Alice was actually Essie's daughter. I can tell that now because they all passed. And Alice's little son Albert, known as Pops Whitman, worked on the show with Billy Yates. Had a hell of a duo act.

Essie retired long before I joined. Stayed in Chicago and made all the costumes. Sometimes when there was no work to do, she came back for

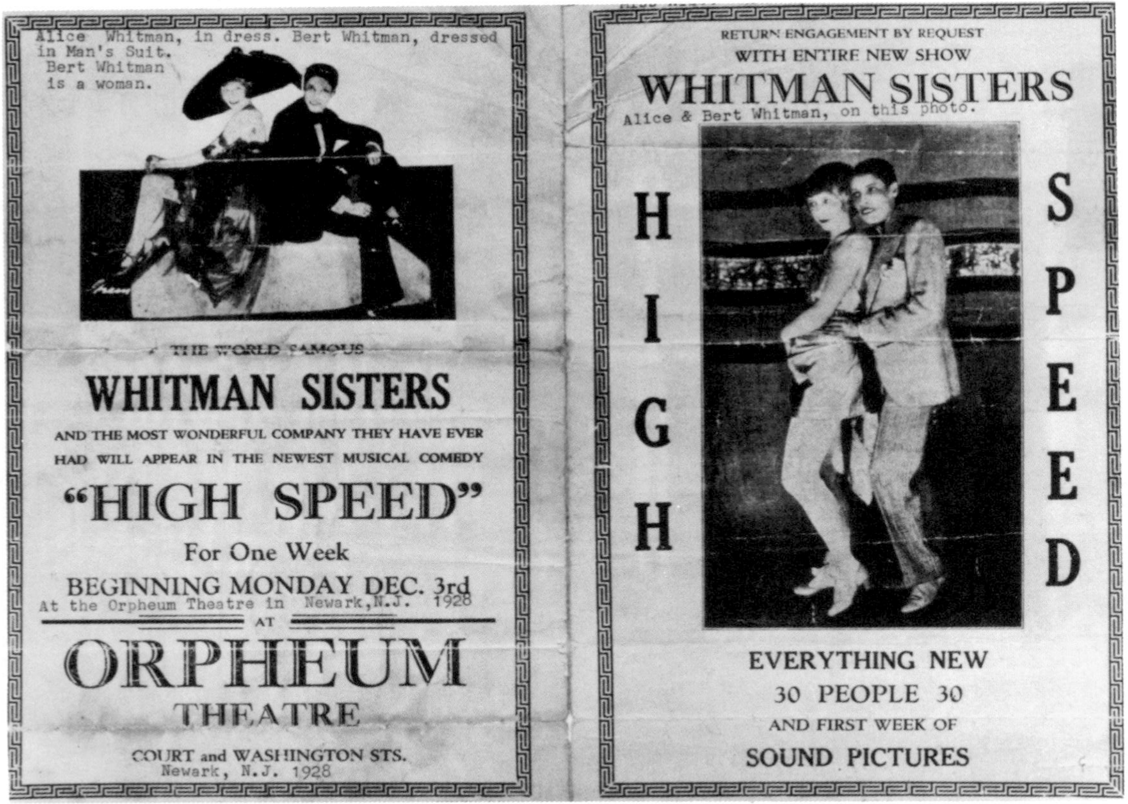

(See caption, facing page)

MABEL WHITMAN

PRESENTS

WHITMAN SISTERS

IN THEIR NEWEST AND PEPPIEST MUSICAL COMEDY

Earnest Michael Comedian & Clarinet player
Willie Bryant, Willie Toosweet.

HIGH SPEED

A GREAT
SINGING & DANCING
REVUE

1928

IN CONJUNCTION WITH

FIRST WEEK OF

SOUND

PICTURES

TWO BIG SHOWS IN ONE

Billy Yates & Pops Whitman

Pops(Albert) Whitman & Billy Yates
was two Great little Tap Dancers

Two advertisements for the famous Whitman Sisters' show at the
Orpheum Theater, Newark, N.J., for the week of Dec. 3, 1928.

*Clyde Bernhardt while
appearing with the
Whitman Sisters' show,
May 1929, St. Louis, Mo.*

a two-week turn with the show, never no more. Essie had a strong voice
that reminded me of Sophie Tucker, and her comedy routines was a
riot. When she did her famous skit about a rich society lady that gets
drunk, the audience broke up every time.

The Whitman family goes back a long way. Old man Albert Whitman,
who looked white, was a Methodist bishop and first cousin to Walt
Whitman, the noted poet. The Whitman girls started out singing gospel
with him on the church circuit before the turn of the century.

The sisters were very religious—everyone on the show *had* to go to church every Sunday, no matter where we were or what we was doing. Somebody miss a service, they be fined and the money given to the church.

We always had to wear our best clothes at all times—if any of the sisters saw a show member walking down the street not looking neat and clean, they raise holy hell. Wanted us all to look successful, like we had money. Or at least making some.

The Whitman show was always a big production and changed about every six weeks. Was almost two hours long, a matinee every day, two shows every night. Had usually over thirty-five people in the show, plus the band.

After the band overture, the curtain rise and the chorus danced out singing happy songs. It alternated boy-girl-boy-girl, about sixteen in all—working like a well-rehearsed team. Their costumes was always neat—the boys had on satin shirts and pants, the girls had satin tops and short satin skirts. Later in the show the girls came out as models wearing gowns trimmed in lace with big, fluffy ostrich plumes coming out the top of their big hats. They walk across the stage, turn and pose, hold out their skirts full. The Whitmans been presenting this kind of fashion show ever since they changed over to musical comedies back around 1905, long before Irvin C. Miller and his Brown Skin Models.

They had a soubrette dressed in tails and silk pants, wearing a silk top hat and carrying a long evening stick. She do a hot jazz number. Later she sing a sad ballad wearing a evening gown with one of them small bands around her head with feathers all in it.

I remember Bernice Ellis, a leading lady and soprano whose specialty was semi-concert songs. She and Dick Campbell, a tenor, sometimes sing duets like *I Can't Give You Anything But Love*. In later years he was the head of the U.S.O., in charge of black acts.

Margaret Watkins also sang on the show. Willie Bryant did some comedy work and danced in the chorus line. Willie Toosweet was the blackface comedian, and his nephew, Wilbert Toosweet, worked in the chorus.

Sambo Reid was the other blackface comedian but was so naturally black he never had to cork up because nobody could tell the difference. Sambo was a Geechee from Charleston, South Carolina, and it was very hard to understand what in hell he was saying—that's what made him so funny. He usually wore a black derby and gray spats.

Leo Watson and Douglas Daniels worked together as a team. Leo was only fourteen and Douglas, thirteen—neither of them grown. They sang and scatted all kinds of songs. Both played banjo, mandolin, ukelele, and

Rare photo of the famous Whitman Sisters' company appearing at the Dunbar Theater, Philadelphia, Pa., Dec. 27, 1928. Roman-style names are members of George "Doc" Hyder's house band that augmented the show. Front row, left to right: Sambo Reid (comedian), Billy Yates (dancer), Princess Wee Wee (singer/dancer), Albert "Pops" Whitman (dancer), Willie Toosweet (comedian); middle row, left to right: Maurice Wilson (dancer), Leo Watson (singer/g), Alfreda Allman (dancer), Dolores Payne (dancer), Myrtle Fortune (dancer), Troy Snapp (ldr/p), Ellis Reynolds (p), Doc Hyder (ldr), Alice Whitman, Bert Whitman, Bernice Ellis (singer), Katie Franklin (dancer), Ethel Frye (dancer), Douglas Daniels (singer/g), Margaret Watkins (singer); back row, left to right: Charles Anderson (yodeler), ——— Fitzhugh (singer), Alex Stevens (t), Bernard Archer (tb). ——— Mason (t), unknown (tp), Clyde Bernhardt (tb), unknown (tu), Leslie Towles (d), unknown (d), unknown (bj), Sterling Payne (as), Josh Saddler (vio), Puny Gray (as), Archie Anderson (vio), Ernest Michall (cl), unknown (ts), unknown, ——— Hubert (singer).

other stringed instruments. Another youngster I remember was Alfreda Allman, only thirteen but worked the chorus line with the grown girls. They put her on the end because she was such a good dancer. There was other acts and the audiences loved them all.

The Whitmans was the stars of the show of course. Bert and Alice worked together as a team—Bert in a man's neat, striped jacket, pants, and shoes. Hair cut short and combed back like a slick processed dude. Alice was all satin and lace with the latest wide-brimmed summer hat flopping in the breeze.

They work a long act together, maybe Bert singing *It Had to Be You* to Alice as both walked and danced, holding on to each other. Making eyes. Being happy and laughing. They made the perfect male-female couple.

The audience always went wild over them. But I swear nobody seemed to know Bert was really a woman. She always had young, excited girls waiting at the stage door for her. Some of them be no more then eighteen. But Bert was straight. She came out in her street dress and those silly gals be still peeping in the door for her. They ask when the "Whitman brother" was coming out and she say he slipped away and was long gone.

The gals all go away mad and Bert would only laugh.

One time I was talking to her when some gal got backstage and came in her dressing room.

"Somebody said you is a woman dressed up as a man," the kid said with big eyes. "But I don't give a damn what you is, I just love the hell out of you."

"Get out gal, I'm goin' on soon," Bert said, not even looking around.

"I do anything you want, even work for you."

Sister Bert winked at me. "Honey," she said, turning to the little gal, "you can't work for me, 'cause I got a husband working for me now. One is enough."

We both had a good laugh. She had more trouble with stage-door gals then stage-door johnnies.

The sisters were always looking for beautiful girls to add to the show. In those days, theaters in Cleveland, Columbus, Newark, and New York had black amateur shows and dance contests. If somebody was good, girl or boy, the Whitmans came and took them in. Only the best and only the lightest high-yellas, no blacks. Then they made them up to be the same light complexion as all the rest.

Ma Rainey would pick up the good blacks the Whitmans passed by and give them a spot in her show—that made Ma very popular in the South.

Troy Snapp was the leader of the Whitman show band and played piano; Ernest "Mike" Michall, a good New Orleans clarinetist, was also one of the blackface comedians on the show; Sterling "Buddy" Payne played alto; a boy from Cleveland I knew only as Mason was trumpet; Leslie Towles, drums; Archie Anderson, violin; and Mae's husband, Mr. F. B. Payton, played tenor and helped out with the luggage and props. We all paid him a dollar a week to deliver our trunks wherever we wanted.

The band always worked in tuxedo, white shirt, and bow tie. Buddy Payne was a bad dresser and once picked up a old tuxedo somewhere. When he came down front to take a hot solo, the lining in his raggety-ass jacket fell out on the floor. Oh man, sister Mae got mad. Pitched a bitch.

"Come out on my stage, will you, looking like a damn old buzzard? Embarrassing the Whitmans. I won't have it!"

She went out the next day and bought him a brand new tuxedo and duct it from his salary. They were very strict on how we looked—at all times.

The band played in the pit except for the fast finale when we finish up on stage. Sometimes the band augmented with the house band like Irving Hughes' orchestra at the Royal Theater in Baltimore. That damn pit was full of musicians and made one terrific band—sounded so rich and heavy. Snapp never changed arrangements when we augmented, but alternated parts or had us play duo solos.

We augmented at the Howard Theater in Washington, D.C., the Elmore in Pittsburgh, the Globe in Cleveland, the Koppin in Detroit. Once worked with Doc Hyder's band at the Dunbar in Philadelphia. They had a much better group then Snapp ever had.

The show traveled by railroad car. In those years, the railroad company gave us our own private coach and baggage car if we had over twenty-five in the show. Then our special car got connected to a train going to where we were going, and we be on our way. Move those coach seats down flat, make them like beds, and stretch out. Much better then Grear's touring cars. Oh Lord yes!

We played a lot of white theaters and some black TOBA places—only the biggest ones that had flyers to take the large drops the show carried. We toured from New York to Atlanta, then down to New Orleans and out to Indianapolis, St. Louis, and up to Detroit.

The Whitman Sisters' show was big news wherever it went. The audiences couldn't get enough of the blackface comedians, the coloreds laughing the loudest. And all the singing and dancing. Much applause. Family people came, both black and white, bringing their children.

This was a quality show—clean, no smutty jokes. The Whitmans wouldn't allow that. I saw the best-dressed men and women in our audiences, even preachers.

Once, when we played Philadelphia, I went over to see Professor Harris, my old teacher. Kept asking me how I was getting along with my studies, but before I could answer, said he saw this fellow in the Whitman Sisters' pit band that looked just like me. Made me feel very good to say it *was* me.

"You were my best student," he said nodding his head. "I'm not surprised."

I kept getting other job offers during my tour with the show. Doc Hyder wanted me for his band. Dewey Jackson in St. Louis give me a offer. Neal Montgomery in Atlanta, too. But I was learning so much with the Whitmans, I turned them all down.

I was with the show about six months when it all came to a fast end. We arrived in Atlanta after a long ride, and Bert called a dance rehearsal for two hours later. Dance rehearsals was necessary as theaters are usually different sizes and it was important the chorus get a feeling for the stage.

But I was dead tired, fell asleep, and never got to the 81 Theater till after rehearsal was well along. She fined me two dollars.

By union rules she should have paid *me* for those dance rehearsals, but never did. Many times I fibbed to the union delegate, telling him I was paid, but I was not.

Besides, I felt those kind of rehearsals could of been done just as well with only a piano.

I'm a funny person, don't like being taken advantage of, and I don't take advantage of anybody else. So I gave my two-weeks' notice.

A few days later I saw sister Mae in the barbershop having her hair trimmed in the chair next to me. Asked me not to leave the show, but I gave my notice and it was too late.

I left the Whitmans in Cincinnati sometime in June of 1929 and went to Detroit to visit a old girl friend. Sister Mae paid my train fare.

While I was there, I stopped over at a club on Saintoine Avenue where all the local musicians jammed and hung out. McKinney's Cotton Pickers was working at the Graystone Ballroom, and some of the guys started to drift over around two in the morning. Ed Cuffee and Todd Rhodes walked in and sat off to the side. They spotted me as a stranger and started to signify, like daring me to play.

"Is that a real horn in the case, or you carryin' your lunch?" Kept teasing me. "If there is a horn in there, I hope the boy know which end to blow." Things like that.

Musicians can be cruel sometimes, especially to newcomers. Tease and laugh. But I was sort of shy and didn't answer. A few guys started to jamming so I went up and hit a number. While I was playing, Rhodes came over and sat in on piano. Cuffee, a good trombonist, stopped his jiving.

When I finished, I had two pickup jobs waiting for me. One was with Bob Cruzette—had a fancy Fourth of July party lined up. Teddy Wilson was in the band—he was going to college then and came to Detroit to make some extra summer money. That man could play piano like nobody's business.

Then I took a job with Lou Hooper because his trombone player got TB and had to lay off a while. I really didn't want the job. It was way out at a lake pavillion some eighty miles from Detroit, and Cruzette had other jobs lined up for me. But Hooper needed me bad, he said, and I felt sorry for him. After a few weeks, Hooper wanted me regular, but I was homesick and came back to Newark.

It felt nice being home again and I didn't take any more work until after Labor Day when that crazy roller rink job came along.

12. *Dinah and His Orchestra, 1929*

My family was always helping and advising me. I respected them, as they were older and much wiser then me. They knew how hard it's been for coloreds to get ahead and was giving me the benefit of their experience.

I remember my uncle used to say: "Clyde, just 'cause these musicians after you to play jobs, don't think you the best horn player in the world. Some damn blower out there might play like hell, but nobody know nothin' about him. Always stay down to earth," he added, "because then you won't have to *come* down to earth." I thought that was good advice.

After soaking up Mama's home cooking and talking about all the places I been with the Whitmans, I took this job with Dinah and his orchestra.

Now, that's a odd name for a man. Years ago, when his name was George Taylor, he did a stage act dressed as Topsy in a spit-tail wig and dress. Always clown and fool around. Jump all over. Called himself Dinah and it stuck on him the rest of his career. Even after he became a drummer he kept jumping all around his drums, sometimes laying on the floor, pitching his sticks in the air, catching them on his back, and never miss a beat. A real flash drummer. He once worked with Jimmy Cooper's Revue on the Columbia Burlesque Wheel circuit.

Dinah had about seven pieces in his band. One was Chalmers Harley on trumpet—I worked with him in the Pearl Smothers' orchestra back in Harrisburg.

Dinah's gig was at a indoor roller skating rink up in Yonkers, New York. It was a fairly large place with bleachers all around the sides. We were hired to play intermission music while the skaters rested. But when we start to play, the manager come out, wave his hand to stop us, and make some announcements. Then we start again but here he comes running out again waving and the skaters come back on. We never played when they were skating.

The rink must of made money when the skaters skated, because we never got to play more then three choruses of any song. I get up to take a solo and have to stop right in the middle because the manager was waving. Couldn't finish the number. The people all applauded, especially when old Dinah did his thing, but there wasn't time for nobody to do much of anything.

The manager was the busiest guy there—always running out, waving.

I hated the job. The other guys didn't seem to mind—as a matter of fact, they liked it. It was easy and they didn't do much. But I thought it was *too* easy.

After the first week, I gave my two-weeks' notice. That wasn't a job, that was a embarrassment.

13. Honey Brown's Orchestra (Willie Wilkins' Band), 1929–1930

I used to hang around the Rhythm Club that was in the cellar next door to the Lafayette. I was living across the street at the time and used to run over often because it was the hottest after-hours place in New York where a guy could play just for himself. Sometimes it was so crowded with musicians I had to wait in line to get up on the bandstand to blow. All the greats came to relax and talk music. And jam.

One night in September of 1929 I was sitting there enjoying myself when Red Elkins came over. We met when he augmented the Whitmans at the Palace in Dayton, Ohio. Said that Honey Brown's trombone player was always drunk and hard to get along with, so she was looking for a new slide horn player. I was on my two-weeks' notice with Dinah so I walked over to the Bamboo Inn where she was working and got the job.

Honey Brown made a name for herself as a ballet dancer in some Buffalo night clubs. She been hired the year before in Memphis to play the lead in the first all-black musical film, *Hallelujah*. During the baptizing scene, Honey got pneumonia, so they brought in Nina Mae McKinney out of high school to temporarily fill in. When they saw how much better Nina sang and danced, Honey was out. Nina just *took* that part.

Honey was twenty-three years old, a keen looking, light gal with sharp features. She was very small and petite, usually wore a evening gown and always had a baton in her hand. Sometimes she go into a little dance act, up on her toes, doing high kicking and singing in her little kitty-cat voice.

The Bamboo Inn had a floor show and Honey was in charge of the acts. One of them was Race-Horse Smith, a long, tall, brownskin from Chicago—Jesus, could she dance. She throw out her long legs, jump up, twist about, and do the biggest split you ever saw. She couldn't sing a lick, but man, could she dance. Her real name was Mamie Smith but was not related to the famous blues singer.

Honey brought in a yellow gal from New Orleans by the name of Billie Adams, a very good entertainer. Her grandmother was a Creole voodoo queen, and she must have inherited some psychic power from her. Billie was always telling me about myself—that I should have more confidence, things like that. I always been attracted to people with those powers, so we got along good.

Another act was Jerry Hall, a female impersonator that billed himself as Jarahal. Could sing baritone and turn right around and sing soprano.

The orchestra went under Honey Brown's name, but it was really Willie Wilkins' band. We backed all the acts and played for dancing, too. Herman "Red" Elkins was on trumpet; Melbourne Scott, alto; Edgar "Spider" Courance out of Cincinnati, tenor; Charles Harkless from Meridian, Mississippi, on bass tuba; William "Bill" Burford, drums; John Marrero, one of the New Orleans Marrero boys, on tenor banjo; and Willie Wilkins, piano. A nice, tight eight-piece group, and Wilkins gave me as many solos as I wanted. No hassle. He ran a good band.

The Chinese owners of the Bamboo liked Jarahal better then Honey and finally put him in charge of the show. The first thing he did was fire Honey, and the orchestra became officially Willie Wilkins' band. Everyone liked it better that way.

The Bamboo Inn was a block-long restaurant located on Seventh Avenue between 139th and 140th. Was famous for dining, dancing, and having a good floor show. Some of the best Chinese food in Harlem was served there, and King Oliver used to come in two or three times a week. He loved Chinese food.

Once he came in looking for a second trombone for a Kansas City tour he had coming up. Shook me up by asking me to join his band. I didn't really think I had that much experience or was good enough for him. I was flattered, but turned him down. I liked my job at the Bamboo. It was clean with good working conditions. And all the Chinese food I could eat.

I was good friends with trombonist J. C. Higginbotham. Sometimes he came over from the Saratoga Club and we both drift over to the Rhythm Club where Fats Waller usually hung out. Then the three of us went around the corner to the old Catagonia after-hours club on 133d to hear the great stride pianist Willie "The Lion" Smith. He was backing singer Mary Stafford at the time.

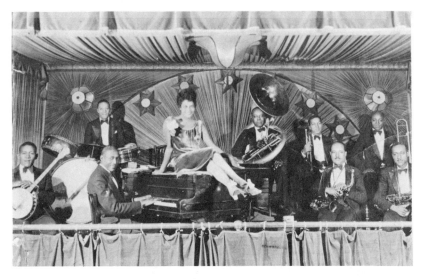

Honey Brown's orchestra at the Bamboo Inn, New York City, 1929, just prior to my joining the band. Left to right: *John Marrero (bj), William Burford (d), Willie Wilkins (ldr/p), Honey Brown (v), Charles Harkless (tu), Herman Elkins (t), Melbourne Scott (as), "Bones" (tb), Edgar Courance (ts). (Photo courtesy of David Griffiths.)*

Out of the corner of his eye, Willie spotted us coming in and let out a low growl, "Arrrrrr. . . ."

"Yeah, this is me," shouted Fats. And The Lion growled again. "You may be king of the jungle," Fats said, "but I come to get your damn crown."

Then they both rocked the place until sunrise, having one hell of a ball. Those two pianists was so equally great, it was just a matter of taste who was better. I know they both respected one another. Sometimes Higgy and I take out our horns and blow hot choruses behind them.

Yes Lord, that was good music!

After about four months with Wilkins at the Bamboo, one night everybody showed up for work to find a big padlock on the door. Couldn't understand what the hell this was all about. Just stood in the cold and kept peeping in the door. Never did find out what happened, but we knew we had no job.

Laid off about ten days and then in January of 1930, Wilkins got us a gig at the Sphinx Inn, down on Second Avenue near 11th. Outside the club was a big doorman and nobody could get in unless he give the OK. On the second floor there was two more musclemen standing by. Must of been seven feet tall, had punchy faces, and wouldn't let nobody in unless they got the nod from the doorman downstairs.

Inside was all decorated with pictures and statues of pyramids, sphinxes, pharaohs, and other Egyptian things. The place had room for about four hundred people and featured a floor show and a nice chorus lineup. Only whites allowed in.

On our first night we knew it was a speakeasy run by racketeers—it was written all over the place. This was Prohibition time, but they served all the booze you wanted if you willing to pay for it—and I mean the *real* stuff, only the very best.

Mean-looking guys with big shoulders always strolling in and out, wearing long black coats, hats pulled down low over their slit eyes, and bumps coming out from under their arms—when they sat down and their coats opened, you saw two gats under there.

It was just like that "Eliot Ness" television show, that's exactly how they looked.

One time a white councilman and his wife was there drinking and having a good time. When the check came, the lady started talking loud about being overcharged, and two giants came over and took them in the back office. When the door shut, I heard a lot of scuffling going on and loud talking. Never did see anybody come back out, but the next

day I was told a man and woman was found back in the alley all beat
to hell.

This was a bad bunch.

We never knew when a fight would break out in the audience. Or
maybe a shooting. Rival gangs was everywhere, some sitting in the shadows back there, checking things out. A lot of known hoods came in
regular but I won't call any family names, because even if they dead and
gone, they still liable to rise up and hang hell on me if they knew I was
telling their secrets. No, I won't call any family names.

I will admit we was all scared as hell. So damn scared, we gave our
notice soon after we started. Two giants came right over and asked the
band to go in the back office to talk about it, the same room the councilman and his wife never came back from. We walked in all bunched together real tight.

The room was dark. The only light was from a low, gooseneck lamp
on the desk, and it was shining right in our faces. Heavy, stale cigar
smoke was drifting around the light. Somebody was behind the desk,
and about five or six others was next to him all sitting quiet. Couldn't
see nobody clear. But I did feel giants standing there in the back, near
the doors.

Nobody was talking. We shivered silently for a while.

"So, what's the trouble, boys?" a deep voice said. I thought he
sounded sort of friendly.

"Ah . . . nothing, boss. Nothin' at all," Wilkins lied. "Just got another
offer."

"Ya want more money, ya got it," he snapped, banging the desk. He
wasn't friendly anymore.

"No. No. That's not it." We was still standing all tight together.

Felt like a hour before he answered. "We sure like this band, don't
we, Bruno?" That wasn't the name he used.

"Yeah, Rocco," another deep voice in the dark growled. "I sure don't
wanna see these boys leave."

My palms was sweating now. I never knew they could sweat.

"Louie, I don't think they should leave, do you?" The question was
going around the room, from shadow to shadow.

Finally, way back in the dark behind us, a raspy, bad voice answered
slowly: "Naw, *I* don't."

"No problem, man," someone in the band managed to cough out. "No
problem."

With that, the door opened quickly and we stepped back in the club fast. Before I knew it, we all up on the bandstand stomping off a number.

We had decided to stay.

So everybody hung in there for about six weeks, and one night we showed up for work and there was a padlock on the door. Just like at the Bamboo, only now we got the hell out of there fast. Didn't even peep in the door. I heard later the bulls found loads of hot furs stashed in the back and put two of them hoods in Sing Sing.

After that, the band worked some dates here and there around New York. I had some time off so I took a few music lessons from Earnest Clarke, a German that had a studio up on 86th Street. He used to teach Meredith Germer, my old Harrisburg teacher. Mr. Clarke was rated high and only taught advanced players. I always felt there was still much to learn, and I wanted to learn it.

Around the first week in July, Wilkins' band went in the Quogue Inn out at Quogue, Long Island. Was in a resort area and owned by Elliot Jamerson, a black man. He built the place with rooms in the back for a band to stay in. The pay was thirty-five dollars for a seven-day week, room and board. Alfred Pratt, a New Orleans tenor from Barbados came in to replace Spider Courance, and Eddie Carr took over for Burford.

We backed the floor show and played for dancing. Mae Barnes worked there all the time, and Mabel Scott, a classy singer, had her first job there. Sterling Grant was in also. He was a Harrisburg singer. Garland Howard—I met him when he was producing the famous "7-11" show in Columbus in 1923—produced the Quogue floor show and his wife, Mae Brown, worked in it.

The old racketeers came in often. They had most of the spending money in those days and practically supported clubs like this. People like Jack Legs Diamond was a regular customer, sitting right next to the state police that also came in regular. Jack Legs was a flashy tipper, always tossing big bills around for the entertainers. Once he gave Mabel Scott a hundred dollars to split with the band, but she "forgot." He found out and Jamerson had her ass on the next train and she never came back. In 1932 Mabel became a sensation in Paris and all over Europe.

Al Smith, the politician, often had his parties there. I saw Daddy Browning and his many friends several times. Our trade was mostly rich people.

After Labor Day, the season ended and the inn cut back on entertainment because the people all closed their homes for the winter and went south. The band got cut to a small combo for weekends only. That was like a part-time job for me, so I left and went back to New York.

Jobs wasn't much better there. Took a week with Cecil Scott at the Savoy Ballroom. Trumpet man Bill Coleman, who was going by the name of William Coleman Johnson, was with Scott along with Hoagy McFerran, alto, and Gus McClung, trumpet.

That's the way the music business was—good for a while and then maybe slow. If things got real bad, there was always the Tree of Hope to fall back on.

14. Ray Parker's Orchestra, 1930–1931

Word got around that Ray Parker was rehearsing a band to audition for the Shadowland Ballroom. Don Christian was on trumpet; Alfred Pratt from Wilkins' band, on tenor; Carl Frye, alto; Buster Eady (no relation to Bill Eady), on drums; James Drayton, a West Indian, bass; and Arnold Adams, guitar, tenor banjo, and singing.

Ray Parker played piano. He was born and raised in New York—don't think he ever worked nowhere else.

I went to see him and hit it just right. Got the job and the band got the Shadowland gig, open-ended. Paid fifty dollars a week for seven nights, damn good pay even though they always ducted three dollars to pay Parker's agent.

This was during the time some black doctors was pulling in twenty-five a week and thought they doing good.

Ray Parker had a *reading* band and that's what I liked. Like a lot of other New York musicians, if a guy wanted me for a gig but his fellows was not good readers, hell, I rather not take it. Not good for your rep to play those bands and I knew it.

The Shadowland was a white taxi dancehall located on the northwest corner of 44th and Eighth Avenue, on the second floor. It was big and had a large revolving glass ball hanging down over the center of the dance floor, all sparkling with lights bouncing off that made moving spots all over the walls.

There be always fifty or sixty pretty dance hostesses dressed in gowns sitting around. Buy a ticket and take a choice. Some patrons came in regular and had steady hostesses to dance with.

Bandleader Ray Parker had a good reading band and that's what I liked. (Photo courtesy of Frank Driggs collection.)

It was a heavy gig, plenty music and lots of room for me to get off with solos. Don Christian start a riff and I was right with him playing head arrangements. Everyone treated each other nice and that relaxed me.

The guys like to call me Peach Brandy. We go up to this after-hours spot at 142d near the Cotton Club so I could get a pint of that special peach brandy I liked now and then. Everyone knew I carried some on me, so they gave me that name. We had lots of laughs over that.

My whole life people always giving me different names. Guys used to call me any damn thing they wanted, except Barnhardt. It was not a difficult name, but they call me Bernstein—others say Heartburn. And dozens of odd names in between. Some even called me Bernhardt.

I liked the name Bernhardt because Professor Smith, a psychic I knew, advised me to change it to that. Said Sarah Bernhardt had great fame and it do the same for me. So, from 1930 on, I became Clyde Bernhardt. After a while, people started calling my mother, Mrs. Bernhardt.

Wherever there was good musicians, there was after-hours jam joints. It was almost part of the business. We quit the job about two in the morning and head for a place to cool down and play for ourselves. Li-

quor was always available. We sometimes pay as much as $5 a pint for
real New York still whiskey—good corn whiskey was popular too. The
racketeers was usually on the level when they sold their stuff. Genuine
imported rye whiskey like Golden Wedding and Silver Dollar all came
from Canada. And Mountain Cream Scotch was in big demand also. A
musician usually get that stuff for $2 or $2.50 a pint.

The bathtub gin they sold up in Harlem dives was poison—might
be turpentine, shave lotion, or antifreeze all shook up with colored
water—many drinkers went blind and died from that. Some guys
messed with beef-iron and wine they bought in the drugstore. Got sick
off that too.

You rarely saw anybody fooling around big with drugs then. The only
ones that did was money people. While some of those wild Grear guys in
1927 had drinking problems, hell, even *they* didn't know what drugs was.

This was Depression time with a lot of day workers losing jobs. Things
was hard, but not that hard for New York musicians. The Savoy was
open. The Saratoga Club, Smalls Paradise, the Lafayette Theater. And
people with money, or people that knew people with money, supported
these clubs and dancehalls.

New York always been a lucky town for me. So is Washington, D.C.
And Los Angeles, Chicago, and Pittsburgh. All good towns for someone
born under Cancer. Yes sir.

Freddie Moore, the drummer with King Oliver's band, came in the
Shadowland one night and told me Oliver was looking for a good get-off
trombone. I had a little more confidence since the year before, so I
thought I might go over and see what the man had in mind.

He was living at 208 124th Street near Seventh Avenue. The famous
brass man welcomed me in and introduced me to his wife. He was a
plain, down-to-earth person, had no superiority air about him or anything. We got along good and talked about a hour.

"Son," he said, "I liked your playing ever since I caught you at the
Bamboo. You got a nice tone and play a damn good swing solo. Lot of
guys today don't like to play no straight solo."

Told me he turned down about five trombone players in the past
month, and I was surprised because some of them was much better
then me.

I was not sure of working with Oliver but got a leave of absence from
Parker, told him I was sick, and tried a few out-of-town dates with him
in January. Worked the Pithian Hall in Washington and a big white dance
in Delaware.

When we returned to New York I met up with Jonas Walker, one of the guys Oliver rejected before me. He thought I stole the job from him and acted like he wanted to fight me. Sure was hollering mad.

Oliver had a big southwestern tour coming up, something the Frederick Brothers Booking Agency set up. He offered to pay me the same flat fifty dollars a week I was making with Parker, but there was no agent fee.

When I told Parker I was considering the offer, he said working regular with the great trumpet man was something big. If Oliver ever offered *him* a job, he said, damn if he wouldn't give up the band and grab it. Fast.

I liked Ray Parker and all the boys. Knew what I had, what I was expected to do, and that the boss liked me.

Some of the guys in the Rhythm Club said I must be crazy to hesitate, said Oliver would go down in jazz history like Duke and Fletcher and here I was still thinking it over.

I really wasn't sure I was good enough to go with Oliver but kept reminding myself of the bad mistake I made turning down Bessie Smith.

Just like Tillie Vennie, Cancer people are hard to move. It's a holdback. It held me back many times in my life.

My family finally pushed me, told me how important it was for my career, and gave me confidence when they said Oliver would not hire me if I was not right for the job.

It was the first of March 1931 that I joined Oliver for his big tour. I never regretted it.

15. *King Oliver's New Orleans Creole Jazz Band, 1931*

King Joe Oliver was a heavy man, about 250 pounds and kind of chubby, but not flabby looking, slouchy, or anything like that. He was neat and clean as a pin. Stood about just under six feet. He was fifty-four years old in 1931, and I remember I gave him a pack of Chesterfield cigarettes on his birthday and he told me how old he was. Was born in New Orleans, he said that too.

His hair was crew-cut style, kept real close. His feet was not as large as the average man his size—looked like he wore a ten at the most. Had no scars that I saw, only this one bad left eye that stuck out like a frog's and was bigger then the other. It was not noticeable unless he had his glasses off, and he made sure to keep them on almost all the time. Never heard him say he was blind in that eye, so I think he could see something out of it. Probably the reason he was not a good sight reader.

"I'm the slowest goddamned reader in my band," he would mumble in his low voice. "You guys might read faster but damn it, you better wait for me."

Oliver was a very dark man and always seemed conscious of that. "There three kinds of blacks," he once told me. "A *black*, a *lamb* black, and a *damn* black." He laughed at his joke and then added, "I'm black and I only seen two other damn people in the world blacker'n me," and then he laughed some more.

Oliver often said things like that. When he see somebody real dark he strike a match and whisper: "Who dat out dare? What dat movin'?" All that kind of stuff.

Everybody laugh and he laugh the loudest. Some New Orleanians have peculiar ways. You just have to understand them—they critical of others and very critical of themselves.

He just loved to play the dirty dozens—a kind of insulting game. The more insults tossed back and forth, the better he like it. Herman Elkins and Walter Dennis always try to dozens him back but they didn't stand a chance. He tell them something bad about their mother or sister, about sleeping with them and what they did and how they did it and what they said about it and things like that. Everybody would die laughing, but the guys always let him go. He was no contest. His dozens won every time.

And man, could he *eat*. The only person that gave him competition eating was Fats Waller. Yesssss Lord. Oliver eat a dozen fried eggs for breakfast and then say how he could eat more. He take about a pound of bacon, fried real crisp, and chew it piece by piece, then drink down maybe ten cups of coffee.

And he loved his grits and rice. Yes he did. And sweets—jam, preserves, and jelly piled high on bread and butter. Then sop everything up.

Once I saw him drink a half gallon of lemonade and twelve bottles of Coca-Cola.

"I know I'm not the smallest eater in town," he growl, "but damn it, I enjoy what little I do eat."

And the guys all laugh. "Well," they say, "we hate to see you when you hungry." Then everybody went into the dozens again.

Oliver never allowed any of us to drink on the job. He didn't either, although he smoked heavy. Sometimes we slip outside where there was a pint or quart jar of corn whiskey hidden. He was watching and sneak around back of the bus and peep in the window. "Alright," he shout, "if I catch any of you mothers drinkin' on your rest period, I'm gonna fine each of you two bucks."

He always watched us but never did catch us.

A couple boys once bought some reefers in Dallas, a whole paper bag for a quarter. That was the first time I ever seen that stuff. Never saw it out east. The guys all talking about getting a Target Cigarette wrapping machine to roll their own, but didn't know where to buy it.

"That's one thing I like about this band," Oliver said, "ain't got no goddamn big reefer smokers in it."

Told me he tried it once. "Some ol' Mexican boy sold me some for a dime. I inhaled, did every damn thing, and that shit didn't bother me no kind of way. How in hell they get their damn kicks from that?"

He always used a gold-plated horn, a Conn I think—they cost more then a brass- or silver-plated one. Back then, really big name bands wouldn't hire unless the musician had a gold-plated instrument. Man, it sure looked class.

Oliver used three mutes: a wah-wah—he was very good on a wah-wah—a cup mute, and a straight mute. I never heard any trumpet player take a wah-wah plunger and play *Sugar Blues* like he did. Sounded like he was crying and moaning—it was magnetic. The horn really talked.

I asked him once what it was saying. "Goddamn it, I was cussin' you mothers out."

He had all his teeth extracted in 1927 because of pyorrhea. Sometimes his denture plates hurt his gums after playing about a hour, and he have to stop, get off the stand, and stay alongside for a while. They had no paste in those days to hold the plates tight like they do now, but as long as they didn't bother him, his playing was not affected. He could hit a high D—never did play those high F's and G's like Louis Armstrong—the highest he go was around C and D. But he scream on a D.

I say King Oliver still played more and was more exciting then a lot of younger men in their twenties and thirties. Of course he didn't sound the same every night. He did have his off days, but so did all of us.

Sometimes he was feeling terrific. "Goddamn it, I feel *good* tonight!" And he came up on the bandstand. "I'm gonna play you all a 1923 solo." And knocked everybody out. Every time.

I always liked the way New Orleans musicians played a solo. Listen to certain riffs played by Oliver, Louis, and Kid Ory and copy after them. A little bit of this, a little bit of that, and soon it set me up with a style of my own.

King Oliver and his New Orleans Creole Jazz Band, New York, N.Y., Mar. 1931. Left to right: Clyde Bernhardt (tb/v), King Oliver (t/ldr), Ernest Myers (g/bjo), Red Elkins (t), Freddie Moore (d), Hank Duncan (p), Lionel Nepton (tuba/b), Paul Barnes (as/ss/cl), Alfred Pratt (ts), Walter Dennis (as).

Oliver had one good-sounding band on this tour. It just so happened that everybody been playing with top-quality orchestras and they all knew the latest music, and that's what the public wanted. Oliver could not afford to have musicians that did not read well.

Except him of course. "You all better not laugh at my slow readin'," he kept repeating. "If you do, I'll fire your goddamn asses."

It was every man on his own in the band, nobody to hold him up— he had to hold himself up.

Red Elkins from the old Wilkins band was on first trumpet; Joe Oliver on second; Paul "Polo" Barnes, a Creole from New Orleans, alto and clarinet; Alfred Pratt from the Parker band, tenor and clarinet; and Walter Dennis, alto and clarinet. Dennis had a weakness for the ladies, always had two or three at a time. Some even followed him as the band moved on. We called them Miss 802's because they preferred New York musicians—and we all members of local musician's union 802.

Henry "Hank" Duncan, our piano man, was a little more selective with his women. Liked only schoolteachers and professional women like that.

Ernest Wilson Myers, the guitar and arranger, was nice and quiet but had real thin lips that Oliver always teased him about. "Goddamn," he say, "your mouth so sharp it pick beans out of a bottle!"

Lionel Nepton was on tuba and string bass—he played both and carried them along with him—Freddie Moore on good New Orleans backbeat drums, and myself on trombone. His nephew Dave Nelson was not in the band but gave Oliver a lot of arrangements.

Early in the tour, Walter Dennis got sick for two months, and Herschel Evans joined in Fort Worth as third alto. Later, Nepton was replaced by the terrific bassist, Simon Marrero—another of the Marrero brothers out of New Orleans—and gave the band a booming drive. In Kansas City, a boy named D. Stewart—his lady called him Prince D. Stewart— was added on trumpet.

The Frederick Brothers Agency also sent over Tiny Taylor, a big fat boy out of Kansas City. He fronted the band and sang. Oliver never did like Taylor's attitude, and he was gone in a short while. Then he sent for Clara Eaton, a nightclub singer from New York. She was tall and thin and sounded like Ethel Waters. In fact, a lot of people, especially whites, thought she was.

The band left New York about the latter part of March on the Nevins Bus Line and went direct to Wichita. That was a trip of at least fifteen hundred miles and took us only three days through small towns, so we were damn near dead when we arrived.

We got there on a Thursday evening, I remember, and opened the following night at the Shadowland Ballroom, the same named hall I worked in New York with Parker. I knew that was a good sign.

This place was bigger then the one in New York and could take care of a big seventeen-piece band. I worked better-known halls but this was really beautiful: crystal chandeliers, expensive draperies, a long, wooden dance floor that shined like glass, polished oak trimmings, large mirrors everywhere, colored lights flashing, everything fancy. All the way, a *class A* ballroom.

I thought we looked terrific sitting up there on the stand in our salt-and-pepper gray uniforms, black shoes, plain white dress shirts, and black string ties. For formal dances we had black tuxedo suits.

The band was jumping that first night. This was *the* famous King Oliver and his New Orleans Creole Jazz Band playing a top job, and I was part of it. I took some long solos, got off some extra triple tongue passages, all that fast stuff. I was showing the King all my tricks and that I was worthy of him.

After the set, he came over and said softly, "Son, you don't have to do all that shit to impress me. You got a good swinging style and all them snakes you makin', loses the flavor. It don't mean a damn thing."

That surprised hell out of me.

He continued: "I like the way you was blowin' before, otherwise I wouldn't of took you."

I started feeling good and bad at the same time. I appreciated his advice, but here I was doing something a lot of other trombone players couldn't, and he didn't like it.

Then I remembered what my uncle told me before I left. Said Oliver was the guy paying me and to listen to the man. And if he told me to play *Shoo Georgia Rabbit*, I should damn well play it and smile. So I followed that advice.

The tour lasted over eight months for me. Wherever we played, the audiences went crazy. We had to be good, because we were playing the finest, biggest white ballrooms in the Midwest and South: The Lakeworth Casino, ten miles out of Fort Worth; The Frog Hop in St. Joseph, Missouri; a whole gang of private rooms in Kansas City and New Orleans; Spring Lake Park, Oklahoma City; and The Coliseum in Tulsa.

I remember one job we played at the Lakeworth Casino. The hall capacity was about fifteen hundred, but on the second night they had sixteen hundred packed in, and on the third there was seventeen hundred. The man had to stop selling tickets or we all been suffocated.

Oliver's was the first colored band to appear in that huge Coliseum in

Tulsa. That was really a big place—three times larger then the Roseland in New York and just as fine, if not finer. Was so modern—had amplifiers on the bandstand! Never seen microphones before. Always used the old megaphone horns in New York and couldn't understand what the hell they supposed to do. The damn things scared me, they were so loud.

King Oliver broke the ice almost everywhere he went—played where others could not. Name bands such as Bennie Moten, Jap Allen, Jesse Stone, McKinney's Cotton Pickers, George E. Lee out of Kansas City, and the Oklahoma City Blue Devils all playing good, heavy, special arrangements. But not for Oliver's audiences.

"They can't get nowhere near them big white ballrooms I play," he often laughed.

He played the songs the audiences asked for. Hot numbers like *Tiger Rag* so the guys could show off; the *St. Louis Blues, Beale Street*, and the *Memphis Blues*; waltzes and standards such as *My Wild Irish Rose, Danny Boy*, and even *'O Sole Mio*; Oliver originals like *Mule Face Blues* and *Boogie Woogie*. We also did *Lazy River, Stardust*, and other new tunes and introduced many songs just as fast as they came out. Publishers sent music to Oliver before they published it. I don't know how many numbers in his book—must have been over three hundred.

He often used Archie Bleyer arrangements and some by Will Hudson and had Ernest Myers and sometimes Paul Barnes make suggestions. And we all did plenty head arrangements. One thing made the band cook was Freddie Moore's push-drumming. Another was the strong rhythm section and the solos the men played in there. They never overplayed themselves.

Oliver knew just the right songs, just the right tempo, and just the right length to make those people get up off their behinds and fill the floor. Never forgot that he had a *dance* band.

Sometimes we did funny bits during the numbers to entertain the people. Ernest Myers had a thing where he came out dressed like a tramp in a long coat all torn and tattered. Wore a beat-up old hat falling to pieces and carried a raggety traveling bag in one hand and his guitar in the other. Man, he looked bad, just like he came out of a rag factory.

When he walk out on stage asking to join the band, we wave him away. The audience laugh. After begging and pleading for a chance, Oliver call *Tiger Rag*. Myers stomp off and play the damnedest solo you ever heard, taking hot choruses behind his back and on top of his head. The audience all cheered and wanted more. Myers was one heck of a solo man.

Freddie Moore had a bit when we did *Sing You Sinners*. Get up during the number and start to shouting and praying, like he found religion. Suddenly, he start to weave and hold his head. As he was falling over in a faint, Myers run out behind and catch him just in time. The audience would roar. One night, Myers didn't run fast enough and Freddie fell back off the bandstand, behind the drums. Oliver almost died laughing. The audience thought it was part of the act and wanted more. Cheered for five minutes.

Oliver was a smart band leader. When he worked white dances, and at least 95 percent of our jobs were white, he knew they all wanted smooth, sweet modern numbers, and that's what he usually played. Whites were not as hip to hot music then as they are today.

When we worked colored places, which was often on our Mondays off, we played a lot of blues and jazz numbers—unless a guy came up and asked us for something else. Some black places did have whites, but they were not allowed to dance. Called them the "white inspectors." They just sat and watched.

I respected King Oliver and learned a lot from him. He usually called me "son" and I called him "pop"—spoke to him just like I did my Papa and my family. I always found time to talk to him and I think he liked that. Regardless of his nasty words, I respected him.

He was always pushing me to have more confidence in myself. "Son," he say, "you play much better trombone then you give yourself credit for. I can get almost any damn motherjiver for the price I pay you. If you couldn't play, you sure in hell wouldn't be here now."

Like the time he heard me singing *St. Louis Blues* on the bus. We just came from a little restaurant where I drank two coffee cups full of moonshine—cost about fifty cents. I was feeling real good, started fooling around, and broke out in song. I never sung on the bus before.

"Who the hell's singing back there?" Oliver said, turning around.

"That's old Clyde," somebody answered.

"I thought it was that big, black son-of-a-bitch that sings with Moten's band," he mumbled. He meant Jimmy Rushing, of course. "Goddamn it, you hadda get drunk so everybody know you can sing."

Well, I been hearing blues all my life. Always sang around the house as a kid, trying to make like Mamie Smith, Mary Stafford, Ma Rainey, and some of the others. But I never took it seriously.

"I'm gonna put that number in tonight, and you sing," he said.

"Aw pop, I can't sing nothin'."

"Goddamn," he shouted through the bus, "if you can't, I'll whip the livin' hell outta you."

I was not sure he was kidding.

That night we played the Lakeworth Casino. I thought he forgot all about it, but late in the set he called *St. Louis Blues*. It always been a instrumental number with him.

"Now get up there and holler them damn blues," he said, turning to me.

I was not about to argue with the boss. Like my uncle told me, do what the man say.

I'm not bragging, but I broke up the house. After the set, pop came over and poked me in the chest with his stubby finger. "Keep at those damn blues, son, and someday you make a bigger name singin' then playin'."

I knew he meant that because he was outspoken and wasn't the kind of person to tell me something just to make me feel good. After that, I always sang on the show and he gave me a ten-dollar raise.

Many people said he was hard to get along with, that he was evil a lot of times. Well, he had his habits, but I understood them. Never did look for him to be perfect—I'm not perfect myself. I was taught to have respect for older people, so he never had no trouble with me.

He didn't take to any b.s.ing on the bandstand while we worked—wanted us to always pay attention. When he call a number and have to repeat the same damn thing two or three times over, he got hot.

Like some guy be up there talking worse then a woman—ya-ya-ya-ya-ya—paying him no mind. Suddenly, the guy wake up. "What'cha gonna play? What'cha gonna play?" he ask, looking around fast.

And Oliver lose control. "Goddamn it, stop runnin' your fat mouth off and you'd know what in hell I'm gonna play." Say that loud, right on the bandstand. Only he was rougher with his words.

See, a lot of musicians, like many other people, they *try* you. Like when guys come walking up ten minutes after nine and we supposed to hit it at nine, he call a meeting.

'You gonna do shit like that, you in the wrong band." And if the guy come late again, he get fired.

No, Oliver wasn't tough. He was right.

I remember one time down in Louisiana, he really lost his temper bad. It was because we always had young gals come running up to us, trying to make time. Some young toughs at this black dance be jealous and tried to start trouble. This one guy run up and knocked down a music stand. Oliver got real hot and turned to the white policeman the house hired.

"That goddamn nigger there knocked over my music stand," he

shouted at the cop. "If the black bastard comes back up here again, I'm gonna blow his motherjiving head off."

Then he pulled out his black .38 special he always carried and waved it around. Everybody froze.

"That's alright, King," the cop said, "you don't have to bother none. Leave him to me."

With that, he took out his nightstick and beat the living tar out of that black guy. Chased him out in the hallway and beat him some more and told him if he ever came back, he kill him himself.

"Everything was goin' good," the policeman said as he wiped off his stick, "and here come this nigger starting trouble, chasing out the girls, pickin' on you boys. I fixed him good, King. Go on with the show."

We run into a lot of things like that in the Deep South but never had trouble at any time at any of the white ballrooms we worked.

Pop never shot anybody as far as I know. Maybe at some old birds flying while we rode along in the bus, but he missed all of them.

We traveled in a little private bus. Only held about twenty-four people, but it was more then enough for us. Roy Johnson, a white fellow, was the bus driver and also did some road managing.

As we rode along we usually be drinking our corn, talking loud, jiving or playing our wind-up record players in the back. Oliver called it the "Red Light District" back there.

On the outside of the bus was a big sign that read: "King Oliver and His New Orleans Creole Jazz Band." When he worked New York it was called The Harlem Syncopators, but he used the other for this tour.

Every place we went they put up sign posters with our picture on them and had advertisements in local newspapers.

We usually opened a dance by playing live on the radio—they put a wire in those big halls and we broadcast all over. The program took a half hour and was transcribed. Then, about two weeks later, they put the transcription on the air to promote our return.

We did that in Tulsa, Fort Worth, St. Joe, and other places. Sometimes they put on a radio show we did somewhere else, but made sure we didn't play the same numbers at the dance. We did a lot of that.

I never made a studio recording with King Oliver, although he wanted me to. That was before the tour, in February of 1931—to be second trombone with Jimmy Archey—but I didn't take the date. So he got Benny Morton for the session. A lot of people tell me my style is similar to his.

Morton had a good solo on *I'm Crazy 'bout My Baby* and after I got with the band, Oliver wanted me to play that exact solo just like the record. So I copied it note-for-note, and to this day people ask if that is me on the record. But it's not.

History books say Oliver's last record session took place on April 15, 1931, in New York. Well, I heard that lie before. I was with Oliver in Wichita, Kansas, on that date, and pop did not leave us at any time to go any place. The recording was much earlier. I say sometime before I joined the band, maybe even 1930.

His last recording was the one I was suppose to be on but wasn't.

Oliver was very critical about a lot of musicians. I heard him say that Fess Williams and Wilbur Sweatman, two highly rated jazzmen, sounded like a bunch of chickens.

"Hell," he told me, "if you put 'em both in a damn bag, take 'em out there in the ocean, and throw 'em in the water—I don't know which one come up first."

He also did not like J. C. Higginbotham or Coleman Hawkins. Put Walter Wheeler and Castor McCord over Hawkins, and I did not think either of them blow as much as Hawkins. But to Oliver, they did.

He always praised Fletcher Henderson but said someday young Duke Ellington get ahead of Henderson, that Ellington's band was built a lot on the New Orleans style. He was crazy about Bob Holmes, but I never saw the day Bob Holmes play as much as Charlie Holmes, and Charlie couldn't get a job with Oliver. I think Bob was from Jacksonville, Florida, and Charlie from Boston. They were not related.

I often heard him say he liked Buddy Bolden. And that Keppard played more trumpet then he himself ever did, but everybody called Oliver the King. Said Keppard and him used to have horn battles back in New Orleans, sometimes for hours, and nobody ever gave up.

He also liked Jimmy Archey and Big Charlie Green and idolized Louis Metcalf, I know that. But he did not like Johnny Dunn. He had his strong likes and dislikes.

We had long, relaxed conversations during that tour. Many times while sitting out on the cool front porch at the Johnson Hotel down in Fort Worth, we talked about just everything. Like the time the Oklahoma musician's union tried to keep us from returning to Tulsa. Or how worried we all were at that fancy white party in Vernon, Texas, just after the Klan lynched a colored man in the next town. I spoke to him about my family. He remembered his early times in New Orleans. And in Chicago. And New York.

Told me about the time in 1927 when Irving Mills wanted to put him in the Cotton Club.

"No damn people gonna build a band around me and I just front it."

There was few things we did not talk and laugh about. It was like talking to Papa again.

One time late at night he heard a noise inside the hotel.

"Who that?" he asked.

"I didn't hear nothin'," I said.

"Somebody go in your room."

I looked around in the hallway, but nobody was there. The next night we both heard the same noise.

"Nobody gonna play tricks on this old nigger," he grumbled as he went back to get his big .38. But he couldn't find anybody either.

When I told him about all the hants I known in my life, he only laughed. Later, when I asked the maid about the noises, she whispered about how Mrs. Johnson, some seven years before, shot her young lover and that he died right in front of that very room and they been hearing noises ever since. Oliver laughed again when I told him. But I didn't.

I can't call all the things we spoke about, but I found him to be very open with me although sort of shy around other people. I think he had a inferiority complex.

"Goddamn," he say, "they only invite this black, ugly nigger to parties 'cause they know they get the whole damn band to come."

It was in Fort Worth that I met Barbara. After work, the band always went to eat at this colored after-hours restaurant. I usually had the house special—smothered steak with a couple vegetables. Cost all of thirty-five cents, including coffee and rolls, but the man let us have it cheaper because he drew a better class of business with us in there.

Barbara followed me back to the restaurant from the Lakeworth Casino.

"Man," Oliver said, "she one good looking broad."

And I thought so too. Bobby, as I called her, lived in town and worked as a hairdresser in white beauty parlors. Had two years of college, and a young colored girl with that kind of schooling then was somebody. She could of been a teacher but didn't have the patience.

Bobby said she liked to be around musicians, liked our band, and especially liked me. I thought she was a hell of a gal, gave her my mother's address, and they wrote long letters to each other. And to my sister, too.

Oliver kept getting some repeat bookings around Fort Worth so I got to know her pretty good.

When we got married in a civil ceremony about a month later, I knew I had myself a special woman. But the band kept moving around so I didn't get to see her as often as I wanted.

It was that western weather that finally caused me to quit Oliver. Hot in the summer and so very cold in the winter. In October, when pop told me he was extending the tour through the year, I wanted no part of it. I gave him my two-weeks' notice.

"Now, don't be so damn sure," he said, looking very serious. "Back when I played the riverboats, if a good musician wanted to quit, he goddamn have to slip off the job."

I asked why.

"'Cause the old boat captain liable to frame you, say you stole somethin', then make you sign a paper to keep working. If not, he put you in jail."

I looked at him.

"But I don't think I do that to you," he laughed.

Four weeks later, November 10, 1931, after the last set in Topeka, I came off the bandstand and extended my hand.

"Well, son," he said, "I damn well hate to see you go."

I thanked him, gripped his hand tightly, and looked straight in his face. He seemed sort of tired. I really hated to leave.

"If those motherjammers in New York don't treat you right," he mumbled, "let me know and I'll send you a ticket to come back."

I hesitated a little, then nodded, turned, and walked quickly away.

Never saw pop again.

16. *Marion Hardy and His Alabamians, 1931–1932*

I kept writing to Bobby to come with me to New York, but she wrote back she meet me there later. Had some business to take care of, she said. So Freddie Moore and I took a bus out for New York.

On the way, we stopped over in Harrisburg for a couple days. Tillie Vennie was working a dance at the Odd Fellows Hall the next night. She could not pay what Oliver did, but we took the job because she needed us.

Shortly after I arrived in New York, Bobby came up. I was staying with my people but got her a nice place in a uptown rooming house.

I was happy we were back together again.

Wasn't but a short time she started running her mouth off. "Clyde," she said, "why don't you stay here in town regular and get yourself a day job?"

That's the way with some women. Get you in a come-on, say they like you as you are, and after they get you, try to make changes.

"No, Bobby," I said, "I'm a musician. That's what I wanna do. Better get used to it."

Then lightly and politely she smiled. "Well, I guess I'm the luckiest girl in the whole world."

"Why's that, Bobby?"

"Because no other girl has two good husbands like I got."

I stood for a while and looked at her. I thought she was joking, but she wasn't. When I finally realized what she said, I knew I been played for a sucker. I felt so very hurt knowing she lied to me, lied to the judge that married us, made a damn fool out of me. I was so ashamed that I never, ever, let my people know I was suppose to be married. Not even my mother.

Deep down I really liked Bobby and couldn't just put her down and walk out. So I came and went whenever I was in town but most of the time I didn't know where the hell she was or what she was doing. We drifted apart in later years, and I heard she died in California in 1944.

I had many girl friends since, some very compatible and some not worth two dead flies. But I never thought of marriage again. Never.

Just before Thanksgiving of 1931 I went over to the New Amsterdam Club at 107 West 130th Street where Marion Hardy was trying out different trombone players.

Hardy had a organized band he called his Alabamians. It had good readers that could play any rehearsed arrangement, had style and appearance. The band featured novelty, show, and entertaining songs as well as jazz numbers and special concertized pieces.

Hardy used some hard arrangements by Benny Carter, the same ones Fletcher Henderson and Don Redman used. Also had a difficult Bob Sylvester arrangement on *Rhapsody in Blue* with about five manuscript sheets full of crescendos and decrescendos, different tempos, and all that stuff.

This was new to me and I don't mind saying, it stopped me cold. Hardy laughed, told me not to worry and go over it a few more times to get it under my fingers.

Told me it stopped even the sharks. He meant trombones like J. C. Higginbotham, Lawrence Brown, Jack Teagarden. They were the sharks. Never considered myself one, just a regular player that could read, fake some, play a good solo—take care of business.

Hardy once gave me a little background on the Alabamians. Said when they backed Blanche Calloway at Chicago's Sunset Club, it was known as Lawrence Harrison's Alabamians. He was the son of Richard B. Harrison, the great Negro stage actor in "The Green Pastures." Blanche asked the club owner to give her brother Cab a chance—he was a strong singer, light-skinned, made a nice appearance, and had good hair. When Cab got in there, those people went crazy over him. So they fired the regular singer, Roscoe Simmons. I heard Simmons got hot and jumped Cab and gave him a hell of a fight.

After Cab got in, he began directing certain band numbers, clowning around, jumping and shouting while he sang. Soon it was Lawrence Harrison that got fired, and Cab took over. Marion Hardy—he was a sideman then—became the real leader because he was the coolest one there, very quiet and conservative. But Cab was the front.

I remember seeing them in the Savoy Ballroom in 1929 billed as Marion Hardy and His Alabamians, featuring Cab Calloway. They were advertised as having a Battle of Music with Lockwood Lewis and the Missourians. Lewis was a very popular entertainer at the Savoy, but nobody knew nothing about Cab.

We all went up to see Lockwood teach the new boy a lesson, but it was the other way around. Cab had salesmanship that was out of this world—got up in his slick white tux, waved his long baton, tossed his head, let his hair fly around—and the audience just went wild. When he sang *Minnie the Moocher*, his jiving, smooth walking, and shouting just *upset* the Savoy.

The Alabamians won the battle that day, and it was the making of Cab Calloway. Cab left the band after that and Sonny Nichols took over fronting. Later, Cab got hired by the Missourians and Lockwood Lewis got let go.

When I got with the Alabamians late in November, Jack Butler was on first trumpet—he was known as Jacques after he went to Paris; Walter "Jock" Bennett was on second with some singing; Artie Starks, from Fort Worth, first alto and clarinet; and Warner Seals, tenor and some singing. Seals was always clowning around, carrying on, talking foolish at times, making the guys laugh. But he was a nice guy.

Ralph Anderson, a good reader, was on piano; Charles "Fat Man" Turner, who later opened his own Fatman's Club in Harlem, bass fiddle; Arnold Boling, drums; Leslie Quarles from Texas but looked Mexican, on guitar; and Sonny Nichols, front man and singer. Marion Hardy was third alto—he could read anything but was not a good soloist.

Man, that was one entertaining band. We used to do a number, *Oh*

Lord, Oh Lord, Let Me See the Light Again. All the light got put off and Sonny Nichols sang under a single spot. The band had on radium gloves, and we chanted in the dark while our radium-lit hands moved in circles and back and forth in rhythm. It was a heck of a specialty for a theater and always went over big.

When we worked the Lafayette, we did a funny bit where Hardy came out dressed as a handkerchief-head mammy and Seals the old pappy. One of the guys was suppose to be their daughter in a tight, short skirt and blonde wig. The band rolled its pants up and were the "children."

I think the song was called *Lackawanna*. We all chorus, "Hello ma, hello pa," and Hardy and Seals answer in song. Then we chorus questions about Lackawanna and they answer again. The "daughter" kept wiggling and smiling all the time. Finally, "pa" ask her if she been good in Lackawanna.

Taking out a fat roll of bills she squealed, "Pappy, with a roll like this, you gotta be *damn* good in Lackawanna."

We did that specialty in New York when we worked six weeks in the Florentine Grill of the Park Central Hotel and got loud laughs. Noble Sissle picked the Alabamians to replace his band there, and we broadcast live coast-to-coast over WEAF in the evenings and WMCA at night.

For a little over a month we worked the Arcadia Ballroom, Broadway and 53d, right across from the Broadway Theater. Then the Renaissance Casino, alternating with Vernon Andrade's orchestra. We also played the Savoy Ballroom and the Lafayette, where we knocked them out with our *Rhapsody in Blue* arrangement.

Some time in the spring of 1932, Walter Bennett and I went down to the Wurlitzer Music Store on West 42d Street, off Sixth Avenue. They had a recording booth in the back and I thought I might make a demonstration record to see how my voice sounded. Bennett also played damn good piano and backed me for the session. The studio and a two-sided disc cost me about three bucks.

I did two numbers: *Some of These Days*, that I sang with Oliver's band, and *Waitin' for the Evenin' Mail*, a hot blues Sissle and Blake used to do.

The record sounded better then I thought it would. I took the demo home and played it over and over on my record player, then tossed it in the drawer.

The most unusual gig I ever had took place in May of 1932. Marion Hardy got some of the boys together one day.

"Fellows," he smiled. "I got a great job lined up next week." I always liked great jobs. "We booked for the 'Lucky Strike Cigarette' radio show!" That did sound good. "But," he added, "we not broadcasting from the studio, we gonna be up in a airplane flying around over New York."

Now, that scared the living hell out of me. Yes, sir. I never been in a airplane and told him he would definitely, *definitely* have to get someone else in my place. No way would I go up.

When my mother heard I turned the job down and it paid thirty-two dollars, I thought she take a switch to me again.

"You should be ashamed of yourself," she said. "People all scuffling for jobs, men in bread lines, and my boy turning down work."

"But Mama," I said, "I could die on this job."

"Nobody dying until He want you to die—then nothing you can do about it."

So I went up in this little old single prop airplane that didn't hold but twenty-six people. Hardy had a few other guys up there that day. I saw Doc Cheatham on trumpet; Craig Watson, alto; Leroy Harris, another alto; and Mack Walker on bass. The rest was the regular guys: Hardy, Jack Butler, Warner Seals, Arnold Boling, Leslie Quarles, and Ralph Anderson on a little piano.

I was nervous as hell and everybody else seemed to be shaking and sweating, too. We went up so high I was afraid to look outside. Then the light plane hit a air pocket and drop two hundred feet down and then shoot right back up again, maybe three hundred feet. Oh Lord, I knew it was my time for sure.

A space been cleared, and we sat on folding chairs around a single standing floor mike while the engineers gave us instructions. I tried to play the parts but my tongue kept getting in the way.

After about two hours of sweating and struggling, I was happy to see the plane landing—but the man said it was all just a balance test and the live show was in a few hours.

I had to do it all over again.

After a nervous wait, we took off from Newark Airport and circled over Manhattan. I peeped out the window this time and saw what looked like little toy trains going back and forth in the dark. The plane went up higher and higher and then the announcer came on.

"Ladies and Gentlemen," he said in the floor mike, "we are broadcasting high over the Metropolitan area of downtown New York. Marion Hardy and his Alabamians are up here circling twenty thousand feet in the air, and all the boys seem to be smiling and nobody's scared."

He was telling all those sweet lies about us. I been scared for a week and when he said that, I felt worse.

"This," he continued, "is the first coast-to-coast remote ever broadcast from an airplane to be heard by radio all over the great United States, from Canada to Florida, from New York to sunny California."

I heard later some foreign countries picked up the program, also.

We played up there in the dark sky for about two hours, alternating with Rudy Vallee and his Connecticut Yankees that was safely down in the studio. The announcer also gave the names of everyone in the band.

The next day all the musicians in Harlem and all my friends said they heard the show, and everybody kept talking about it for weeks. I was glad I played that broadcast *after* I played it.

We also worked many one-nighters out of town, barnstorming in a private bus. Played the college circuit like Yale University in New Haven, Connecticut, and Keystone College in Pennsylvania. There was a good two-month stay at the Fawn Barn Club at Lake Placid, New York, late in 1932, another class A place, catering only to rich white people, the very wealthy. We got fifty-five dollars a week there, plus room and board.

By this time Hardy had replaced drummer Arnold Boling, who left to go with Lucky Millinder, with Tiny Bradshaw and featured him on vocals; Craig Watson, a good alto and clarinet, took over regular for Starks; Don Christian replaced Jack Butler; John Swan for Walter Bennett; and a good bass player, Olin Aderhold, came in for Charley Turner.

The Alabamians was one of the many bands then that carried a state or city name. And like so many others—none of us was from Alabama.

Once, when we played a private dance in York, Pennsylvania, this white man walks up to the bandstand—had Alabama written all over him. Spoke very slowly.

"Where . . . yawl . . . from?" he drawled.

"We booked out of New York, but the band organized in Chicago," Hardy said politely.

"Yawl one of them Yankee bands?"

"We play all over the South," he lied.

"How many of yawl in here from Alabama?" Nobody answered. "I said, how many of yawl in here from Alabama?" We weren't about to say anything. "Yawl got the name Alabamians and I want to know who they are!"

By now we were scared to say no, and scared to say yes. The man was getting angry. He pulls out this fat roll of big bills and holds it up.

"Whoever here from Alabama gonna get ten dollars," he shouted.

Everyone raised his hand. Somebody raised both hands.

"I don't know why," he said as he passed the money among us, "so many damn colored boys ashamed to admit they all from the South. Just give 'em some money and they fess up fast."

I stayed with the band for over a year. Hardy was a wonderful guy, just like a big brother and very friendly. He was stocky built and fat, a brownskin man born in St. Louis, Missouri. Told me when he was a teenager, he was in Mexico fighting Pancho Villa.

When the band laid off, I played some pickup one-nighters with Sid Watson, Milton Cole, Alfonzo Steele, and even Cecil Scott when he had some work.

One time, Ellsworth Reynolds had this black band on a white theater show in New York and needed a fill-in. The band all dressed to look like Arabs, and when I went backstage to audition, the first thing he did was look me close in the face. Up and down.

"Sorry," he said, "you take too long to lighten up."

I didn't get the job.

17. Billy Fowler and His Society Orchestra, 1932–1933

Billy Fowler was a terrific alto and clarinet player and a handsome-looking guy in front of a band. As far as complexion was concerned, he was so light many whites used to ask if he was Jewish and thought he was just passing for colored. But I only went by what he said, and he said he was black.

I first saw Fowler when he came through Harrisburg in '26 working in Mary Strain's package show.

I joined him in September of 1932 after he was in France about three years and came back to form this new group. He usually had about twelve to fifteen men and billed as a society orchestra. Can't call everybody, but Fowler was on reeds. Jack Butler, Cliff Bryant (in later years he dropped the *t*), and Gus Aiken was all on trumpet. Butler also did some singing.

Leslie Carr, from Louisville, Kentucky, took first alto and vocals—he used to copy his singing after Russ Columbo; Herbert Johnson was tenor; Lionel Nepton from Oliver's band, string bass; and Egbert Victor—we called him Sharkey—on piano. Man, he was a shark—could play a whole lot of piano. Wherever he played, people sure knew he was there.

There was another boy by the name of Blunt that played tenor. Can't call his first name. Drummer Herb Cowens, who I worked with in 1928, did specialty songs—especially a funny imitation of the famous black

Bandleader Billy Fowler was a damn good director and could bring a band through most any type of show. (Photo courtesy of Frank Driggs collection.)

pantomimist, Johnny Hudgins. Clarence Holiday, Billie Holiday's father, came in on guitar later.

For a time, Fowler backed Fats Waller at four different ballrooms in New York's Astor Hotel and on other jobs until Fats formed his own band. We be billed as Fats Waller and band under the direction of Billy Fowler.

Even though this was still Prohibition time, Fats never had to worry about drinks when we worked downtown. Always a big table in the bandroom lined up with all kinds of Canadian whiskey, scotch, gin, everything. Don't know where it came from, but it was always there.

Fowler was a damn good director and could bring a band through most any type of show. Once we were rehearsing in the upstairs hall next to the Lafayette when the famous Maceo Thomas, of Chilton and Thomas, walked in. He was all excited. Said our music caught his ear as he passed by and wanted us for his first Lafayette date on February 18 next. Benny Carter's band been booked, but Thomas let them go.

We often went downtown to work good-paying jobs in those private mansions on Fifth Avenue and also Park Avenue. We arrive in tuxedos and set up in the parlor. The guests wore the latest-styled fashions all the magazines wrote about.

The homes was decorated expensively, and there was always servants around to keep things going, serving the finest delicacies and mixed drinks. Some of those wealthy families was Irish, some Jewish and Italian.

We played plenty of hot music, more then we would at a hotel dance where people often just sat and ate. We played what they wanted, and Leslie Carr maybe sing something like *When Irish Eyes Are Smiling* or we play *'O Sole Mio* to make them happy. Those fancy socials was something else again—nothing but the best.

There might of been a depression going on, but it was going on some-place else.

Fowler was a good guy to work for, but he had a sweet line of jive that sometimes got too slick. Like the time we auditioned in some down-town place. Nobody was there, but he told us some big shot white man was listening to us on a wire in a hotel room across the street. We played about six numbers, then Fowler went out, and when he came back, said we didn't get the job. Wasn't but a few weeks later I heard our numbers playing on this radio show.

See, we all dumb, didn't know we made a transcription that was put in a commercial. Of course, the only guy got paid for the records was Billy Fowler. He was a slicker, not as slippery as Charlie Grear, but he had his habits.

Advertisement for Billy Fowler's orchestra at the Lafayette Theater, New York City, for the week of Feb. 18, 1933.

I loved my music so much I often worked jobs on my night off. One was in the spring of 1933 when I went up to the Cotton Club to take Henry "Red" Hicks' place in the Mills Blue Rhythm Band. Red been working a seven-nights-a-week schedule, and his lip fell out.

It was the only time I ever played the famous club. Ethel Waters was appearing in her "Stormy Weather Revue" and just wowed the audience. Mae Diggs, a Creole from New Orleans, was suppose to sing, but Ethel didn't allow her, so she did a dance routine and talked her music. Pete Peaches and Duke was the class-act dancers on the show, and the great precision dancers, the Cotton Club Boys, was also on the bill. Winnie Johnson and Lena Horne was some of the show-girl models— they just walked the stage looking beautiful in their slim, flashy gowns. Lena wasn't but sixteen.

Fowler often worked split weeks in RKO theaters in New York and New Jersey, playing behind vaudeville acts like Moms Mabley and Amanda Randolph. We played off and on in white theaters in Trenton, Asbury Park, Engelwood, Teaneck, and through New Jersey until April when Fowler decided to disband and move to Akron, Ohio. I heard he became a town alderman.

I gigged around New York for a few months, taking some one-night pickup work with Cass Carr, Earle "Nappy" Howard, and Edgar Dowell.

And I did my share of house-rent parties, too.

Rent parties, chitlin' struts, or breakdowns as some called them, was popular in Harlem and other places where times was hard.

The landladies pass the word around, sometimes even print a little card to let everybody know a food party was going on at a certain apartment, maybe a walk-up or brownstone. A couple tables and chairs be set up in the front room and everybody came from all over to get at the great Southern food just waiting to be tasted. Was as good as any restaurant in Harlem. People paid for what they ate and drank, and that went to help pay the rent and other expenses.

Those women were mostly old Southerners that was used to serving large families. They cook chitlin's, blackeyed peas, rice, candied sweet potatoes, boiled pigs feet, barbecued spare ribs, sauerkraut, and pigs' knuckles—fresh or smoked—turnip or collard greens, and cornbread. And plenty of bootleg whiskey, hard-cutting corn, home brew, and root beer.

They charged fifty cents a huge meal, and the landlady still made a profit. In those days, she could go out and buy pigs' feet for five cents a pound, and spare ribs three pounds for twenty-five cents. You could do a lot with your money in the early thirties. If you had any.

People didn't go to rent parties unless they brought their appetite with them. Some ate as much as three of those fifty-cent orders. Oh Lord, could they pack it in.

Most of the time they had dancing also. Musicians came over or they got hired. Never over four pieces—a piano, sax, trombone, and drums, and if they put in a trumpet, it was muted. The job didn't pay a hell of a lot, maybe five dollars for the night and all we could eat and drink.

Sometimes the party start about eight at night—go right through to the next morning. It was always crowded. People wait on line until one came out, so the next could get in. The lines go all the way downstairs and spill out in the street.

Upstairs, everybody was squeezing around, eating, drinking, dancing between tables, through the rooms, in the kitchen. I rarely saw any fights. Oh, some of them old notoriety women with a couple drinks in them let their hair down and raise all hell. Or maybe a guy be feeling happy, jump up on the table, and mess up all the food.

Many white gals out of the big downtown shows always came in. So did some of them Park Avenue swells. Taxi cabs pulling up, some limousines. Many black servants that knew what was happening uptown might bring in seven or eight of their white bosses.

But those parties was illegal, and if you didn't slip the cop on the beat his twenty to look the other way, he come and raid the place. Then you saw all those dignitaries in tails and top hats, their ladies in evening gowns with diamonds and furs being loaded in the old patrol wagon and taken away.

We just minded our business. But it was always good for a laugh.

18. Ira Coffey and His Walkathonians, 1933–1934

Walter E. Tebbett produced a walkathon that was a popular kind of presentation during the tough Depression years. Was like a dance marathon, only the contestants walked around and around on a circular track until everybody fell out except the last couple. Then they got a prize.

Tebbett went from city to city and used only locals for his walkathon. It was great fun and entertainment for the many people that needed smiles so badly.

Ira Coffey had a little six-piece group and worked the walkathon exclusively—was Tebbett's right-hand man. On the recommendation of Marion Hardy, Coffey hired me, and we all took off for Atlantic City, New Jersey.

Coffey was no heck of a jazz pianist but could play behind a singer. Edgar Battle was on trumpet and did some singing—we called him Pudding Head, I don't know why. Norman Mason was alto and Edmund Duff, a light-skinned boy out of Chicago, was tenor and Red Saunders, drums.

The walkathon opened at the Convention Hall on July 4, 1933. On the first day, the union delegate came in and gave Tebbett a bad time. Didn't want no black band in Convention Hall, he said. The union was all-white, the management was white, the production was white, and the walkers didn't take to blacks walking alongside of them, either. So I was not surprised.

But Tebbett was allowed to keep Coffey because he was the musical director and knew the cues. We all got our two-weeks' lay-off notice that first day, and white musicians took over under Coffey. Some whites wouldn't work with him, so they got others that would.

So I came back to New York and did pickup weekends with Milton Cole, a good pianist. Sid Stratton was well-known in the Jersey area, and we also did some club work together. I took whatever I could, never had no problems making a week's salary.

During that time I also got a week with the Whitman sisters at the Lafayette. New York local 802 required the sisters to hire four extra musicians, and Mae was glad I contacted her for the job.

The Whitmans was still a top attraction. Troy Snapp was there leading the band as was Leslie Towles on drums. George Hunt, the trombone player—we called him Rabbit—said he got his lip vibrato from me when I was with the show in Kansas City back in '29. Said he practiced damn hard to get the style down. That made me feel good knowing I influenced somebody. He later went with Count Basie.

One of the top headliners on the show that week was Princess White. She been with them for a couple years. The last time I saw the lady was in 1920 when I delivered telegrams to her at the Brooks Dreamland Theater in Badin.

She didn't remember me at first, especially since I was small for my age as a boy. But after I told her it was me, I got grabbed and hugged. Just about squeezed to death.

"This old boy," she said to her husband, "used to be one of my children when he was growing up. I knew him as a little snot-nose rascal," she laughed, "and here he is playing in the show band."

Princess White was still a very attractive woman, about fifty-two years of age, but easily passed for thirty. She was a true legend in black show business, played in New York before I was born, and worked internationally before that. In 1933 she was still performing like hell, doing lead-offs and solo spots of three numbers in a row.

Her feature with the Whitmans was *Stormy Weather*, and every time I looked out in the audience, Ethel Waters be sitting right up there in the front box seat.

Princess was one of the greatest jazz, blues, and popular singers I ever heard, and I heard most of them.

Early in October, when Coffey's Atlantic City job finished, Tebbett opened another walkathon at the Airport Inn in Camden, New Jersey. All the guys came back except Red Saunders, and he was replaced by Harry Dial. Coffey also didn't like Pudding Head—his attitude was bad, so he later sent to Milwaukee for Joe Thomas.

The Airport Inn was actually a big hangar at Central Airport with a large track going around inside on the ground floor. A bunch of local youngsters, maybe seventy or eighty of them with numbers pasted on their back walk as partners around the track and with only short rest periods try not to fall out so they might win the hundred-dollar first prize. And in those days, that was some money.

Everybody started out fast and kept at it twenty-four hours a day, day after day, week after week. But soon their legs got weak and gave out. They stagger about trying to fight against the pain, sleepiness, and all that, bump into people, fall down unconscious. Their partners try to pull them up, drag them a while.

Then guys ran out with stretchers and carry them back to the dressing room where the doctors were—and nurses too—but they were finished. Others stronger kept going, sometimes for a month or two months, even longer. These were all young kids, nobody over thirty.

The audience paid admission to come and watch and have a good time. The bleachers always packed with people cheering their favorites, betting on who fall out first or who would not, and they laugh and scream. The whole family be there, kids and all. Eat lunch and supper right in their seats—spend all day, maybe all night too—while the walkers kept walking around and around. Even local newspapers reported what was happening, just like a race report.

Sometimes people not walking come out and pose for pictures. Once, during the walkathon, they had a full-dress formal wedding with flowers, flower girls, bridesmaids and all. A big event. Another time, everybody got dressed up in Halloween costumes. Even the band. And all the time the walkers kept on walking.

Ira Coffey and his Walkathonians, Camden, N.J., 1933. Left to right: Clyde Bernhardt (tb), Harry Dial (d), Norman Mason (as), Ira Coffey (p/ldr), Edmund Duff (ts), Edgar Battle (t).

The band sat up in the back and entertained the audience. We got forty-five dollars a week sideman pay and worked from 2:30 to 5 in the afternoon and from 8 to 11:30 at night.

They usually had about three regular masters of ceremony on the show to keep the fun going. Earl Fagan and Johnny Cahill was two. But the top M.C. was young Red Skelton, who was only twenty at the time. Oh man, could he put on a show. Make funny announcements, joke and clown around with the audience, talk to the walkers, fool with the band.

I remember one time he came out dressed in evening tails, starched white shirt, white tie, top hat, and carrying a long baton. Supposed to be a concert maestro billed as the "Mad Genius."

Our little band struck up *Poet and Peasant Overture* and Red led us with great flourishes. Then, gradually he started making mistakes—changing tempo, misdirecting, getting confused. Soon he was tripping over chairs, knocking down music stands. His hat kept falling off, and he chase it around while leading the band with his other hand. The people all hysterical laughing, rolling out of their seats.

After a fast and furious finale—his hat lost, coat torn, tails hanging—he take a low bow and one of the guys in the band blow this rubber "bronx raspberry" toy real loud just as he bent over. The audience fell out screaming, kept laughing long after he left the stage.

I laugh right now, just thinking of it.

The walkathon in Camden lasted almost three months until everybody fell out but one pair. The show closed January 14 and went on to Atlanta, Georgia, but without me. I decided to stay in New York.

Started getting good offers from Charlie Johnson's Smalls Paradise orchestra and Luis Russell's Saratoga Club orchestra. Kaiser Marshall's Connie's Inn orchestra wanted me and so did Vernon Andrade and his Renaissance Casino orchestra.

With so many bands after me, I felt I was now accepted as part of the New York dance-band scene.

19. Vernon Andrade and His Society Orchestra, 1934–1937

I heard a lot about Vernon Andrade. Had a well-respected, established band. Played one of the best location jobs in New York, but so many musicians said he was hard to please. Very strict, with mean, hateful ways. I just knew he wouldn't hire me to play in his orchestra and was thinking of taking Luis Russell's offer.

George Wilson was filling with Andrade at the Renaissance Casino until a regular trombone was hired, told me Andrade tried out four different trombones and didn't like any of them.

"Clyde," he said, "you play the straight, sweet solos with that singing tone he's looking for. Pays the best in Harlem—give it a shot, man."

So I put on my best light-brown double-breasted suit with matching tan suede shoes and went up to the Renaissance to see him. I knew he liked his musicians to be well dressed.

The Renaissance Casino is at 150 West 138th Street, on the corner of Seventh Avenue. Used to have a long, tall sign sticking out from the red brick building. There was a bar inside, and the large dance floor had this reflecting glass ball hanging right down over the middle. The place was the most famous ballroom in Harlem, at one time more popular for big-name society dances then the Savoy.

Bob Douglas was the manager of the Renny. He's the one that had the basketball team called the Renaissance. Was a great black team long before the Globetrotters became known. Held all their games right there in the casino. That's how big the place was.

Andrade said he heard me with the Alabamians over the radio and also with Fowler at the Lafayette. Told me to sit in for a few numbers during a dance set. By the time it was over, I had the job. The date was January 23, 1934.

In brass, he had Chico Carrion, a Puerto Rican trumpet man that also did some arranging; Don Christian, who I worked so good with in Ray Parker's orchestra, on second trumpet; Allen Brown, a exciting high-note man on third—could hit F's and G's. Ulysses "Shorty" Scott was lead-off man on first alto and clarinet; Claude Greene from New York, sax; Wington Thompson, third alto, flute, and clarinet; Joe Thomas from Tulsa, Oklahoma, on tenor; and one other guy on reeds whose name I can't call.

Jimmy Parker, the drummer, was a pretty good professional boxer—

Clyde Bernhardt in 1934. (Photo courtesy of Frank Driggs collection.)

had trained with Tony Canzoneri. A couple times he got another drummer to take his place and just took off to fight somebody.

Leo Julian was on piano. He was the brother of Colonel Hubert Julian,
the famous black aviator. Peter Briggs recorded with Louis Armstrong's
Hot Seven, was bass, and Andrade played guitar and tenor banjo. Don't
know if he could play a solo—never saw him do that—just stomped off
numbers.

Half of Andrade's band was West Indian. Since I worked in a few West
Indian bands myself, a lot of guys thought I was West Indian too.

They used to tease me, tell me I was passing for colored. "You really
one of us," they laugh.

Bandleader Vernon Andrade worked at the Renaissance Casino for twenty-seven years. (Photo courtesy of Frank Driggs collection.)

Even Andrade, who was from Panama but his people came from the Islands, teased me. "Barnhardt," he say, "what part of Barbados you from?"

He still called me Barnhardt and never did believe I was American-born.

We were the dressingest band in town—Luis Russell and Duke Ellington were also—nobody dressed any better. Looked like a top-class band *should* look with different combinations of suits, jackets, and tuxedos for any occasion.

Private organizations gave regular affairs and receptions at the Renaissance—mixed black and white political clubs, leading West Indian and Panamanian social groups, and high-powered colored associations. Andrade played for them all. He was the regular house band and sometimes worked seven nights a week, plus maybe two or three matinees. Bob Douglas often turned down social parties because the band was booked solid.

Although Andrade was a hard man to work for, he carried a good name among musicians. Never tried to cheat anybody out of money. Told him right up front what he suppose to get. Some of those social clubs couldn't afford to pay as much as others, so then we got less. When the heavy groups like the Cosmopolitan Tennis Club or the Cricket

Club, the Carolinians or the United Sons and Daughters of Georgia came in—they pay more. We sometimes got as much as eight dollars a night for each of those good affairs.

If Andrade thought the job didn't pay enough—like maybe a little old women's club wanted to hire us—he ask if we wanted it, and if the answer was no, turn it down.

He paid by the shift, plus all the extra dates we worked. Most leaders paid by the week, and if they felt like throwing in a couple extra jobs, we play them and keep our mouth shut. That is, if we wanted to stay in the band. So Andrade was good that way.

The few times Andrade played the Savoy and Rockland Palace, we got twelve dollars for the dates. I knew we were easily making double what the top Savoy bands got—some of them lucky to be pulling in thirty a week.

Andrade knew his business. I gave him credit, because he knew how to call a set: usually four songs, different tempos, maybe a waltz, then a sweet number, a calypso, and then a hot number. Sometimes we did a beautiful twenty-minute waltz medley like *Tales from the Vienna Woods* and the people just loved it. Kept asking for that over and over. Waltzes was popular then in Harlem, and if you didn't play any at colored social affairs, you didn't play for that club anymore. Hell, no.

Just like King Oliver, he spot a crowd and know exactly what the people wanted to dance to. That's why he stayed at the Renaissance for twenty-seven years.

Everybody in the band was a good reader. Andrade had a copy of all Jimmie Lunceford's top numbers—and we could play hell out of them. Horace also brought over all the arrangements he made for his brother, Fletcher. We regularly played *Rug Cutter's Swing*, *White Heat*, and *For Dancers Only*. If Andrade liked a hot record hit of some band, he got Joe Thomas or someone to take it off in the same key and make the exact arrangement.

We did Stuff Smith's *Ise A-Muggin'* just as good as he did, maybe better. We sound so much like that record, people all cheered and stomped. We even played *What Are You Gonna Do When I'm Gone?*, a song I wrote in 1932 (and dedicated to my "wife"), and had Eddie White make up a band arrangement.

Andrade rarely smiled. During dances he sat up there and looked like a sour puss. People came over and ask if he was angry.

"I been coming here ever since 1925 and he still look mad," they say.

"No," we answer, "that's just his way."

"Well, he ought to get some personality."

He did have personality, but it came out after he had his whiskey. Then he was one of the jolliest, happiest guys you ever want to see— smile and laugh, and when we be playing, shout encouragement.

"Oh play it, Clyde," he holler, "let's go, Shorty!" On the final bar he wave his hands: "Take it out fellows, take it *out*." He sure loved his drink.

The busiest time for the band was usually from Labor Day in September until around Independence Day. By the first of May, he call us all together.

"If you guys haven't been saving your money, you better start now. I'm taking no jobs after the Fourth of July. If you broke, you gonna have to root, hog, or die. Take a rest and be ready to hit it in September. Me? I'm leaving for Saratoga to play the races."

And that's what he did.

He was very strict about any of his guys playing outside jobs. I found that out after I took this little one-nighter with Charlie Johnson over in Montclair, New Jersey. Went there because I had the day off. Paid five dollars. The place was packed, but when it came time to pay, the boss had run off.

I told that to Andrade and he got hot. "Clyde, you damn ungrateful and greedy, that's what you are," he growled. "You working the best job in town and still not satisfied. Guys all sittin' around the Rhythm Club waiting on jobs and you bustin' your ass for more."

Told me all I had was a ride to Montclair and back and got paid just what the job was worth.

We once worked the Apollo, playing for the same Chilton and Thomas act that Billy Fowler backed. But they didn't like Andrade's orchestra— said he was good only for dances and not for playing a act. Andrade never took another Apollo date again. He had plenty offers for out-of-town dances but was satisfied with his steady location work at the Renny.

During my time with the band, I kept up my music lessons, taking advanced trombone from Manuel Grupp, a Russian Jew that had a downtown studio. He was also teaching advanced lessons to Tommy Dorsey at the same time. Mr. Grupp was good and kept me from losing what I learned from Meredith Germer.

One Friday, Harry Dial stopped over my house. I worked with him in the Walkathonians and he was looking for a extra trombone for a Alex Hill recording session. The job paid ten dollars. Hill's regular trombonist, Claude Jones, was sick.

Now, I knew Andrade wouldn't like me to take no other job. That mess-up with Charlie Johnson in Montclair was only a few months back and it still worked my mind. But I wanted the record date bad because it would be my first, and I figured Andrade would never find out. This time I wouldn't tell him.

It was Monday noon, September 10, 1934, that I showed up at the famous Brunswick Recording Studios at 57th and Broadway. I had heard so many Brunswick records, so many good bands and singers, I rated them up with Columbia and Victor, the two major record companies then.

When I walked in and looked around, I was very, very disappointed—it was the saddest looking place I ever seen in my life. All run down, old and shabby, looked like they been out of business for years.

Chairs all scattered about. The rugs—I think they were rugs—had the floor coming through. Things peeling off the walls. The few music stands they had were the tall, old-fashioned kind that symphony orchestras used.

Couldn't believe what I was seeing. "Is this where Isham Jones, King Oliver, and all those others recorded?" I asked Alex Hill.

"This is the place," he said, looking around.

"I don't believe it."

"Man, this son-of-a-bitch place been here since time began."

We had a good laugh over that, but the studio was sure all beat to hell.

At the end of the long room in the back was the control booth. I saw Irving Mills, the big-time music publisher and producer, talking with John Hammond that somebody said was a multimillionare jazz buff.

The band went by the name of Alex Hill and his Hollywood Sepians. Albert Nicholas from New Orleans, was on clarinet; George James, alto; and Eugene Sedric, tenor. Fonley Jordan took first trombone and I was second. This was the first big-time job Jordan ever had and I saw he was scared to death.

Dick Green and Joe Thomas were on trumpets—this was not the same Joe Thomas that was with Andrade; Eddie Gibbs, guitar; Billy Taylor, bass; and Harry Dial, drums. They hired pianist Charlie Beal, who worked with Noble Sissle, but Mills thought he was too "modern" for this session, so Beal got paid off and Hill took over the piano part.

They put us all about—I was here, two trumpets way over there, rhythm someplace else. Some old beat-up mikes stood on the floor here and there.

We rehearsed from noon for two hours. But every time the little red light went on to start a record take, Dick Green and Fonley Jordan got nervous—seemed like they was playing out of tune. Mills come running out to calm them down, tell them not to be scared of making records, they should be brave and strong and pay no mind to the little red light.

After a few more false starts, Mills gave me the first trombone part. Don't recall how many takes we made, but they finally got some good sides. Worked until about six that night and recorded four Alex Hill jump originals: *Functionizin'* was one; *Ain't It Nice* and *Harlem Living Room Suite* was two others. The fourth had no title, just a number. They tell me only two songs came out on Vocalion that was the subsidiary label of Brunswick. Don't know what became of the others.

After the session, I had dinner and came back up to work a dance with Andrade. Suddenly, one of the guys way at the other end of the bandstand hollered out: "Man, how that record session go today?"

See, all the guys liked to jive and word got around. I didn't know what to say.

Andrade turned around and looked over the band with those suspicious eyes of his. "What session? Who made what session?"

"Old Barnhardt there went downtown and made a session with Alex Hill."

He turned and looked at me. "That so? Still ain't satisfied what I give you here? When you work in my band, 'spect you to work *only* in my band. The first damn Tom, Dick, or Harry come along, you with him." He was really hot. "Barnhardt, if you wanna work with that guy, then you damn well better go stay with him."

That scared hell out of me. I knew I had a very good job and was afraid he fire me. He didn't, but I never took another outside job again the whole time I was with him.

And when those Hill records came out, people wouldn't give me credit for my solo work on *Functionizin'*. Said it was Claude Jones. Now, Claude played one of those technical styles, fast passages and all that. I played like Jimmy Harrison, more in a swing style.

Around the first of February of 1935, Cecil Scott came in on tenor and worked about a year until he left to go with Teddy Hill. Also during early 1935, Horace Henderson replaced Julian on piano and Teddy Wilson filled in for Henderson whenever he was out. But Henderson was out once too often, so on Christmas Day, Sharkey Victor came in regular. Once, Fletcher Henderson sat in on fourth trumpet and improvised the entire part. I never heard the famous pianist play a horn before.

I remember early in 1935 when Ella Fitzgerald used to come up to the Renny two and three nights a week. She was working with Chick Webb, who was on and off at the Savoy. Everybody liked her. She wasn't but sixteen then—just out of the orphan home—and won a amateur contest at the Harlem Opera House. That's how she got with Chick's

band. Webb didn't pay her any regular salary, but he let her have a couple
bucks now and then.

She always sang with us in her street clothes because that was all she
had. Andrade wouldn't let her work formal dances without a evening
gown. And she didn't have any. We all felt sorry for her and always gave
Ella money before she left.

I liked working for Vernon Andrade. It was solid, steady work, good
money, and I was home for all the holidays. But on looking back, I think
my three years with him hurt my career. Before Andrade, I was gigging
around New York and usually available for extra work. Now when Sy
Oliver came and tried to get me for a Jimmie Lunceford date, I had to
turn him down. Got recording offers again from Alex Hill and some
from Red Allen and others and turned them down also.

So I was lost to a lot of people, especially when swing was getting to
be popular and other musicians all making reputations on records and
radio. Many important white writers and fans couldn't get uptown to
hear me because Renaissance dances was usually private.

Kept meeting people during this time that thought I died. Didn't
know where the hell I was.

One time we were rehearsing in the Renny when Edgar Hayes came
in with his band. The Original Blue Rhythm Band that Lucky Millinder
fronted disbanded early in January of 1937 and Lucky took half the
guys. Hayes took the rest and formed this new band. Bob Douglas was
nice and let Hayes rehearse up there for nothing. He always gave guys
just starting out a break, tried to help if he could, maybe give them
jobs to keep their heads above water.

Hayes had three trombone parts, and sometimes he was short or a
guy was late to rehearsal so he ask me to stay and fill the part. Just for
rehearsal—wasn't asking me to join up or nothing. And I wasn't thinking of joining. But I always told him I couldn't do it. I knew Andrade
get hot again.

At home I talked about it. "Uncle Jim, that Andrade don't like his men
sittin' in nowhere."

That got *him* hot. "This is America," he shouted, waving his arms,
"and what you do on your free time is your own damn business. That
West Indian think he owns a band of nigger slaves—they all too scared
to look back over their shoulder. Maybe he scare you, but not me."

My uncle was three-quarter Indian and had a temper.

"But Uncle," I objected, "he liable to fire me."

"Let 'em fire you—you don't have to kiss ass. You not alone here, we
all working, nobody on relief. The hell with that damn monkey-chaser!"

Mama was a little calmer. "Don't be selfish, Clyde," she said. "If he asks your help and you want to do it, do it. God will open doors for you, don't worry."

So I rehearsed with Hayes a few times when he needed me. No money, just sat in to help the man out.

Andrade caught me one day, got hot, and sure enough fired me. On the spot.

20. Edgar Hayes' Orchestra, 1937–1942

I left Vernon Andrade Sunday night, February 21, 1937, and Edgar Hayes immediately hired me, and by Wednesday we all in Philadelphia working some weekend jobs.

The next time I saw Andrade was in the Alhambra Ballroom where Hayes was rehearsing.

"Barnhardt," he said, "I made a mistake when I let you go."

"No, Vernon," I interrupted, "it was no mistake. You did me the biggest favor you could of done for me."

And that was true. I was now with another good band—do whatever I wanted, when I wanted. And damn sure wasn't scared of the boss.

I liked the sound of the new Hayes orchestra: swing, jazz, sweet, popular, everything well balanced in a style between Jimmie Lunceford and Duke Ellington.

Hayes had one hell of a book—all original arrangements and very tough. We rehearsed those difficult numbers over and over, some seven or eight times until we got it just like he wanted. But once we got it down, we were a smash. Count Basie always said Hayes didn't know how great he really was—he often hired Edgar as his rehearsal leader and then go home and leave him in charge.

Like the guys used to say, the Hayes band was the "college," and when you came out of there it was like graduating. You go anywhere after that.

Hayes was also a hell of a pianist—played everything, even the classics. Played great stride just like James P. Johnson and had the articulation of Earl Hines. To me he was one of the greatest piano players and band leaders in the business.

This was the line-up when I joined. I'll start with the trombone section: R. H. Horton—we called him Robert but his real name was

Redius—was the same man I heard in Sam Wooding's band back in 1923; Wilbur De Paris was there too, but David "Jelly" James replaced him after a few weeks. Jelly and I handled both first and second trombone parts.

Scad Hemphill was first trumpet. I remember he was always laughing, like a old Cheshire cat, especially at how people all dressed—hell, I thought he looked like a damn dressed-up groundhog himself.

Bernard Flood was second trumpet and Henry Goodwin, third with some jazz solos; Joe Garland, tenor; and Tab Smith, first alto, but Rudy Powell came in from Fats Waller to replace Smith after a few weeks when Tab went back to Lucky.

Crawford Wethington was third alto and Roger Boyd, fourth; Kenny Clarke, drums; Elmer James, he pick and slap string bass very well; Andy Jackson, guitar; and Edgar on piano. A solid fourteen-piece band.

Joe Garland wrote and arranged many of the numbers including *In the Mood* that Hayes recorded in 1938. That piece was heavy music—had four big manuscript pages just for the trombone parts. We called it his Black Symphony. When Glenn Miller heard the song, he had Garland put stop breaks in, cut out some parts, and recorded his own big hit the following year.

A lot of people tried to put a claim on that number, but after a lawsuit, Garland won out.

Edgar and Crawford Wethington had been trying to get a good booking-agent for some time. Often went up to the second floor office of the Lunceford and Oxley Bureau at 17 East 49th Street but kept getting the cold shoulder. Need more experience, they said, do more rehearsing and all that. Promised us a audition someday, but we never got one.

In those first few weeks, Hayes wasn't working regular, so I picked up some dance dates with Tommy Lindsay in a white orchestra, the first time I ever worked in a mixed group. There was also some club jobs with Lil Armstrong's orchestra around New York and New Jersey. She was one beautiful person to work for. Would sit at the piano and play Louis' big hits, even imitating her husband's hoarse style of singing. She was a good piano player, but I didn't think she was as good as Tillie Vennie.

Hayes was taking whatever work he could find. On some jobs, singer Orlando Robeson fronted and then we be billed as his band. Some of the guys resented that arrangement but Hayes did it anyways. Later, Orlando joined us regular and after he left, Hayes got Ruth Ellington. A lot of people thought she was Duke's sister, but her real name was Joyce Tucker.

We did some Connecticut jobs under Fess Williams and played the Astor Hotel under W. C. Handy. Handy's daughter Elizabeth sang *Beale Street Blues* and *Memphis Blues*, but we only allowed to play stock arrangements of his numbers. Gave strict orders not to put any high-powered stuff in his songs while he was directing.

We also found work playing on the "Sheep & Goat Club" radio show with Ralph Cooper in New York. Amanda Randolph and Juano Hernandez did a hilarious takeoff on a black Romeo and Juliet.

"Romeo, oh Romeo, where is you at?"

I still remember how we all broke up at that, missed our cue, and almost messed up the whole show.

When I think now of all the dialect shows taken off radio and television, I can't help but call how many black people really liked those programs. And how many black performers got knocked out of work. Didn't seem right because they were damn funny shows. Yes, they were.

So Hayes kept scratching for jobs until Easter Sunday, March 28, 1937, when he took the band in the Renaissance.

There was three bands there that day: Jimmie Lunceford just back from Sweden, Vernon Andrade, and Edgar Hayes. It was a triple Battle of Music. The place was packed to capacity. Big shots sitting up in back of the bandstand. Booking agents, club owners, important white people. Didn't know them all, but somebody pointed out Mr. Harold F. Oxley of the Lunceford and Oxley Booking Bureau to me. The very important white booker.

Vernon opened the show and played the first hour. Then Hayes came on—he knew this be a good opportunity to show his stuff so he pulled out his hot numbers. Opened with *Stomping at the Renny*, and I'm not bragging, but we blew Andrade away. Old Henry Goodwin, he was screaming on trumpet, Edgar was stomping, just playing his ass off, and the band was riffing like crazy.

Man, those dancing jitterbugs went wild—all hooting, hollering. People started standing up to watch the band.

Sy Oliver, who was working in the Lunceford band then, came over and asked who did the arrangement.

"Joe Garland," I said.

"Man, I'm telling you," he whispered, "you cats got something."

Next we did *In the Mood*, then let it all out with *Meet the Band* and other great swinging numbers. We wrapped it up with *Swinging in the*

Promised Land, and the audience was so hot they wouldn't let Vernon come back on. We had to do a encore and still had to beg off. Made such a impression that Andrade never did come back, and we alternated with Lunceford for the rest of the show.

One of those white fellows in back of the stage got hold of Oxley and asked who was booking our band. He quickly said he was, but he wasn't. This was the same Oxley that kept putting Hayes off and promised him a audition some day. Now he couldn't get Hayes signed up fast enough. Jimmie Lunceford, who was partners with Oxley, came over and shook Edgar's hand.

After we got with Oxley, he sent us down to London Tailor's to have new uniforms made, then booked us a week in the Apollo, and we came back there two more times during the year. A hell of a lot of good bands couldn't get in there but *one* time.

And Oxley got us a one-year contract with the Decca Record Company. About a month before, we recorded some numbers under Orlando Robeson's name for Variety Records. Did that in the same New York building where the Brunswick Studios was located. Irving Mills was at that session too, but Robeson selected all the songs.

On May 25, 1937, we all went in the New York Decca studios over at 50 West 57th Street and made our first sides under Hayes' name. Leonard "Ham" Davis replaced Scad Hemphill on first trumpet.

We put down some of our best numbers: *Stomping at the Renny*, *Edgar Steps Out*, and *Caravan*. Now, here's something I never did understand about that session. Bernard Flood took a vocal on the fourth number, *Laughing at Life*. There's no doubt in my mind about that, only the record books credit Ralph Sawyer as singer. I never heard of such a person.

When I later listened to that Sawyer record, it was not Flood, it was Jimmy Anderson. I think somebody slipped that fake name in, because I know it is not a legit recording—was never done in a studio—and definitely not at that May session. Anderson's first job with Hayes was early in 1938, so he couldn't possibly recorded with the band in 1937.

The cut must of been taken from a aircheck or one of the many radio remotes the band was always doing in 1938.

We also made *Satan Takes a Holiday*, *Queen Isabella*, and other records during 1937 that helped the band tremendously. Sold like hot cakes in the United States and Europe.

Sometime in July I made another vocal test record. Edgar backed me on piano. Just something I wanted to do for myself because I had some original numbers. One side was called *Without You*, a song I wrote in

The great Edgar Hayes band of 1937. Front row, left to right: Andy Jackson (g), Kenny Clarke (p), Rudy Powell (as), Crawford Wetbington (ts), Roger Boyd (as), Joe Garland (ts); back row, left to right: Edgar Hayes (p), Ruth Ellington (v), Elmer James (sb), Henry Goodwin (t), Bernard Flood (t), Leonard Davis (t), Clyde Bernbardt (tb), R. H. Horton (tb), David James (tb). (Photo courtesy of Frank Driggs collection.)

1936 (and dedicated again to Bobby). The other side was *Gate You Swing Me Down*. Didn't take it serious, but Hayes sort of liked them. Rudy Powell made a big band arrangement of *Without You*, and Hayes featured me as singer on it occasionally. Went over big at dances and in those days it was unusual for band singers to get a hand for anything.

During 1937, Hayes made extensive road tours playing one-nighters through Virginia, Tennessee, North Carolina, Ohio, Kentucky, Indiana, and Washington, D.C. Everywhere we went the band was a sensation.

I remember one black place in Columbus, Ohio—it was a jammed-packed Sunday night, just as many people outside as inside, and they was still coming in. The dance floor was so crowded you couldn't stir those niggers with a stick—many dancers was right up on the band-stand next to us, and I could hardly leave to go to the toilet.

They had us back there about ten days later and it was the same thing all over again.

One restricted white place, somewhere in Ohio, had us in three different times in a six-month period. They loved us. But the owner made it clear we could not have our girl friends or wives come in the hall, or anywhere on his property. Said if they did try to come in, he make them all stand outside. We were not to fool around with any white girls either, even if they made passes at us first. Said if we didn't go about our business, he let the whole damn band go. Oxley told us to put our jobs first, and we never had no trouble.

Lodging was usually a problem for bands on the road. Places always filled up or the band having to split in different hotels. Many times they were nothing but ratty old flea bags.

But I solved that problem by joining the Harlem branch of the YMCA, which had a traveler's aid service. It recommended private families all over the country that took in boarders. I go out and find these homes and have some of the best rooms in town for myself. Private. Quiet. Some owned by doctors and teachers and I was treated like family. Served me breakfast. Got drives to and from the job.

Guys in the band all thought I had relatives living everywhere.

"That old Clyde knows somebody in every town," they moan. "Goddamn!"

When we came back for a October eleventh Decca session, Bob Stevens had a hell of a time with Ruth Ellington. He was the head studio engineer—recorded Ella, Bing Crosby, and others—and was trying hard to tell Ruth what he wanted from her. Said her volume was wrong. Diction wasn't clear. Stuff like that. Couldn't tell her a damn thing, and finally Oxley told her to leave. Right then and there in the studio. Ruth was finished with Hayes.

So Bill Darnell came running down and took over Ruth's part just as if it was written for him. This white singer looked like Willie Smith, the first sax with Lunceford—they could have passed for brothers, only Smith was a light-skinned Negro.

Around the first of 1938, Hayes brought in young Earlene Howell to handle the girl vocals. Earlene just won top prize in a Apollo amateur contest and it was her first band job. I called her Tater Mae—a name all the guys called a ugly chick. We had a good laugh over that. She liked the name, but one day Henry Goodwin told her what Tater meant and she got mad for a couple days. But she kept the name. Yes, she did.

Shortly after, Jimmy Anderson was added as male singer. Hayes also replaced Crawford Wethington with William "Happy" Mitchner, Elmer James with Frank "Coco" Darling, and Andy Jackson with Eddie Gibbs.

After a heavy Midwestern tour, we got back to New York on Sunday, February 13, and went right in the Renaissance.

Now, I hadn't been doing much singing since I left King Oliver except when Edgar let me do my *Without You*. I never went in bands pushing myself—just kept my mouth shut and did the job I was hired for.

That night, Edgar called my song in the first set and it went over good. During our break, Oxley told me he wanted to record the song.

"But Mr. Oxley," I said, "Edgar thinks the number is too weak and I have no name as a singer."

"I'll fix that," he said.

At the next record session on February seventeenth my song was recorded even though Edgar's lip was dropping down his chin. It was my first vocal record and opened plenty of doors for me, all due to Mr. Oxley. The band recorded a total of eight numbers that day, including a Hayes instrumental arrangement of *Star Dust* that became his biggest-selling hit.

Two days later we were all on the big Swedish luxury liner S.S. Drottingholm heading for a European tour.

The newspaper reporters and photographers from the black press was there to see us off. Big buffet spread, sandwiches, drinks, all you wanted. Lots of flowers. My mother, brother, and his family came down to give me courage. I never been on a ship before and read all about them sinking and things like that. Kept thinking of the song about the Titanic and sixteen hundred people going down when they hit that iceberg. So I was deathly afraid of boats.

In 1929, Ed Swayzee, Joe Hayman, Herb Flemming, and that bunch wanted me to go over with the Blackbirds' show. Begged out of it, wouldn't go. No sir.

But I couldn't get out of it this time although I damn sure tried. Held up getting my passport and my mother raised all hell. Told me not to make her ashamed and said everybody wanted to see if I was good enough to play in Europe.

So here I was. I was happy to see so many people all going to Europe but was still scared as hell.

The trip over was scheduled for eight "easy" days—like the travel advertisements said. Two days out of New York we ran through a awful storm. The wind and rain started blowing hard, the thunder was rumbling terribly, and bright lightning kept shooting through the sky. I was with Edgar in a outside stateroom, and stewards came running in to lock up those little portholes where the water kept smashing in.

The ship rocked and twisted all around, and I could hear the propeller spinning out of the water every time the back end came up. Then the boat fell fast and I try to grab hold of something, anything. Then, up it came again. Knew for certain I was going down—there was no doubt about it.

After three very rough days, the storm moved away and things got calmer. Walked in the dining room that morning, but weren't many people eating, maybe only a dozen or so. Ate me a nice breakfast and felt much better.

A few days later, the captain invited the whole band to dine at his table. We put on our tuxes and became honored guests for the evening. All the people came out. Had a Swedish band there but we took over and played some of our best dance numbers—damn near got that ship rocking again.

Then the captain took us on a tour, showing us everything from the control room down to the shining boiler in the engine room. It was a beautiful, grand old ship. I wasn't afraid any longer.

After eleven days at sea we arrived in Göteborg, Sweden. That's when the road manager told us the trip took three days longer because we gone four hundred miles off course to avoid some big icebergs sitting out there. If I known that before, damn if I wouldn't of had a heart attack. That's for sure.

After our first job in Göteborg, we bussed on to Stockholm for some theater dates and played a special party for King Gustavus. When we walked in that long hall, the Swedish band struck up the American national anthem and everybody stood up, including the king. People bowing—thought their noses was going to hit the floor. As we sat at our special table, there was a great big American flag hanging above us.

Later they asked us to do a couple American jazz numbers and we almost set the place on fire—the people all dancing and clapping to hot jazz. I saw the king back there applauding along with everybody else.

When he came up to shake our hands, I felt proud to be a American.

It was while I was staying at the Grand Hotel in Stockholm that I had one of my terrible dreams. Just as clear as ever, I thought I received a cablegram that Mama died. It was a shock and I felt very bad. The message said they couldn't keep her out of the ground until I got back so they had to bury her. The dream continued with me going out to the cemetery to pay respects. It was nice grounds, and Mama was buried right there next to a medium-size tree. Saw lots of flowers on her grave. Someone was telling me the ground was too soft to put up a stone so I should remember the spot next to the medium-size tree.

When I woke up, I was sweating and crying. It was dark and I was still in Sweden. Knew my people at home let me know if anything really happened so I tried to get back to sleep. But it worked my mind bad, and I couldn't.

The next morning, R. H. Horton wanted to know why I was making noises and was so fitful all night. I couldn't tell him. I had enough strange dreams as a kid so I tried to take it off my mind. When I later returned to the states, I couldn't rush over to Newark fast enough to see Mama. She was fine—it was only a bad dream.

Or so I thought.

So we kept working in and out of Stockholm and for longer trips chartered busses. We rode over to Oslo, Norway, then down to the National Scala in Copenhagen, Denmark. Never saw a club as large as that in America—was so big they featured circus acts in there. Played many theaters and concert halls through Sweden, Norway, Denmark, and Finland.

When we went to Belgium and Holland, the band traveled by train, riding through Germany to get to the lowlands. I remember there was a lot of military activity going on at the time. Soldiers everywhere—coming, going, marching, lining up. Sometimes the train stopped and we get off to allow the military on. When we get back, our seats be gone. Once, we got put off in Frankfurt and they packed in soldiers and took off without us. Waited two hours in the cold for the next train.

Many times uniformed Germans was sitting right next to us in our compartment.

"You are American jazz musicians?"

"Yes we are."

"We would like to have some of your records, but we are not allowed to listen to your music."

I noticed that every German soldier I met spoke English. Once, a very blond one was sitting nearby. It was the time in 1938 when Joe Louis was training for his second fight with Max Schmeling.

"That Max," said the soldier, "he going to knock him out in the first round this time. Joe Louis not fight all that good."

R. H. Horton was sitting next to me and didn't take kindly to that remark. "Goddamn, you just wait," he said, shaking his finger. "Old Joe get him this time."

"Wait a minute, Robert," I said, "he just trying you."

"Someday we will be in America," the soldier suddenly said. "We going to *take* your country, and the first thing we will do is send all you *schwarzes* back to Africa."

"Yeah?" shouted Horton. He was standing up now. "Well, just let your Hitler fellow start something over there, and we got stuff that will stop him before he even get started."

The other soldiers all laughing now.

"Shhhh, shhhh," I whispered to Horton.

"The only damn way you come to America," Horton added, waving his fist, "will be as a prisoner of war!"

"You damn fool, keep quiet," I said, pulling Horton's sleeve. "You in Germany now. Put the soft pedal on it. Won't take much for them to pull us all off the train and toss us in a concentration camp. Take it low, man, take it *low*."

Horton sat down, but the soldier kept saying how Americans were not ready for war. "Unprepared, untrained, soft and lazy," was how he put it. "We will whip the world," he said as he got up and left.

So we rode through Germany, past train stations where long rows of rifles all stacked like corn stalks, past pretty little towns with dozens of dark Army trucks just standing around, waiting.

I thought of what that soldier said and hoped he was just boasting on a lie on sand foundation.

We stayed in Belgium and Holland almost two weeks and was very well received everywhere we played. Long applause. People shaking everybody's hand. Kissing Tater Mae's hand. One time a man bowed low to kiss her hand, and she turned to me with her chin up, "Clyde, from now on you can call me *Madame* Tater!"

The Edgar Hayes European tour was scheduled for four weeks but lasted almost twelve, with more offers coming in then Hayes could handle and plenty of holdovers. We got a terrific offer to play Monte Carlo in Monaco for a twelve-week residency, but the guys started grumbling. Said they knew how good we going over, that Jimmie Lunceford been to Europe in '37 with a hell of a band and come back after only two weeks.

So the boys held a kangaroo meeting, talking about getting more money, thinking about going home to their families right then. Some

The Edgar Hayes orchestra in Copenhagen, Denmark, Mar. 1938.
Kneeling, left to right: *Frank Darling (sb), Clyde Bernhardt (tb),*
Bernard Flood (t/v); back row, left to right: *Kenny Clarke (d), Joe*
Garland (ts), Happy Mitchner (as), Henry Goodwin (t), Earlene
Howell (v), Leonard Davis (t), Roger Boyd (as), Rudy Powell (as),
R. H. Horton (tb), Eddie Gibbs (g), Jimmy Anderson (v). Not shown:
Edgar Hayes and Jelly James. (Photo courtesy of Frank Driggs
collection.)

guys even pulled a strike one night in Sweden, wouldn't go on unless
they got more money. All that kind of stuff.

I kept out of it because I was wanting to go to Monte Carlo. Would
of been on location in some casino, so I was in no hurry to get back.

When Oxley and Hayes heard about all this they decided to end the
tour and everybody come back to the states together. Didn't want the
band breaking up.

We sailed from Bremerhaven, Germany, on the big S.S. Bremen. The
trip was smooth this time and the food delicious, but the Germans
wouldn't allow us to visit the engine room—seemed to be very se-
cretive about that. And since they didn't allow no American music, we
didn't play no dances. And of course, there was no captain's dinner for
us, either.

During the eight days it took us to return, some of the guys got bored
and started looking around for something to do. Eddie Gibbs had
bought a new suitcase to replace his beat-up, ratty one. So the guys
decided to bury the old suitcase at sea.

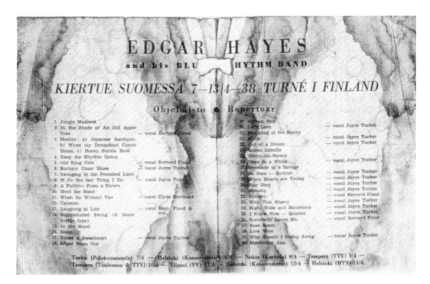

Both sides of musical program used by Edgar Hayes' orchestra on tour of Finland, Apr. 7–13, 1938.

Four of them carried the case while the rest walked slowly behind
in a single file, humming a dirge. Around and around the deck they
marched solemnly, finally stopping by the railing. Henry Goodwin began
shouting a funeral sermon, carrying on about how good the case been
and how it was going to a better world. And the guys all holler, "Amen,
brother" and "Glory to God." Eddie Gibbs sob loud each time.

Everybody came over to see what was happening. The Americans all
laughing. The Germans didn't know what the hell to make of it. One old
German in a deck chair nearby turned to me. "Is this a real funeral?" he
asked.

"Yes," I answered sadly.

"Who died?" he whispered, showing concern.

"A suitcase," I said. "It was all wore out."

"Ohhhhh, just like a old man, it wear out."

"That's right," I said, just as Gibbs pitched the case over the railing
and in the water below.

Then the guys formed a single line and slowly marched back to their
cabins, jiving on a spiritual. It was one big laugh.

When we returned from Europe in May of 1938, Hayes left the
Lunceford and Oxley Booking Bureau. I thought that was a mistake,
but some guys in the band kept running Oxley down, and Hayes wasn't
strong enough to say no. So he dropped Oxley. After he did that, wasn't
too long before those very same bad-mouthing guys then quit Hayes.
Just a rotten thing, all around.

I was surprised when Oxley asked me to form my own small group.
Said he would handle the booking and get me my own recording dates.

Well, I never wanted to have my own band because I seen the headaches some leaders had from their guys, no matter how nice they were.
Those guys just like to give trouble—step on you, try you, late on the
bandstand, borrow money, not pay back—do all kinds of dirty things.

I didn't need that kind of trouble so I turned Oxley down. I was
happy with Hayes and stayed with him.

But Rudy Powell, R. H. Horton, and Henry Goodwin all went over
to Charlie Johnson's orchestra. Hayes picked up Louis Jordan on first
alto and Norman Green on third trombone. Jimmy Wright, tenor, came
in later when he got Cyril Newman on third trumpet. Newman wasn't
as good as Goodwin, but he was a light-looking boy, and Edgar was very
particular about having light ones in his band.

He was as bad as King Oliver regarding color. I once recommended
a good horn man but Hayes said he was too short and much too dark.

"Damn it, Edgar, you lookin' for a Rudolph Valentino band?"

"Oh man, shut up," he answered. "We playin' fine white places and chicks might turn their back if they see all them ugly niggers up there. I'm gonna get somebody that look like somebody."

I never did go for that kind of stuff. Louis Jordan told me he had that trouble when he came to New York. Some of those black guys in Harlem wouldn't give him work because he was too dark. And, he said, the problem was worse in Chicago. I heard it happened to Sylvester Briscoe when he came to New York in the thirties. He was one hell of a trombone player.

Hayes was being booked now by the Gale office. They put Teddy Hill's orchestra against Hayes and toured the two bands as a Battle of Music playing dances all down through the South.

While Hayes was working the band at the Savoy in June, most of the guys took a special recording session with Luckey Roberts. Roberts was always helping New York musicians and getting those high-powered, high-paying gigs, so we were happy to help the man out. Musicians always helped one another in those days. To me, Luckey was one of the all-time great piano players. Didn't take a back seat to nobody.

Roberts said this was a special charity recording so we contributed our time and got permission from the union for the session. Had his wife there, singing in front of this big choir. We did gospel numbers, some jazz and pop tunes, all Roberts originals—about eight or ten sides. A great session, but I never seen or heard nothing about those records to this very day.

Early in July we were rehearsing to go in the Apollo Theater to open on the fifteenth for a week.

We had two new numbers. One was Eddie Durham's *Slip Horn Jive* and the other was a hell of a arrangement by Hayes on *Bugle Call Rag*. Had some four-bar breaks in there for the brass that was rough—all written in harmony—cut everybody at first, but after a few days we started getting it. All but this Cyril Newman fellow. He couldn't make it. The guys started grumbling that the band was too fast for him, that he played a weak trumpet and was hurting everybody, holding us up.

A few days before we scheduled to open, a twenty-year-old Dizzy Gillespie walks in our rehearsal and sits down in the back. He was carrying his horn in a velvet cloth tucked under his arm. Drummer Kenny Clarke was good friends with him.

"Goddamn, there he is!" shouts Kenny. Hayes didn't know much about Dizzy. "This here boy'll play your goddamn music," Kenny said, "and he'll take it apart."

Hayes needed a trumpet bad, but didn't know if this Gillespie fellow was any better then Newman. Asked Diz to sit in and told Newman to stay in the back.

Diz walked up. "Gimme a A," he said. He tooted his A and a few other notes. Wasn't but a minute that the band lit out on *Bugle Call Rag*. Old Diz played every damn note that was written there.

Edgar started laughing. "Take it down again for me," he said looking over at Diz. And we all ran through it and Diz played flawlessly again.

"Fess," said Dizzy, "now take it down again for *me*. I think I got it now."

Edgar was shaking his head in disbelief. Knew Diz *already* had it. So we ran through it a third time, only now Diz turned his back to the music and played the entire number from memory. Everbody about fell out. Damn, that man *was* dizzy. He got the third trumpet spot that day and Newman was out.

Everyone got to like Diz, kept a lot of life in the band. He wasn't known yet, but was swinging like hell, not bopping. Didn't have that bent horn then nor did he blow his jaws out either—got that showmanship much later.

Diz was a born comedian—had the guys laughing all the time. Breaking everybody up. Like a mischievous kid, he be doing devilish things on the job. One time during a number he slid off his seat and sat on the floor, blowing and turning his horn all kinds of funny ways.

Another time, he rose from his chair while playing, came down, and pushed Hayes halfway off the piano bench. With his right hand he chorded some extra harmony, then slowly walked back to his seat and sat down, not missing a note the whole time.

"That's the biggest fool I ever saw in my life," Hayes said. But the audience loved it, thought it was part of the act, and had a good laugh.

One time we all staying at this hotel in Detroit. Every night before we left for the club, Dizzy play fingering exercise runs for about twenty minutes. Jimmie Powell was in the band then, and we shared a room right above Dizzy's. Bassist John Drummond was in our room at the time. We kept hearing Dizzy's runs echoing loudly up and down the courtyard outside our window.

"That old Dizzy down there," said Drummond, "he always messing with somebody. I'm gonna fix his ass."

So Drummond calls Diz on the hotel phone and puts a handkerchief over the mouthpiece. In his best old-lady voice he squeaks: "Hello . . . hello . . . is this Mr. Gillespie?"

"Yes, ma'm," Diz said.

"I wish to hell you would stop blowing that damn horn. You about

drive me crazy. If you continue to play that thing, I'm calling the manager and have him put you out."

"Yes, ma'm," said Diz.

"You should be ashamed of yourself disturbing my rest. You nothin'
but a damn nuisance." And wham! He hangs up.

We were starting to break up.

Drummond calls the number again. "And I mean everything I said."

"I'm sorry, madam," said Diz, "I didn't mean to bother you."

"And I don't want you to blow that damn horn tomorrow either."
Wham! He hangs up again.

That night on the bandstand, Diz looked mad.

"What's the matter, Diz?" we asked. The whole band was in on the
gag, of course.

"Man, some old bitch called my room. Told me I can't play my horn
no more."

"What you say, Diz?"

"Hell, I cussed that mother *out*. Told her off and said to go to hell
if she don't like it. Man, I laid that bitch's ass out."

"You gonna practice again tomorrow, Diz?"

"I don't know, said she cause trouble for you guys. Maybe I'll practice
in the basement."

That broke the band up. Here he was telling us how much he cussed
the woman out and we all knew he was humble as a lamb.

Nobody ever told Diz the real story. Doesn't know till this day.

The Apollo Theater had some of the greatest entertainers in the
country at that time. It was the "Palace Theater" of Harlem. Singers,
comedians, dancers, great bands, and MC's all played there for blacks
and whites that expected only the best. They were tough audiences,
but when you played the Apollo, you knew you played the top.

When Hayes took the band there in July of 1938 with Diz, Jordan,
and the rest of us, he had a funny accident. Edgar was a card player,
always getting a game of Tonk together and playing everywhere he
went. That night, the stage manager hollered, "All on stage," and we
took our places. But no Edgar. He was still in the dressing room playing
Tonk with some sucker.

The curtain went up and we hit it. Still no Edgar. Suddenly here he
come running out from the wings and the audience just howled. He
forgot to take off his stocking cap that was holding his process down.

All he could do was stand there in open-mouth astonishment. "Wa . . .
wa . . . wa . . . ." was all that came out.

The show that night was great. We did all our special arrangements.

Jordan sang *Flat Foot Floogie*. I sang *Without You*. The blackface comedian Pigmeat Markham was on the bill, along with Ralph Cooper, Vivian
Harris, George Wilshire, and others.

I remember Pigmeat did one of his crazy court skits that was
hysterical.

As the "judge," he came out shouting: "I feel so good! *Everybody*
gonna do some time today."

George Wilshire, as the policeman, brought some street girls in
Pigmeat's court.

"Who are these luscious looking broads?" said Pigmeat, smiling wide
at the gals and popping his eyes.

"I picked them up soliciting," said the policeman.

"What's your occupation, mama?" said Pigmeat to the first woman
who had on a short, tight skirt.

"I'm a seamstress, your honor," she said sweetly, adjusting her stocking and snapping her garter, "and I do my business after midnight."

"What? How this nice old gal get picked up? Case dismissed." The
audience loved Pigmeat and laughed loud.

"And what's *your* occupation?" he asked the second.

"I'm a seamstress," she said, rotating her big butt to a drum roll as
Pigmeat followed every movement. "And I do my business after midnight, too."

"Another honest working gal! Case dismissed." More laughs. "And
what's this?" Pigmeat asked, looking down at Ralph Cooper in drag as
the third gal.

He was the worst-looking old broad you ever saw—messy makeup
smeared over his face, a big fright wig on his head, stocking falling low.
Skirt hanging off. Had these huge rubber bubbies under his sweater, and
every time he walk, they bounce up and hit him in the face.

"I picked her up on 135th and Madison," said the cop.

"What's your name?" asked Pigmeat.

"Cleota Runabout."

"And what's your occupation?"

"I'm a streetwalker," he answered, "and I do my business after
midnight."

"How's business?"

"Well judge, I was doing all right until these damn seamstresses
come in."

Pigmeat bops him loud on the head with a big air bladder and the
lights go out to fighting and bopping. Roars of laughter. Even the band
broke out.

Bill Robinson, the greatest of all black tap dancers, toured often with the Edgar Hayes band. (Photo courtesy of Frank Driggs collection.)

Everybody liked Pigmeat's burlesque blackouts, especially Diz. For months after that show, he point to a loverman in the band and whisper: "Cleota Runabout. Cleota Runabout." And we break out all over again. Became a inside joke.

Louis Jordan left the band after the Apollo date and took a small group over to a Brooklyn club where his wife, Ida, was singing. That was his startup as a name.

Jordan knew of Oxley's offer to me and often said I should go out for myself just like he did.

"You hid in that band, man," he say.

But I stuck with Hayes.

Late in 1938 Hayes took us out on a five-week package tour headlined by the greatest of all black tap dancers—Bill Robinson. We played the RKO circuit that was big-time white theaters. He traveled in his own Duesenberg, but most of the time he be in the bus with us and his chauffeur followed behind.

The first time we went out, he called a meeting of all the boys. "We gonna play white-time on this tour fellows," he announced, "and I want you all to know up front what I expect."

I knew we rehearsed his routine down pat so didn't know what in hell he was talking about.

"I had a damn hard time getting where I am," he said. "I'm accepted wherever I go—hotels, restaurants, clubs, theaters. All white places. You boys are part of my tour and therefore you go where I go." I knew what he was getting at now. "If anyone in this show disgraces me by being loud, arguing, getting drunk, and acting a damn fool, I'm gonna beat the living hell out of him. And after I get through goin' upside his head with my fists, I'm gonna pistol whip him to finish the job." He flashed that shiny, gold-plated automatic he always carried.

"Then I'm gonna personally boot his no-good black ass off my show."

He was serious and everybody knew he could do it too, even though he was close to sixty at the time.

"I got a reputation to maintain," he finished, "and no black cat gonna tear that down for me. *Nobody.*"

He was very clear and never had no trouble with the band. And every year after that until 1942, he take the Hayes band out on another package show. Tim and Freddy, singer Ada Brown, and dancers Moke and Poke came along on some of those tours.

Diz worked steady with the band for about four months through 1938, then go out on other jobs when the band laid off. He left to work with Cab Calloway early the next year, and I recommended Eddie Roane to take his place.

Hayes took the band out on a new seven-week package tour in the spring of 1939. Had June Richmond, the Dandridge Sisters featuring Etta Jones, the famous Nicholas Brothers, and dancer Honi Coles and the Ubangi Club Boys. It was one hell of a show.

The Ubangi Club Boys were female impersonators and looked more beautiful then a whole lot of women I seen. The boys came out of the pansy show, as it was called, at the Ubangi in New York. They tore it up wherever we went.

Hayes then laid off the big band for about three months and took a few pieces in small New York clubs. So I gigged around with Joe Garland's brother, Moses, and with other bands that didn't even have no names.

I did pickup dates with Teddy Hill at the Savoy, and one time when I sang *Basin Street Blues*, Doc Cheatham whispered I wasn't taking a serious bow. Said my quick head nod might kill the number and if I bowed from the waist, with a good flair, it would show more appreciation. I always remembered that advice.

Hayes took the big band out again in September playing Jewish and Italian dances in Brooklyn and down to the Howard Theater in Washington, D.C.

By 1940, Hayes been in and out of the Savoy, the Renaissance, and the Apollo. Don Byas and Earl Bostic came in for a time. They were in when we worked the Golden Gate Ballroom in New York opposite Charlie Barnet.

During Edgar's many layoffs in 1940, I worked the Savoy with the bands of Stuff Smith, Hot Lips Page, and others—and many times again the following years.

It was September 24, 1940, that my mother died. She was buried in Rosehill Cemetery out in Linden, New Jersey. I took it very hard but was shocked to see her grave right next to this medium-size tree. A lot of flowers on the mound and there was no stone. Lord, it looked exactly like the dream I had in Sweden two years before.

When I saw my dream in front of me, I'm afraid I broke down. My uncle rushed over to hold me up but I couldn't tell him what I seen— they all liable to think I was crazy or maybe having a breakdown like when Papa passed. But it worked my mind bad, very bad, seeing that sight once again.

In January 1941, Hayes took the band down to Washington, D.C., for President Franklin D. Roosevelt's Inaugural Ball. It was one of many being held, but I never did see any president and was disappointed.

Joe Glaser, the big-time manager, booked Hayes to go out with Louis Armstrong's band on a Battle of Music tour sometime in March. Glaser had Don Redman on the tour so the band was billed as Edgar Hayes and His Orchestra under the direction of Don Redman. Redman would take over his own special arrangements. Then Edgar came on and did the rest.

Velma Middleton been singing with the Hayes band about two months and was also on the tour. Velma was heavy, you know, and she sing and dance, get to jumping and stomping, then make a long running split across the stage to loud cheers. Glaser caught the show in Roanoke, Virginia, and before Hayes knew it, Velma was working in Louis' band. Edgar damn near died.

I suggested he go up and catch this new singer that was working at

the Crystal Caverns in Washington, D.C. I seen her in Harrisburg at the
Ivancock Boys Place working for nickels and dimes. She was good.

"Who's this old gal, Clyde?"

"Her name is Pearl Bailey and she wants to be a band singer."

"You mean Eura Bailey?"

"No, this is Pearl, her sister."

"Oh, you mean that long, black dancin' gal that won the Apollo
contest?"

"That's her."

"Don't want her, too black."

That got me hot. "Edgar, you don't look like no damn glass of milk
yourself. Why in hell you always bringing up that stuff? That gal can
really work."

So he went up there. Savannah Churchill was the headliner and Pearl
was stealing the show every night. Edgar said he liked Pearl better then
Velma and took her with us the next day to New York's Roseland. Hayes
even made a special arrangement for her on *St. Louis Blues.*

The day before we opened, Joe Brecker, the owner of Roseland, said
he wasn't about to pay for a girl singer. Edgar got all excited knowing
he took Pearl out of a paying job. She was staying someplace over near
127th and Seventh where Pop Collins was charging her a quarter for
breakfast and Pearl couldn't pay it.

Hayes asked if I had any ideas. I suggested he take five dollars out of
everyone's salary and ten out of his and pay Pearl with it. Thirteen guys
plus him meant seventy-five dollars a week for the singer. Hell, we only
making sixty-five ourselves.

He wasn't sure that would work but all the guys agreed to the deal.
So we paid Pearl and she was a hit. Those white people went crazy for
her. One time, Count Basie's singer, Helen Humes, got sick and Basie
borrowed Pearl with all her arrangements. When she got back, Brecker
agreed to pay her fifty dollars a week.

"Honey," she cried, "the man done put me on salary and now I ain't
gettin' as much as you all paid me. I'm fallin' back!"

By midyear of 1941 Edgar was starting to be off more then he was
working. In July I went out with Horace Henderson's orchestra for a
month playing one-nighters in Virginia, Tennessee, Georgia, and other
points south.

In September, Hayes took out another package tour for two weeks,
working first-class ballrooms and halls through North Carolina and
Georgia. Savannah Churchill was on that tour, also comedian Rochester,
who did fancy dancing in his checkety pants. Kitty Murray, a heck of a

entertainer, worked with Rochester. Smiles and Smiles, a man-and-wife act, was also on the show.

One Sunday afternoon at the Savoy, Pearl and I was practicing a song we did together called *Barefoot Blues*. The date was December 7, 1941.

"Lord have mercy," she wailed, "I just heard on the radio them Japanese done bombed Pearl Harbor. Lord, if they drop one on New York I damn well better not die in the Savoy Ballroom."

Everyone knew we might get in a war. I tried to volunteer back in February. Noble Sissle was the head of my draft board and called to tell me they needed young men for the 369th Regiment Band. All the World War I musicians was being let go. I went down to the induction office to get my physical and found out I had hay fever and sinus trouble.

The top doctor, who was a Regular Army colonel, brushed me aside. "Sorry boy, we can't take you sick people in the Army. You'll get to sneezing out there in the trenches and give the whole damn regiment away." I got put in 4-F.

Pearl stayed with the band through the spring of 1942, when she went out with Cootie Williams. I was sorry to see her go but was glad to follow her success in show business and later in politics, although I never received even a postcard from her in all that time.

Hayes went in the Savoy on February 20, 1942, for a two-week stay against the Jay McShann band from Kansas City. Everyone knew Edgar had a damn good band. He worked against Lucky Millinder, Charlie Barnet, and Tommy Dorsey up there and cut them all. Even the Savoy dancers liked him. .

But that McShann gave us a house cleaning. I mean, every night he ripped us to pieces. When Jay turned his boys loose, he had hellions working. Just roaring wild men. Of course, he didn't have readers like we had, so he couldn't take care of a show. But as a dance band, he had it all.

In the early part of 1942, my good friend Cliff Jackson, the pianist, went with me over to the Brill Building in the heart of Tin Pan Alley. Had a little recording studio there, and I sang a couple songs: *Lay Your Habits Down* and *So Long Blues*, two of my originals. I titled that first number *Lay Your Body Down* but was told to change it. Like all the other tests I done, I didn't take it seriously.

I once brought the demo over to play for Sox Wilson and his wife, Coot Grant, old-time vaudevillians living up on Lenox, near 134th. Often went up to see them and thought they were nice people. Sox liked the sides and told me to take them over to Mayo Williams, the black talent scout for Decca.

So I got up my nerve and went down there with Sox.

"Yeah," Williams told me, "I know Hayes had a good selling B side with your *Without You* number. But you just a old trombone player, Clyde."

"Give the boy a chance," Sox told him.

"I don't take no chance on somebody not known," Mayo said raising his voice. Then he smiled. "Tell you what I'll do. I'll fix it with Louis Jordan to record your songs. They fit him good."

Sox was sitting sort of behind him, shaking his head no. But he didn't have to tell me that. I knew how it worked—take the songs and goodbye.

I got up and left, went home, and threw the record in the drawer with the others. Didn't make no more tests for a long time after that.

Through most of 1942, I worked the Savoy with Franz Jackson, Dave Nelson, and other bands while Edgar was laying off again. Sometimes I doubled on both bandstands and though I was young, it was a damn hard thing to do. I liked to work hard. Do my job. All the Savoy bands knew I took care of business, so I got a lot of work up there.

I was with Dave Nelson when he recorded some twelve sides but never heard nothing about them coming out—maybe because the people that paid for them was South Americans.

I was now with Hayes over five years. Although he had a top reputation as a pianist and band leader, by June of 1942 he wasn't working at all. Even other bands couldn't understand his problem.

Then a strange thing happened.

One day I was walking down Seventh Avenue and saw Edgar standing on the corner. Looked depressed as usual.

"Man, this is a tough town," he moaned.

"What's the matter, Edgar?" I knew what the matter was—he was a Gemini and those born under that sign just cannot make it in New York. Not his fault, he simply not compatible. I knew that.

"I'm at the end of my rope," he said. "I done everything I can. Double and triple booked, booked myself, cut prices, took all the shit jobs. But I still can't make it. Everytime I get my band started goin' good, these damn people—if they ain't them niggers then it's the ofays—take my jobs, take my men, gimme a bad time. You the onlyest one that's sticking with me, Clyde."

He looked bad. Took his glasses off and held his eyes. I thought he would cry.

I invited him to join me for a Chinese chop suey dinner. We talked for hours, and I soon realized he was going to give up the business completely.

"Got a idea," I said.

"What is it?"

"Jimmy Butts' wife's grandmother is a spiritualist around the corner and I was up some months ago for a reading."

"Aw, Clyde, you don't believe that stuff?"

"Now listen," I said, "she told me things about my mother and father that nobody knew but me. Said they still watching over me, guiding and helping me."

"Well, I don't know . . ."

"Also said the man I work for needed help and she knew what to do about it."

"What it cost?"

"She take two dollars."

"Ain't got two dollars. I'm on my ass."

So I gave him the money, and he went up the next day to see Madam Daisy Harod on 130th, near Eighth. She told him all his problems was due to his first wife that put a bad jinx on him and he been carrying that for years. So she took it off and said things would be better, that his greatest wish would come true.

The very next day the William Morris Agency called him. They never booked Hayes before but gave him a eight-week lounge job playing piano at the Somerset House in Riverside, California—started him off at two hundred a week.

He did so good they extended his stay indefinately, raised him to three hundred, and allowed him to add some side pieces. Moved his family out there, bought a beautiful home, and was never in debt or out of money again. Edgar worked the Somerset for many years until the place closed. Then had his pick of jobs.

I visited him out there many times, and we always talked long about Madam Daisy Harod and her strange prediction that come true.

After Edgar left for the coast, George Wilson, who was in Fats Waller's band, heard I was at liberty and got me to fill in when he went with Charlie Johnson to Atlantic City. Fats had Bob Williams, Eugene Sedric, Johnny "Bugs" Hamilton, George James, Hank Duncan, Herman Autrey, Al Casey, Slick Jones, and other good musicians. We did a week at the Royal in Baltimore and another at the Howard in Washington, D.C., around July.

Ed Kirkeby, Fats' manager, asked me to take a September tour, but I saw Fats only wanted his horns playing parts and that wasn't for me.

Took a quick job with the Sunset Royals orchestra backing Ella Fitzgerald out in Staten Island and at the Savoy. Jimmy Smith was on first trumpet for that date.

It was the Saturday before Labor Day in September 1942. Was playing a week with Dave Nelson's orchestra against Jay McShann at the Savoy.

Jay came over. "Houseman, you done played with just about everybody else up here. Now I like to have you in my band—regular."

Hell, he couldn't say that fast enough. I grabbed the job.

21. Jay McShann's Kansas City Orchestra, 1942–1943

Everybody called me Houseman at the Savoy. Jack LaRue, the head bouncer, gave me the name.

"Man, you here more then me," he said.

The Savoy Ballroom was the most popular dancehall in the world. Had a double bandstand featuring two bands working alternate sets. The Number One stand was for the regular house band and the other for visiting groups. They called that the Battle of Music.

Some of the greatest bands in the country worked there "against" each other: Fletcher Henderson, Chick Webb, Duke Ellington, Benny Goodman, Erskine Hawkins, Count Basie, Glenn Miller, the Casa Loma orchestra, the Savoy Sultans. All the best. And two or three times a week there was broadcasts over WMCA radio direct from the Savoy. And on Sunday, too.

By this time the Depression had died out. People working, more going out for a good time, more people giving dances, and there was more money around. The Savoy was the place to go.

The Track, as we called it, was bigger then Roseland—could take a hell of a crowd, at least five thousand people. Located upstairs on Lenox Avenue in Harlem, the place stretched all the way between 140th and 141st on the right side going uptown.

People always lined up on Lenox waiting to get in, sometimes there be more standing outside then inside. After paying eighty-five cents admission, you walked up the marble stairs to a nicely kept ballroom. Fancy wall decorations all over, thick patterned carpets on the floor, soft benches for sitting, round tables for drinking, and a heavy brass railing all around the long, polished dance floor.

Happy, laughing faces was all jammed in under different colored spot lights. The room sure was terrific. Even the bouncers wore tuxedos and looked more distinguished then most of the customers.

People danced or just sat around watching the wild, sweating dancers do their steps. The Savoy Lindy Hoppers was the feature and was something to see. Came out in special uniforms, each with different colors—the gals in short, crazy skirts. The fellows had on bright silk overalls.

And dance? Man, those jitterbugs just loose as a goose. Feet going all which-ways, hands flapping and waving, partners sliding between the other's legs, frontwards, backwards, bodies tossed in the air, legs straight up, clothes flying—Lord, they were *fast*. New steps. Old steps. Impossible steps. When they did their thing, everybody cleared the floor and watched. Those dancers couldn't be topped.

I especially liked to watch old Twist-Mouth Charlie and Betty, they were so hot they later turned professional. The famous Snake Hips Tucker came in regular, but they had guys doing his whole damn routine just as good as he did. Only they didn't have his name. Every living person up there could dance, and if he was just average, he stayed the hell off the floor because he had no business out there. Liable to get run over and smashed to death.

The Lindy Hop, The Big Apple, Suzy-Q, Truckin', The Bumpy Bump, and other dances became popular all over the world and they started right there at the Savoy. Three or four different Lindy Hopper groups worked around town with some of the original Savoy Hoppers heading each. Jitterbug contests was common, and the prize be maybe five dollars, and those Savoy Hoppers won every time.

People came from everywhere to see the Savoy—Europe, South America, China, Japan. Arrived in busses—come to sit and watch the fun. Downtown people always driving up in limos and cabs. Lana Turner, Jack Oakie, George Raft, Greta Garbo in her dark glasses, all those famous people. Raft was suppose to be a good dancer. Hell, up there he was just ordinary.

From 1931 all through the Depression, there be more whites coming in the Savoy then blacks. When money was hard to come by, local whites came in from everywhere—East Harlem, Columbia University, downtown—and kept the Savoy going. The place couldn't of survived the Depression without those white kids.

Moe Gale was the owner of the Savoy with his two sons, Moe, Jr., and Tim. Charles Buchanan, a West Indian, was the business manager and saw that everything ran good. Hired and fired. Kept order.

If anybody acted a fool, got drunk, made trouble, then Buchanan got rough. No matter who the person was—guest, dancer, bandsman—he snap his fingers and Jack LaRue, Stackhouse, and some of the other black bouncers was all over him. His butt got thrown down those long stairs right to the policemen that was always stationed there. The bulls pitched the guy headfirst in their waiting patrol wagon and took him away.

Sometimes those Southern black servicemen came in and let their hair down. They be gone as fast as they got there. Wham and out!

Once some lesbians got to fighting in the ladies' room with lots of cussing, battling, and those giant bouncers went right in there and threw them all the hell out. The old gals was rough, but the LaRue crowd was rougher—some of them trained with Joe Louis.

Anyone made trouble there, never came back. Barred out forever, black or white. Charles Buchanan and his giants saw to that.

Mr. Buchanan let us rehearse during the day and even allowed bands that didn't work the Savoy to rehearse there. Some bands come in just to have their picture taken. Dancers always there in the afternoon with record players, practicing new steps.

When Jay McShann hired me he paid fifty-five dollars a week when the scale wasn't but fifty. On the road he paid eleven dollars a night, more then a majority of New York bands was paying. We wore special uniforms—tan jackets, brown pants, tan shoes, and dark green bow ties on white shirts.

Jay had a band that was special. Had unknown stars, guys I was sure was going to make names for themselves some day. Damn good solo musicians and all well rehearsed. The band had a Western style: Kansas City jazz all mixed in with rocking, hard Texas swing.

After Jay came to New York from Kansas City and got good notice, he hired Skippa Hall to write for him. Skippa was a terrific arranger and pianist and knew exactly what each guy could do.

My first job with Jay McShann was on the Tuesday after Labor Day, September 8, 1942. Right there in the Savoy. I replaced Frog, who was trying to get in the Army. The first trombonist, Little Joe Baird, was a nice player but was the youngest in the band and wasn't used to playing those hard New York arrangements of Skippa Hall's. Didn't like those numbers with high B-flat and high C and D notes or those straight sweet tunes featuring the brass. Many times I had to alternate the first and second trombone parts with him.

The great Charlie "Yardbird" Parker was feature alto; John Jackson, first alto; Jimmy Forrest took the hell-fired tenor solos; Freddie Culliver, section tenor; and Bo McCain from Oklahoma City was baritone sax.

Bernard "Buddy" Anderson took first trumpet parts and Orville "Piggy" Minor, feature and second trumpet. Never did know why they called him that—maybe because he was so small. Bob Merrill was feature and third trumpet; Eugene "Gene" Ramey, bass fiddle; and Leonard Enois, electric guitar.

Gus Johnson, now he was one hell of a swing drummer. Had a way of soaking his slick hair with a wet towel before one of his wild solos so his hair fly around and water come spraying off like sweat. He was exciting to see.

Walter Brown was feature blues singer, and Al Hibbler, who was born blind, took mostly the pop numbers. With Jay as leader and pianist, that was one hell of a band. Yes it was.

After John Jackson took a war defense job in Kansas City, Joe Evans came in on straight and sweet alto solos.

Walter Brown often sang his *Confessin' the Blues* and *'Fore Day Rider*. Hibbler was doing *Blues in the Night* and a lot of sweet pieces. Bob Merrill was also a damn good singer, but most of the time Jay wouldn't give him a chance. Had to beg Jay to sing his specialty, *Wrong Neighborhood Blues*.

I remember one number we did called *Bottle It*—a real hot, jump-

When Jay McShann turned his 1942 band loose in the Savoy, he had hellions working. Just roaring wild men. (Photo courtesy of Frank Driggs collection.)

ing arrangement. All instrumental. Skippa rehearsed each section of
the band separately, sometimes as many as six times before we got it
down. Some of the fellows was slow readers, so it took a little longer.
We also did *Hip, Hip Horray; I Don't Want to Set the World on Fire;*
and *Roll 'Em.*

Our speciality was *Cherokee,* featuring Charlie Parker. He was a sensational soloist—I thought he was the greatest alto man of 1942. Parker
was playing so much that most people didn't know what in hell he was
doing. Was over the heads of New York musicians, and I'm not going to
lie, he was over mine also.

Parker seemed to be ahead of his time, sort of futuristic, but whatever
he was doing, I knew he was doing a lot of it. Plenty of wild improvis-
ing but still swinging. Placed his phrases just right, and if he got too far
out, got back without getting lost, always on time and it sounded so
good. John Jackson could play the same way but had a much prettier,
smoother tone then Charlie. Both boys came up together in Kansas City.

I always say that nobody teach a musician to play jazz—he needs
something within him to work on. He got to feel it. Got to *know.* Play
around with the melody but don't lose it. Improvise on chords too.
That's how to create ideas of your own.

I liked talking with Charlie Parker. He thought it was very funny
when I told him how so many people always mixed up my name.

Like the time in 1937 at this mucty-muck party, you know the kind—
think they so damned high-toned, get a little too close and they move
away slightly. So the old hostess was high on spiked punch and kept
introducing me as Mr. Bradhurst. Then as Mr. Brandywine. Finally as
Mr. Barnyard.

I couldn't stand it no more. "Please! My name is Bernhardt.
Bernhardt! B-E-R-N-H-A-R-D-T."

"Well," she said sort of stiff-necked, "everybody makes an error *sometime."* Then with this blank face she introduces me to a white gentleman standing there. "Mr. Davis, I'd like you to meet *Mr. Cornbread."*

When I told that to Parker he near fell out laughing. After that, he
started calling me Cornbread.

Told me he got the name Yardbird because he was crazy about eating
chicken: fried, baked, boiled, stewed, anything. He liked it. Down there
in the South, all chickens are called yardbirds. Every house had some.

Most of the time Parker was broke and kept borrowing money. He lay
a line of sweet talk on me and get it everytime. But I knew he was a
good-hearted guy and do anybody a favor if he could.

Jay McShann was one of the best, down-to-earth guys I ever wanted to work for. Just like any other musician in the band. In fact, he was *too* good, and guys took advantage of his easy nature. But he always tried to keep peace and harmony.

We all socialized on our time off, only it was in two groups—the Lushies and the Users. Jay, Joe Evans, Freddie Culliver, myself, and others that liked their whiskey, wine, or beer was the Lushies. I didn't drink much, but sometimes a little whiskey now and then after work.

Charlie Parker, Walter Brown, Little Joe, and some others was in the second group. They didn't drink but was messing with dope and usually kept to themselves. I never been around any musicians in New York that used the stuff, because good bands there wouldn't want them if they got wind of it. No matter how good they were, they just wouldn't hire them.

But Jay didn't give a damn what anybody in his band did as long as it didn't get in the way of the job. And I think he was right. A person has to respect his job and not do those kind of things in the open. When it got in the open, the man had trouble.

I used to talk with Parker about his habit. Told me he been smoking reefers as a kid in Kansas City. Now, he said, he tried everything and it had him good.

"You New York guys," he said, "you got more sense then these Western musicians. You don't mess with this goddamn shit." I really felt sorry for him. "I know it's gonna out me one of these days," he continued, "but man, I'm not a bad cat, this is just my life and I can't do without it."

After we closed the Savoy, the band went out playing the Howard Theater in Washington, D.C., for a week, the Royal in Baltimore for another week, then the Paradise in Detroit.

It was at the Paradise that Parker got in trouble. The band played its first show that Friday night. After we did Mary Lou Williams' *Roll 'Em*, a hell of a band number, Walter Brown sang a blues. When we hit *Cherokee*, Parker walked down front as usual and began blowing real hot when all at once he just fell over. Down on the floor, out cold.

People in the audience screamed. We kept playing but I was dumbfounded—thought he dropped dead. They pulled the curtain and the stage manager dragged Parker off, put him in a back room, and tried to revive him while we continued the show.

After the set we all ran back and Parker was sitting there laughing. "What in hell happened, man?" he was saying. We were wondering the same thing. "Goddamn, must have had too much of that shit."

Jay didn't say anything. He was easygoing.

The next day some guys came up to where Parker and Brown was staying, a rooming house run by a big 250-pound feminine guy, out there on Adams Avenue. Tore the place apart, ripped carpets up, cut open mattresses. Didn't find what they looking for, but that gay guy came running backstage to see Jay.

"I wanna see that damn McShann," he kept shouting.

"That's me," growled Jay.

"Those goddamn men come in my place looking for some shit and tore your niggers' room apart. If I knew they using dope they never get their fat asses in my hotel."

"What in hell I got to do with it?"

"Those mothers are in your band, man. You gotta pay damages."

"The hell with you," Jay said. "What they do off the stand is their business. Everybody here is three times seven. Why in hell don't you see the FBI? They the ones messed you up."

And Jay left the guy standing there cussing.

I think Jay was right about the FBI. I remember a young white guy always hanging around the Users bunch. Once saw him working in Charlie Barnet's band back at the Golden Gate in New York but never heard him play a note—never knew who he was, never saw him before. When the same guy showed in Detroit, I began getting suspicious. After the raid, he was gone with the wind.

Might have pulled the wool over those KC boys' eyes, but I knew the FBI was sniffing close and didn't nobody know it.

So Parker played the rest of that weekend, but by Monday he was high again. The owner of the theater told Jay to get rid of him, and the next day Parker was on his way back to New York. Peck Austin replaced him.

Walter Brown ran into some other kind of trouble in Baltimore. He was a hell of a blues singer, but in the Royal he wasn't accepted.

When he came out singing that line, "Baby, baby, don't you want a man like me?" those old black gals sitting down front laughed. "Hell no," they shouted, "you too black and ugly, child."

That's how ignorant some Negroes were in 1942. His records went over big, but when people saw him in person, they didn't take to his looks or color. It happened in the Howard Theater, too. Those bitches ratted him so, Jay had to take Walter out and pay him for the whole week. I heard Bull Moose Jackson had the same problem.

Never did understand that kind of stuff. No sir.

The band continued traveling, playing mostly one-nighters in the Deep South through the Carolinas, Georgia, Florida, Mississippi, Louisiana, back to New York state, then out west to Missouri, Arkansas, Texas, Oklahoma, Kansas, Nebraska, Minnesota, Wisconsin.

We played mostly dances and the band was a smash. Drew more then

Louis Armstrong, the Ink Spots, and other top names wherever we went. Sometimes we played radio remotes, and when we worked the Band Box in Chicago, broadcast at least four times a week for a month.

While we were in Chicago, Russell Smith, who was first trumpet with Cab Calloway, tried to get me to come over to Cab. But I liked the McShann band. Yes I did.

We were deep in wartime then, so it was almost impossible to charter a band bus because the Army was using them all. We had no choice but to go as regular passengers on the train. Some of the guys never did get used to not having a private bus for themselves—they get to balling around in some city, messing up, and the train be gone. Sometimes they missed three or four straight jobs before somebody thought to call the New York office and find out where the band was. Then they scramble to meet us at the next job.

Trains was so damn crowded in those war years. We wouldn't of gotten on the train at all if our road manager hadn't paid off some of the station masters. When we get on, there barely be room to stand in a corner. Many times I sat on my suitcase for three hundred miles—sleep on it, too. Other riders, mostly soldiers, slept on the floor, and when the conductor came through he had to step over everybody.

In the South many trains be segregated and the problems even worse.

Food wasn't available, so most of the time we did without. Bring on sardines and crackers or maybe some bread and bologna, but the bologna didn't stay fresh long. Sometimes we run outside for a candy bar when the train pulled in a station. But it pulled right out, so we hop back fast. We paid for our own food and accommodations—that was our expense.

Schedules were always getting loused up due to late trains and midnight missed connections. When we got in a town we search for a cab to take us to a hotel that was always filled up. Even my YMCA rooming houses were not always available. Man, it was rough.

I ran into my share of woman trouble one time down in Dallas.

During our last set, this six-foot, 350-pound woman stomps up to the bandstand. She was mahogany color and had jet black hair hanging down her back in two long braids. Man, was she big. Her head was big, she had big shoulders, big arms, big old awkward-looking legs, big feet—*everything* she had was big.

I looked around and she was standing next to me, smiling. She had big teeth, too. I tried paying her no mind, but she kept smiling, like a old, fat Buddha.

"Where yawl come from, honey?" she said sweetly.

I was still playing the set. "We in from Houston," I said between puffs.

"You look tired."

"Yeah."

"Feel like a drink?"

"No, not particularly."

She dragged over a chair and sat herself down heavily next to me. By the time the set was over, this fat old broad had ordered a setup, pulled out a bottle of Old Grand Dad, and put it in front of me.

The guys all started to laugh. "Man, old Clyde done trapped himself a bear!"

I didn't want any part of this deal. Hell, no.

But she looked determined. "My husband in the Army two months now," she said, pouring out a tall drink, "and here I done found myself a new boyfriend."

"Hold on there, gal."

"Drink all you want, honey, we take the rest home with us."

"I ain't goin' no place with you."

"I got salted-down chicken in the icebox I'll fry up."

"Listen woman, I can't go with you."

"What you mean, yawl *can't?*"

"I'm married," I lied fast, "and my wife's at the hotel right now."

"The hell with her," she said, turning nasty and loud. "I'm married also and yawl gonna park your hips in my bed tonight."

"No, I'm not," I said, raising my voice, too.

"Don't tell me what you ain't gonna do. Yawl too damn little a runt to talk that way to me." She was shouting now.

"I'll talk any damn way I please, woman." I tried to sound tough.

"You talkin' like you want me to whup you good, nigger."

People turning around to see what was happening. The band guys were all breaking up, never seen me lose my cool before.

Suddenly, the woman grabs my collar with her big paw and lifts me right up out of my chair. I was just shaking and hanging, damn near choking. Her bloodshot eyes looked straight in mine, waiting for a answer.

"No way," I gasped out.

With that, she hit me upside my head with her other fat fist. WHAM! Then WHAM! again. Stars started moving around inside my eyes. Music stands got knocked down. Chairs fell over. Sheet music flying. With all my strength I hauled off and hit that damn bitch as hard as I could. My hand stung from the blow.

She just grunted. "Now you done made me *real* mad. I'm gonna take your ass apart right now!"

Somehow I twisted away, grabbed my horn, and made a run for the door. All the guys laughing so loud they must of thought this was a damn old Pigmeat show at the Apollo.

"You big, old ugly grizzly bear," I shouted over my shoulder, "your daddy's a hairy gorilla, and your mama's a goddamn baboon."

"Don't dozens me, you little shrimp," she bellowed as she started after me. "Come back here. I ain't finished with you yet!"

As I ran out the front she come bouncing behind me like a heavy sack of mush. Jay McShann's cousin was sitting out in her big roadster in the shadows.

"Lemme in! Lemme in!" I shouted. "Open the door *quick*." As the rear door swung open, I dove in and laid flat on the floor, pulling my horncase on top of me.

Just then Jay came out and looked in the car. "Hey Cornbread, what in hell you doin' down there?"

"Man, get in the car," I whispered, "that old bear is after me and she liable to whup me some more. Let's get outa here *fast*."

As we drove out past the front of the dancehall, I peeped over the car window, and there she was looking up and down the road. Jay drove me straight to my rooming house, but I was sure that crazy woman followed me, so I was too nervous to sleep that night.

I heard later she showed at the hotel where I was supposed to be staying and whupped hell out of the desk clerk, smashed open some rooms, and punched the guys around.

"Where's the damn slide-horn player?" she kept shouting. "Wait'll I get my hands on him."

Man, she was like a cage of apes.

By daybreak I was at the railroad station looking in all directions in case she was still waiting for me. I spotted a white Texas Ranger and explained my situation. He escorted me to my train section and right to my seat. It wasn't until I got to Fort Worth I stopped shaking.

The band caught up with me there, but a month later Jay scheduled a return dance at the same hall in Dallas. I told him I was sick and took the next train out to San Antonio. Never did go back to that town. Ever.

Since that time, I always been afraid of "bears" hanging around the band—even the medium-size ugly gals we called "taters" scared me. I liked the "yams," the real pretty girls, but the "bears" and "taters" always scared the "yams" away.

I worked many more months with Jay, all one-nighters through the Midwest. A very heavy schedule. Somewhere in Kansas, Hal Singer came in to replace Freddie Culliver. He's a great tenor and fit in good.

Clyde Bernhardt on the bandstand at the Happy Hour Nightclub, Minneapolis Minn., July 15, 1943. Seated, *Joe Evans (as).*

By June we were in the Happy Hour Nightclub in Minneapolis, Minnesota. After nine months with Jay McShann, I was beginning to feel the strain of it all. No layoffs. Always tired, my feet swelling up. Plenty of headaches—totally exhausted. Never had no problems like that before, so I gave Jay my two-weeks' notice.

On July 20, after Ira Petiford finally replaced me, I returned to New York and went straight to my doctor.

22. Cecil X. Scott's Orchestra, 1943–1944

Old Doc Desmond told me to take it easy for at least six months. Said the heavy schedule of one-nighters was hurting my health and I should stay in town and take a good rest. Otherwise, he said, being on the road so much might bring on other illnesses, maybe even heart trouble. I didn't want that. No sir.

Just about this time, Joe Glaser, who was managing Louis Armstrong, Andy Kirk, and June Richmond, was looking for me over at my Uncle Jim's apartment up on 129th Street. Glaser was a millionaire and had lots of connections. Drove up to Harlem in his big black limo with the JOE license plates and left a message for me.

When I went to see him, he tried talking me into joining Louis' group. Hot and heavy for me to meet the band in Omaha, Nebraska. Said Louis had a bigger schedule then Jay had, that he pay good money, and even throw in four band uniforms I wouldn't have to pay for.

It sounded good, but I turned him down. I knew Louis was flying his guys around in Army bombers, and as I had a hell of a thing against flying, the whole conversation made me nervous.

I told Glaser I was not going back on the road until I got my health problems together.

Relaxing wasn't easy for me, but I enjoyed it. Every night I slept in my same bed, ate three good meals a day, and all right on time. And if I wanted home-cooked meals, just went outside and took my pick of eating places. Harlem had some of the best barbecue you ever wanted to stick a tooth in.

After a few weeks I got a telegram from Jay McShann wanting me back, but I wouldn't take any regular job with anybody. I was enjoying my rest.

Something came to my mind this was a good time to learn to play the piano. Always wanted to learn ever since Mama got one for my brothers back in the twenties, so I signed up for some lessons at the New York School of Music on 125th Street. I liked all that fingering and learned to pick out some tunes after a while. It was almost like a hobby—kept at it steady for a year or so whenever I was around New York—but never got good enough to play professional.

Later I took a few dance gigs with Cecil Scott's orchestra out in Coney Island and in some Italian halls in the Canarsie section of Brooklyn. Just to keep my lip up.

By the first of October in 1943, Cecil got steady work at New York's Ubangi Club down on Broadway and West 52d and changed the band's name to the Ubangi Club orchestra. Wasn't but nine pieces: three brass, three reeds, and three rhythm. Cecil played tenor and clarinet; Frank Powell, first lead-off alto and clarinet; Al Campbell, third alto and clarinet—he was a good section man; Kenneth Roane, first trumpet; Henry Goodwin, who I worked with in the Hayes band, second trumpet and feature hot-man.

Cecil Scott's orchestra at the Ubangi Club, New York City, Dec. 24, 1943. Left to right: Al Campbell (as), Thomas Barney (sb), Frank Etbridge (p), Frank Powell (as), Clyde Bernbardt (tb), Cecil Scott (ldr/ts), Harold Austin (d), Henry Goodwin (t), Kenneth Roane (t). Unidentified soldier paid to have photo taken.

Also in there was Harold "Hal" Austin, a better drummer then he ever got credit for, read or fake; Thomas Barney from Savannah, Georgia, on bass; and Frank Ethridge, pianist. I took the job on a regular basis— as long as it was only local work. No road tours.

I been knowing Cecil a long time by now and remembered back in the twenties when he was doing that crazy Cab Calloway stuff in front of his band. Like he be leading and playing his sax and suddenly fall in a big split, then rise slowly as he kept blowing a hot solo. The people all loved it. He wasn't doing that kind of business now because of his bad accident in 1931. Cecil often spoke of the woman that took him over to her apartment, and while he was getting undressed, a wild man started punching loud on the door. Banging, smashing, and cussing.

"If there's a goddamn nigger in there with my wife I'm gonna cut that sucker's face," the guy was shouting.

Cecil said he was never so scared in all his life—his heart was in his mouth. The guy was breaking down his only exit, so he panicked and jumped out the window, forgetting it was four stories up and near about killed himself. Smashed up his foot and leg bad—got all pushed together in a bloody mess. Every bone was broken. Then gangrene set in, and they took the whole damn thing off. Wore a cork leg after that.

"Man," he told me, "the Bible tells the truth. I treated my wife and family wrong. God didn't take my life, he just taught me a hard lesson."

Everybody knew how he lost his leg—never hid the story. When you fool around with a married woman, you open up the gates to hell.

Cecil had a six-month contract with the Ubangi but kept working there long after that. It was just a average-looking club, some imitation pictures of Africa on the wall, but not a whole lot of them. The bandstand was suppose to be a old native hut or something. The Ubangi was popular for many years, and about 1949 changed over to be Birdland.

They had a good floor show there, almost two hours long. Chappie Willet wrote the music and Donald Heywood produced. Alan Drew was master of ceremonies and male comedian. Used to have this big cigar stuffed in his mouth all the time—that was his trademark. His jokes was kind of smutty but he had the people laughing.

Moms Mabley was the female comedian at the Ubangi. Mabel Lee, dancer Derby Wilson, and singer Myra Johnson was also on the bill. When Myra left, Margaret Watkins came in—I worked with her in the Whitman's show in '29. Had a heavy contralto voice and could sure holler them blues.

Those female impersonators, the Ubangi Club Boys, got so popular

they went out touring long before I worked there. The club had real
chorus girls then.

It was about January of 1944 that Joe Springer, the owner of the
Ubangi, sent us down to the Center Street police station to get a cabaret
card. This was a wartime rule in New York to make sure you didn't have
no record of using dope and messing up. Checked me out, but I never
even got a citation in my whole life.

The card had my picture on it next to my name and birthdate. Entertainers like Billie Holiday, Charlie Parker, and a gang of others didn't get
a card, and it was damn tough for them after that. The city stopped
those cards some years later, and I still have mine around the house
some place.

After working the Ubangi for about five months, a rumor started
going around that the club was cutting expenses. Something about a
new war tax and they were going to drop a musician or two, maybe a
couple chorus girls in order to break even. I thought they doing terrific
business but heard that's what they were going to do.

Since I didn't know if I was the one to be cut off, I called Luis Russell—
I heard he had a whole lot of work booked—and went up to the Savoy
for a rehearsal. The next night I gave Cecil my two-weeks' notice.

23. Luis Russell's Orchestra, 1944

"Don't know why in hell those other bands didn't feature you as a
singer," Luis Russell told me. "You are damn good."

I explained to Fess (we called all our band leaders Fess), that I always
been hired to play trombone and only did what I was suppose to do.
Besides, after I got through playing some of them hard arrangements,
with high D's and E's and often having to help out other trombonists, I
didn't have a mind to push myself in as a vocalist.

"You gonna make a singing name for yourself someday, Clyde," he
said.

After I joined Russell at the Savoy on the first of March, he had me
doing about nine vocal numbers a night. I never been a feature singer
before and couldn't understand the attention I was getting. When I
walked to the mike to shout my blues after a trombone solo, the audience raise hell, clap, and cheer. Seemed to think a singing bandsman
was unusual, and that probably put me over.

Russell formed this band right after he left Louis Armstrong. Born and raised in Panama, but we called him West Indian. The man was a good piano player, but I wouldn't compare him to Hayes. Hayes was one of the greatest. But Russell was a wonderful musician and great as a musical director—could lead the band through a hard show. Very experienced.

Taft Chandler and Jesse Powell played tenor; Buddy Payne—I worked with him on the Whitman Sisters' show—and Clarence Grimes was the altos. Howard Robertson was baritone sax; Howard Callender, also from Panama, on first trumpet; and Chester Boone took third trumpet and sang a few numbers. Snooky Butler, from Harrisburg, came in a few months later on second trumpet, Gene Ramey on bass, and then Thomas Barney from Cecil's orchestra replaced him.

Russell had another bass player after that, a crazy guy I used to call Smitty. Love to trap pigeons up in the Bronx and make pigeon stew. Had a pressure cooker he said killed all the bugs and the birds tasted as good as chickens.

Eric Henry was on drums and a fellow by the name of Alex "Razz" Mitchell came in after him. Luther Brown, the other trombonist, didn't

Luis Russell was the first to present me as a feature singer, Mar. 1, 1944. (Photo courtesy of Dr. Albert Vollmer.)

have my experience, and I liked to help out. A lot of New York players wouldn't do that, but I remembered how I got helped when I was young, so it didn't bother me none.

Can't call all the others, but there was about fifteen men in the band.

Nora Blunt—she just graduated from high school in New York—came in as girl singer.

After two months in the Savoy, Russell took a package show on the road. Blues singer Lil Green headlined, and the Deep River Boys sang spiritual-type songs.

We traveled by train until somewhere down in Tennessee where Russell hired out a sleeper bus—we lay on beds all the time because there were no seats. The beds all arranged in three decks, and people kept climbing over those on the bottom row to get to the top. It was uncomfortable but Russell couldn't get no better because of the war.

We rode that way working one-nighters through Pennsylvania, Ohio, Indiana, Kentucky, Virginia, the Carolinas, Tennessee, Georgia, Florida, Alabama, Mississippi, Louisiana, and Texas—damn hard touring right to the middle of July.

Lil Green had two big record hits, *Romance in the Dark* and *Why Don't You Do Right?*

"*In the Dark* was what put me over," she once told me. "Made that test in Chicago with a couple local boys, took it home, and played hell out of it. Liked the way it sounded. All my friends played it, too. When I brought it over to the Bluebird Record Company in 1940, the man went crazy."

She damn well knew she could do something better, but the man put that test out with all the gritty noise and everything, and before she knew it, had a smash hit. That was her start up.

Lil kept telling me to do the same thing. I told her how I done that once with Decca and got turned down by Mayo Williams because I had no name.

"Honey," she laughed, "colored people ain't gonna do nothin' for you. Let some of them whites hear you and you'll get someplace."

I appreciated her advice. It was to prove very true for me almost two years later.

When we were down in Chattanooga, Tennessee, we met Lil's aunt, who brought the band two great big cane baskets filled with half dozen hot, roasted chickens, about twenty-five sweet-potato pies, fresh baked rolls, homemade jelly, and lots more. Like a feast in Harlem. Lil's family came from a little old country place down in Mississippi, near the Louisiana line, and that woman sure could cook up a breeze.

Lil Green always wore long gowns on stage with nice jewelry and a pretty band around her hair. Everywhere we went, people knew her, had her records, and liked the way she sang the blues.

But when we got to Florida, she started giving Russell a bad time. "They got too damn much singing on this show," she cried. "Hell, *I'm* the star here."

I knew she was talking about me. I been getting good hands and plenty encores and it had to come out. But I was surprised she made a crack like that.

"We all part of the same show," Russell finally told her. "The better everybody is, the better the whole package is." He was looking annoyed. "If you talkin' about Clyde or Nora, I hired them to sing with *my* band and that's got nothin' to do with you." Then he pointed his long finger at her. "This thing of one star on the show not allowin' nobody to do nothin', I won't tolerate. I'll pull the damn band if this continues."

I admired Luis Russell because he stood up for his band. Most guys wouldn't of backed their men that way—especially when the star was making nine hundred a week and I was getting twenty dollars a night. Hell, she could of made big trouble, and Fess knew that, too. But he had his band in mind all the time.

We came back from the tour almost three months later and finished up at the Apollo for the week of July 21. Besides the Royal in Baltimore, the Apollo was the toughest house in black show business. Saw many good acts, big names, too, get booted off the stage there. And I couldn't forget what happened to Walter Brown in Baltimore.

So I was a little nervous making my Apollo singing debut.

For my spot, I sang Russell's great B-flat blues, *I Need Your Kind of Loving*. It was a heck of a jump number and the band was pushing hard. When I finished, a tremendous roar came rolling up toward me. People whooping and hollering. You couldn't hear your ears.

I was so surprised, I just stood there. Russell was all smiles and quickly struck up a encore, *Straighten Up and Fly Right*, the new Nat Cole hit. When that broke it up again, Frank Schiffman, the owner of the Apollo, came running out of his office to see what was happening.

Then I did Russell's slow *Back o' Town Blues*, and they still wouldn't let me off. I knew Lil Green was waiting to go on, so I closed with Russell's jumping arrangement of *St. Louis Blues*, with all those stop-time breaks in there, and walked off to long applause.

Lil was standing in the wings giving me her mean-mistreater look. "Clyde, you done tore this damn show apart. I'm suppose to be the star here and you makin' it rough for me tonight."

Newspaper publicity for the Club Plantation, St. Louis, Mo., Aug. 1944.

Old man Schiffman came over and patted me on the shoulder. Knew me from the Hayes band. "Where'n hell you been hidin', Clyde?"

"I'll tell you, Mr. Schiffman," I said, "I don't consider myself like a regular singer. I'm really a musician that doubles."

"The proof is in the pudding," he answered. "You're big enough to come in here as a solo act."

That night Schiffman set my photograph out front in the lobby, right next to Lil Green and Luis Russell. And the Gale office put me on regular salary—two hundred a week, work or play. Damn good money when the regular guys in the band didn't get but sixteen dollars a night and nothing when they took time off.

That week at the Apollo was something special for me. Two or three encores every show. I knew my dead father and mother was out in the audience leading the applause—I could feel it.

God did more then I ever expected him to do—I was not only a accepted jazz musician but now *earned* a name as a singer. It still brings a certain thrill to my mind.

The tour ended after the Apollo close, and Russell took the band on location to the Club Plantation in St. Louis, Missouri. Milton Buggs, a Billy Eckstine type, and Nora Blunt sang band numbers, and I did my blues. Ralph Brown was master of ceremonies—he had class, good stage personality, and could back it up with a terrific flash dance act. Ella Fitzgerald headed the floor show; Peg Leg Bates danced hot tap numbers on his wooden stump; Moke and Poke did comical Lindy dances, and Gatemouth Moore from Kansas shouted the blues.

I never did have any trouble with Gatemouth. He liked my singing and was always there to compliment me. "Man," he laugh, "I'm gonna have to take up the 'bone before you out me." I got to be a big fan of his.

After working the Plantation through August, we returned to the Apollo backing the Ink Spots, probably the top black vocal group then. That was about the time Charlie Holmes came in the band, replacing Buddy Payne. We opened the Friday before Labor Day, and that Sunday played eight shows, and on Monday we played nine. The standard was four a day. Don't mind telling you it was a heavy schedule. We could only grab a sandwich and coffee or run to the john when a solo act was out front. Were never off more then ten minutes at a time.

Russell took us back on the road after that for more one-nighters, more crowded trains, more missed meals. By October I was sick again, just like with McShann. Nervous, tired, and now I also had a bad case of bronchitis. I struggled through my two-weeks' notice, then took the next train back to New York.

My doctor was expecting me.

24. Claude Hopkins' Orchestra, 1944

Old Doc Desmond warned me not to go back on the road for a long while and to watch my meals, watch my blowing. Said I had to rest.

After taking it easy for about two weeks, I got a call one morning from Claude Hopkins. Said he was working the best job he ever had in his career: the Club Zanzibar. One of the biggest night clubs in Times Square, right on the corner of 49th and Broadway, up on the second floor. Used to be a all-white place called the Hurricane, and when Joe Howard bought it he made it the Zanzibar.

Hopkins recently opened the club and was needing a trombone. I decided that two weeks was long enough to rest and a steady New York job be no trouble at all. So in November of 1944 I joined Hopkins for a easy run.

The Zanzibar was very beautiful, and it had class. At night they dim the lights down. There was a lot of mirrors in there, and all the reflections looked pretty. Famous black talent like Bill Robinson, Ethel Waters, Bill Bailey, the Peter Sisters, the Nicholas Brothers, and Cab

Calloway worked there often. Chappie Willet wrote the floor show as he did at the Ubangi.

Blacks were allowed to come in the Zanzibar, but they couldn't get a ringside table unless they had a big name—like Joe Louis or somebody in that category. White sports people, movie stars, politicians, and money big shots always came in there. But no Lindy Hopper dancers. It was strictly the fox-trot crowd.

Most of the time ordinary people like tourists, servicemen, and office workers lined up outside a block long, but the place was sold out every night. When we took our intermission break and go downstairs to the Turf Grill, the people we saw early in the afternoon still be waiting to get in. Some never did get in. But the big shots—they got ushered right through—never a line for them.

Of the band members I remember, Kenneth Roane was on first trumpet—I worked with him in Cecil Scott's band. Was one of those guys you had to be on your P's and Q's all the time. Very precise.

Lammar Wright was on third trumpet, and John Letman came in later on second. Lammar was playing even better then when he was with the Missourians. Very loose. James Whitney and Sandy Williams on trombones, but Wilber De Paris took over for Whitney later, and then Ed Cuffee replaced him.

Pinky Williams took baritone and his brother Skippy, tenor; Joe Garland, tenor; and John brown, string bass. Wilbert Kirk, a hell of a drummer, was in there, too, one of the best in New York. Claude was on

I joined Claude Hopkins at the Zanzibar, one of the biggest night clubs in Times Square, Nov. 1944. (Photo courtesy of Frank Driggs collection.)

piano—a total of sixteen pieces in the group. Benny Carter did some of the arrangements.

My two months with Claude Hopkins was clean—no luggage prob-lems, no schedules, no worries—just steady local work. A lot of guys told me Hopkins was very hard and outspoken, but I knew he was a Virgo, and Virgo people are very critical. If you do something wrong, he tell you about it. That's for sure. I thought he was one of the nicest men I ever worked for.

In late December, when he cut down to six pieces because of that damn amusement tax, I took odd pickup jobs around town but re-turned to Hopkins at the Zanzibar many times during 1945 when he augmented.

Joe Glaser started getting after me again for some Louis Armstrong road work. But I wasn't ready. Old Doc Desmond told me to rest, didn't he?

25. The Bascomb Brothers' Orchestra, 1945

I been thinking of making another test record for myself for a long time. Jay McShann was in town looking to line up some work and agreed to back me. Charlie Parker came along, and I also got drummer Gus Johnson and Gene Ramey on string bass. Went down to the Nola Studios, located on Broadway between 51st and 52d, across from Rose-land. A lot of musicians always went there to make their tests.

I paid old man Nola for a two-hour studio session, but Jay, Charlie, and the others wouldn't take money from me. I knew plenty musicians not half as good that wouldn't cross the street without some bread first. I was going to call us Clyde Bernhardt and His Kansas City Buddies— because that's just what they were.

We recorded my own vocal numbers: *Triflin' Woman Blues; Would You Do Me a Favor?* and *Lay Your Habits Down.* Things were going along good until old man Nola started giving Charlie trouble on the fourth number, *So Good This Morning.* First he said he was too loud, then he was too close to the microphone. Finally asked Charlie to turn his back to the mike. Charlie got steamed right in the middle of that last number—told the man exactly what he thought of him. In detail.

That's when Nola got real nasty and threw us all out. Handed me the glass disc, and we were finished. I paid for two hours but barely worked a hour, and the man wouldn't give me no money back. Was damn unfair, and I knew I been cheated—worked my mind for months after that. Never could do anything with that test and it ended up in my drawer with the others.

I knew it might of been a big record for me, but it wasn't to be.

After the New Year, I began to work steady with the Bascomb Brothers' orchestra up in the Savoy for a good location job. Paul Bascomb was a top tenor player and highly rated. His brother Dud was on trumpet but usually stood out front and directed. He was quiet as a mouse. They were from Birmingham, Alabama.

Russell Gillum and a guy we called Popeye were in the trumpet section along with a white player, Larry Salerno. Bill Swindell, from Baltimore, Maryland, was alto and Johnny Hartzfield, tenor; James Whitney and Steve Pulliam, trombones.

I think Robert Harley was on piano. Isaac MaFadden was guitar and Nick Fenton, bass, both out of the Sunset Royals. Sammy Banks was drums, and Dave McRae, the section baritone, also handled the business for the band. It was sixteen pieces, but with guys all coming and going, I can't call them all.

Later the band went under the name of Dud Bascomb—I think the Gale office changed it.

I remember one time, Russell Gillum and Popeye got to arguing bad on the bandstand. Now, the Savoy didn't take kindly to trouble, from customers *or* band members. When they fell out on the dance floor, rolling around, punching out each other's teeth, Jack LaRue ran over and grabbed them both. The guys thought they were tough but hadn't met up with this giant bouncer. He booted their butts hard, picked them up, and tossed them down the stairs. Those notoriety boys never did come back to the Savoy. Or the band. Dud brought in Kenny Dorham and another trumpet the next night.

During March, the Brothers laid off like a lot of other bands was doing, so I took some short road-jobs with Jay McShann and his new band. Some public dances as far down as Washington, D.C. Still had good musicians in there, but it wasn't like his '43 band—didn't have that Kansas City sound. All New York boys now.

When Jay laid off, I came back with the Brothers. Dud lined up a record date with Joe Leibowitz of DeLuxe Records that had offices out in Linden, New Jersey. The session took place in the WOR radio studios, 1440 Broadway in New York, in the later part of May, as I recall. Dud

Dud Bascomb and his orchestra at the Savoy Ballroom, Jan. 1945. Left to right: Kenny Preston (v), Dud Bascomb (t), Courtney Williams (t), Russell Gillum (t), unknown, unknown, Popeye (t), Bill Swindell (as), Steve Pulliam (tb), Paul Bascomb (ts), James Whitney (tb), Clyde Bernhardt (tb), Dave McRae (bs). (Photo courtesy of Frank Driggs collection.)

said he was going to record me doing one of my vocal numbers, but a few days before the date I got a call.

"Clyde," he said, "I got a hell of a number here that Dan Burley wrote. Likes your singing and wants you to do his song." I was a little disappointed that he changed his mind. "I'm giving you the choice," Dud continued, "but if I was you, I do Burley's number. He can do a hell of a lot for you."

Well, I always been a person that liked to please everyone, so I agreed. The number was *Somebody's Knockin'*, and like Dud told me, it did very well.

Dan Burley was the theatrical editor for the *New York Amsterdam News* and a damn good blues pianist. He just came back from India and Burma and was playing my record of his song all over the place. Also got good air play around New York.

September 2, 1945, was VJ Day and the end of the war with Japan. I was playing a special broadcast that night with Claude Hopkins at the Zanzibar. Cab Calloway was the feature band and a act by himself. Dorothy Donegan did her piano act, and Pearl Bailey was the star attraction. It was a night to remember.

But I always thought it a strange coincidence that I was with Pearl the very day the war ended—and also started. A strange coincidence.

The Bascombs took the band on a good six-week location job in September to the Club Riviera in St. Louis, Missouri. Was the biggest black club in St. Louis, owned by Jordan Chambers, and was class all the way. Played the acts and dance sets.

When we got back, the Gale office wanted to take me and James Whitney out to the Far East with the Jeter-Pillars band. Jimmy Jeter and Charley Pillars had this terrific orchestra, but I wouldn't go. No sir. The war was supposed to be over, but I heard some of them Japs was still shooting our boys. I was scared and told them so—I never went out.

I got a call in October from Leonard Feather, the noted jazz writer and producer. Told me he liked that Dan Burley number I did on De-Luxe and wanted to do something for me. We met later at the Famous Door on the Street—West 52d Street, that is.

Gene Ramey and Ben Webster was working there, and Feather asked me to sing a number. When I finished, the club owner offered me a job, but the Bascombs had a good tour coming up so I turned him down. Feather promised to call as soon as he lined up something special.

The Bascombs were booked into Unit 259 on the United Service Organization circuit sometime in October, playing U.S. Army, Navy, and Marine theaters down the East Coast. We got paid over union scale, and our money came in every Saturday noon, wherever we were. If the bank was closed, somebody opened it up just to pay us.

We traveled by train, and when we got to where we were going, government busses picked us up. All reservations made by the USO. Stayed right in the officers' quarters on the Marine bases, and our food was free in the officers' mess hall. A good deal all around.

Besides the full Bascomb band, the feature singer on the tour was Rosa Brown, who been big in the "Hot Mikado" show in New York. Her material was somewhere between blues, jazz, and gospel, and I thought she was a hell of a entertainer. George Williams of the old George Williams—Bessie Brown vaude team was along, working with Smiles, a tall, brownskin guy. He was half the Smiles and Smiles team. They also had Strawberry Russell doing a novelty act, playing something like a cigar box. There was others on the bill, and we had a damn good show.

Late in November I got a call from Leonard Feather to do his Musicraft record date. The USO unit was in Richmond, Virginia, at the time, so I rushed down to the railroad station after the Saturday show and caught a train for New York. By 6 P.M. Sunday I was at Feather's home going over his numbers. The session took place at 9 the next morning, November 26. It was a pickup group with top-name musicians, with Feather on piano and me on trombone and vocals. We did four songs, all Feather originals, and he featured my name large over the band on the record label. I helped him with some lyrics on *Lost Weekend Blues*, and he also gave me co-composer credit.

We finished by 1 P.M., and I was back in Richmond the next day. Didn't get there in time to work the Monday night show, but Dud covered for me—told the road manager I was sick, or I been docked a day's pay.

The USO tour ended in Rocky Mount, North Carolina, right after Christmas. I was glad it was over, because the weather was so damn cold—it was hellish. Dud wanted to play some dances in West Virginia, but I wouldn't go. Georgia maybe, but not West Virginia—that was even colder.

When I returned to New York dead tired, something told me to go up to the Savoy and check things out. Right that very night. When I walked in the hall, Cecil Scott's orchestra was just finishing a set. I went over to say my hellos to the fellows.

"Man, look who's here," said Henry Goodwin, "it's old Clyde Bernhardt." And all the guys came crowding around, smiling, patting my back, slapping skin. I couldn't figure out why they so happy to see me—I knew how to get along, but they all treating me like family.

"Clyde, when you get back from that USO tour?" asked Cecil. In those days, everybody knew everybody else's business. It was in all the trades.

"Came in on my own tonight," I said. "They all still out there."

"Got anything lined up?"

"No."

"Good. We gonna have a opening right now."

And Cecil turned around to Jonas Walker, his first trombone. "Walker, you on a two-week notice from now. And I'm paying you off, so this is your last night."

I started backing off, because I didn't care to take nobody else's chair, but everybody stopped me. Told me this guy been giving all the fellows trouble and was hard to get along with, always drunk and evil, telling everybody to kiss his so and so. Just the night before, he and the other trombone, George Wilson, had a devil of a fight right out there on 140th near Lenox. Even though George beat the living hell out of him, Cecil didn't like that kind of stuff, but good trombones was hard to find. So everyone was damn happy to see me.

All except Jonas Walker. He was the same guy that wanted to fight when Oliver took me over him. "He just a goddamn little slick-ass nigger always stealin' my job," he kept mumbling.

The next night I took over for him working a solid three-month location job. All because I had this feeling to check out the Savoy that very night.

26. The Blue Blazers, 1946–1948

Leonard Feather called me for a Pete Johnson record date he was supervising on January 2, 1946. We did five numbers up in the National Studios on 57th and Broadway. I was only a sideman this time, and Etta Jones took the vocals. The following month, Feather had me in on another session, this time for Musicraft.

It was April when Cecil Scott left the Savoy. Business was slowing down, and he started laying off like so many other bands were doing.

Times were changing—clubs closing, money was low. The soldiers all gone. Working people let out of defense jobs. Bands dropping men and cutting down to small groups. Guys all jumping bands. Even Cab Calloway—and he had one of the most popular bands around— wasn't working steady. As good a band as Jimmie Lunceford had, he

wasn't working most of the time either. Not even Duke—I heard when
he was suppose to be out on the road he was really laying off in Atlanta.

It was a changing time—for everybody. I scuffled around for any job
I could scrape up. Even went with Jonas Walker when he needed a
second horn on a job. Called me and I grabbed it. That's the way musicians are.

One day I went down to the Gale office to see if they might need a
horn player.

"We been watchin' your records, Clyde," said Ralph Cooper, who was
booking bands out of Gale during the day. "Musicraft is promoting and
they gettin' good air play." I knew that and was glad he did also. "Man,"
he said, "I'd like you to put a small group together, maybe seven or
eight experienced men, work up some special arrangements, and I
think I can find you some work."

Now, that surprised hell out of me. I thought about Harold Oxley in
'38 asking me to do the same thing, and how Louis Jordan kept trying to
push me. Damn, I never wanted to be a boss—just too many problems.
I saw hateful guys doing mean things to leaders. Keep trying them. Cuss
them out. And if they did it to them, I damn well knew they do it to me.
I was no better.

But this was 1946. New York City. Job offers getting less and less. I
had to eat, and I was too proud to go on relief.

I liked playing in a smaller band—a guy has to be a better musician.
Use more solo space. So I formed the Blue Blazers. I thought that was a
hell of a name—a blue flame is hotter then a red one, and it sounded so
damn good.

I got Joe Allston on alto; Freddie Williams came in on tenor, and then
Stafford "Pazuza" Simon came in after him. He's another that always
twisted my name around. Liked to call me Heartburn. But if that made
him happy, then I laughed also.

My trumpet was young George Scott, and after he went back with
Luis Russell, I got Willie Moore out of the Erskine Hawkins Band;
Horace Brown was piano; Joe Scott on bass (no relation to George), and
Clay Burt on drums—all damn good readers.

Howard Biggs, who was arranging for Luis Russell, made up some hot
arrangements for me. Knew how to make seven pieces sound like fourteen. Howard "Swan" Johnson did others, and Franz Jackson, Skippa
Hall, and John Drummond arranged the rest.

Then I filled in with stock small-band numbers from the Music Ex-
change Store in the Brill Building. All kinds, not only jazz and blues,
but new fox trots, standard waltzes, rhumbas, cha-chas, and other Latin
numbers that was popular then. I bought some maracas and chop sticks,

and Clay Burt put in a set of tom-toms. It cost me for all that, but I wanted it to be a all-around band, have something for everyone.

If a song was popular, we were going to play it. I eventually had over three hundred titles in my book.

We rehearsed every day beginning Monday, May 13, and I did what I could to make the fellows happy and keep harmony.

I would tell them: "If any of you boys think you can improve a number, let's give it a try. We all gonna work together 'cause everybody's important here. Just because the name Clyde Bernhardt is up front doesn't mean I'm takin' all the solos, like Louis Jordan. In my band, everybody gets a taste."

I learned that from King Oliver. When musicians feel they are wanted and know their leader is a regular guy, that makes them relaxed. And better players. That's what I was looking for.

When Willie Moore came in, he had the reputation as liking to bull-doze people—especially at the wrong time. But he was a Aries, and I knew Aries needed to get their credit. So I had a solution.

"Fellows," I said, "I got a lot of things on my mind. Can't think of everything and need your help."

"What's that, Clyde?"

"If you guys don't mind," I said, "I'm gonna put Willie Moore in charge of the brass section."

"What?" Everybody laughed. There was only Willie and me in brass.

"Willie," I said, "you a damn good blower. You got ideas, and I wanna give you a chance to bring them out. You can set your riffs, make your own changes, take your own solos—man, you in charge of brass!"

Willie was all smiles. "That's it, man," he shouted, "we gonna get this band goin' now!"

Since that worked so good, I put Joe Allston in charge of reeds. That was him and Freddie Williams.

"Goddamn . . ." he said.

We all got along fine.

I tried to develop a good Kansas City sound—a pushing beat, something like a little 1942 Jay McShann band. The guys liked that and we worked hard.

Two weeks into rehearsal, Ralph Cooper called to say he booked us in the Elk's Rendezvous up on Lenox and 134th. A fill-in while Herman Flintall, the regular band, took the night off.

I don't think Ralph Cooper had the confidence in us he said he did, because he didn't show that night. Sent his skinny little nephew to check us out and report back.

There was no acts at the Elk's Rendezvous, so we had a good chance to show our stuff. Opened with our theme, *Gate You Swing Me Down*, the number I wrote in 1937. Then we played some popular numbers like *Cement Mixer*, a few of our special swing arrangements, and finished the set with me shouting *Lost Weekend Blues* and *Triflin' Woman Blues*.

Cooper's little nephew came running up and hugged me, then hugged all the guys. "How in hell you get this great band together in only two weeks?" he kept saying.

I told him how hard we worked every day, about all the good arrangements I bought, the way I run the band, and the KC beat I was working on.

"You got somethin' here," he said.

It was in 1946 that my Blue Blazers worked the Greymore, the biggest white hotel in Portland, Maine. Left to right: *Clay Burt (d), Clyde Bernhardt (ldr/tb/v), Joe Scott (sb), George Scott (t). Three musicians not shown.*

The owner of the place was standing nearby. "Damn, this little old band is better'n my regular boys," he was mumbling.

It was a beginning. After that, word started getting around. We picked up jobs in the Metropolitan area, some up in Harlem, and a lot of white dances downtown. One was backing Maxine Sullivan at the McKinley Theater in the Bronx.

While we were doing one-nighters, Johnny Hart, a downtown booking agent, got us a audition in the Times Square Hotel for a location job up in Maine. We did some of our best numbers, and Clyde Bernhardt and his Blue Blazers was hired.

It wasn't until later I heard they auditioned some eighteen different little bands, black and white, before they took us.

We went up to Maine in July, the first colored band ever to work the Greymore in Portland, the biggest white hotel in town. Got a two-week contract playing just for dining and dancing—six nights a week, nine to twelve midnight. And every night for our last set we broadcast live over the local ABC radio outlet.

Before long we were getting fan mail from as far away as central Canada, Minnesota, and Michigan. People writing for us to play certain numbers. Telling us they liked us. Some couldn't believe how few pieces I had in the band. Even got a letter from a woman that wanted to come to Portland and spend the weekend with me. Obviously she guessed wrong about *this* Bernhardt, because I damn well knew there was no colored people where that letter came from.

Shortly after we got the hotel job, Johnny Hart came up and tried to get me to drop three men.

"Too many ugly boys in your band," he said.

"What?"

"I can see you don't know nothin' about this business," he said, waving his hand. "Even the coloreds don't like too many black faces. You put in more light ones like yourself, and you be surprised the jobs I can get for you."

It was that same old race stuff all over again. I never did approve of it and told him so.

"Then you finished with me," he said. "I can't be bothered with a stubborn fool like you."

After two weeks at the Greymore, they renewed our option for four more. And I didn't hear nobody complaining about how my men looked.

When we returned to New York, I got a call from Mort Browne, a white publisher that put out my *Without You* through his Lewis Music

Publishing Company. He was now a talent scout for Sonora Records, owned by a Mrs. Rubin and her vice-president husband. Their son was the publicity man. They been making popular and children's records and was thinking of branching out. Mrs. Rubin heard the Blazers on the radio and wanted us to audition.

Browne asked me to come to his office in the Brill Building to talk business. I walked in with my pianist and Mort started acting funny. "Uh . . . don't know if I can talk to you today, Clyde." He been positive on the phone, told me the appointment was set. "Go home and wait for my call," he said sharply. "Goodbye."

About a hour and a half later, he called me at home. "Who's that boy you brought down, Clyde?"

"The piano player I'm gonna use."

"Your whole band look like him?"

"What in hell you talkin' about, Mort?" But I knew.

"Well, that fellow is far from good-looking. I know damn well you can get men who make a hell of a lot better appearance then that guy."

"He's a good musician," I protested.

"Doesn't matter, Clyde. Can't use him."

"But this is only for a record date, what the hell does it matter how he look?" My Indian started coming up in me.

"Matters to me. If your record goes over, there's a lot more work in it for you. Don't want any problems then."

I thought about what he said long after I hung up the phone. It was more of the same old line. My guy was good. Wasn't the notoriety kind or anything. At the Greymore I refused because I was working the job. This time, the job depended on it.

After a while, I called him back. "What you think of Jimmy Phipps?"

"I've seen him," he said. "If you can get that boy, you got the audition."

I sure didn't like to be part of this damn color business, but I had no choice. Recording dates for a new band was damn hard to get—meant money for us now and maybe later, too. I had to think of the other guys, so I went along. But I knew what this was all about and felt real bad. Real bad.

Phipps and me went over to the Fifth Avenue offices of Sonora. Mrs. Rubin liked my singing and the songs I selected, and we got a one-year contract.

The Blazers made its first records on Monday, September 16, 1946. Four of my own vocal numbers: *Sweet Jam Jam*, *Triflin' Woman Blues*, *Lay Your Habits Down*, and *Would You Do Me a Favor?*

*Publicity photo of Clyde Bernhardt taken in
New York City, Sept. 18, 1946.*

"If this sells," Mrs. Rubin told me, "you'll be making more for us."

I was the first colored band to record for Sonora. Later, Dud Bascomb and Coleman Hawkins made records for them, but I broke the ice there.

When *Triflin'* came out, some juke box operator in Miami ordered nine thousand records to put in boxes all over the South. Big radio stations started giving it air play. It was the biggest-selling record that Sonora ever had. Mine too.

Mort Browne never told me, but I heard through the grapevine some Harlem musicians went to see him before I got with Sonora.

"Hell," they told him, "we got better bands in Harlem then the Blue Blazers. Don't mess with that Bernhardt."

But Browne laid into them and threw them all out. I knew one of the
guys, and he always been calling himself my friend. Just don't understand some musicians. No sir.

We recorded another vocal session on January 21, 1947, for Sonora.
Four sides again: *Good Woman Blues*, one of my originals; *If It's Any
News to You*, co-written with Walter Hillard; *My Little Dog Got Kittens*,
by co-writer Harry Stevenson, a record salesman up at Vim's in Harlem;
and *I'm Henpecked*, Enoc Martin's number. He was the leader of the
Velvet-tones, a pop group that Mort Browne was booking, and we did
him a favor.

As the records started coming out, I let Mort act as my manager and
booker. I put Skippa Hall in as my regular pianist and picked up some
local white jobs, dances and such. But the big ones all seemed to get
away.

I found out later that Browne was asking more then twice scale for
us. I guess he tried to get rich overnight, so he knocked us out of lots
of good work.

Late in 1946, Leonard Feather wanted me to go on a tour to Spain
with a jazz group he was putting together. Didn't want my Blazers, only
me. And it paid good money. As my band was just getting started, I felt I
owed it to them not to break up. I turned Feather down.

In January of 1947, we played a benefit at Mitchell's Field out in Long
Island. Nipsey Russell was MC. Also had Madeline Greene, she used to
sing with the Earl Hines band. It was a big show with many acts, and
everybody was glad to do Uncle Sam the favor.

About a week later, we found out it was not a benefit after all. The
black officer that booked us pocketed all our pay and even had the
nerve to ask us to do another free show. We blew the whistle, went up
to the top white officer, and just laid that nigger out. They demoted him
or something, but we never did get our money.

There sure are some hurtful people in this world.

Early one spring day in 1947 I was on the way over to see Mort
Browne. Don't usually carry my horn when I'm not working, but just
before I left home, something loud and clear told me to bring it along.

As I was walking in the Brill Building lobby, I heard a voice off to one
side. "Are you a musician, son?"

I sort of glanced around and saw it was a white Army officer speaking
to me. Had on a chest full of medals and plenty of braid on his cap.
Didn't know this man from Adam's house cat.

"Yes sir," I answered.

"What's that you have there?"

"A trombone."

"Where do you play?"

"I have a band uptown right now."

"I'm looking for a little six-piece band to play for a private party in Washington, D.C. I'll pay a thousand dollars and first-class transportation both ways. Can you get me a band for that?"

Now, I always been known as a cool guy. But big paying jobs only fall your way in fairy tales. I couldn't believe this.

"Well," I said thoughtfully, "I got seven men that can do the job."

"Don't want seven. Too much noise."

Then I thought of Ralph Cooper at Gale. Took the officer inside to the phone and called him up. Figured Cooper checking him out couldn't hurt—and I let the man see I was a business man.

After Cooper got a advance, we all went down to Washington. The Army picked us up in busses and drove us over to this outdoor pavillion. It was a fancy dress affair, not more then about fifty people—all rich whites, high-ranking officers and politicians with their wives. Along the side was long tables filled with all kinds of hot and cold dishes, soft drinks, and a lot of hard stuff, all open to the band. It was a class A job.

I told the officer we cut the band down to six as he wanted, but I didn't. Pazuza, our tenor, went along as our "valet," but I paid him the same as the other guys. It worked out fine for everybody, and we all got a good payday.

Never did ask why that officer was standing in the lobby of the Brill Building just as I happened to walk by carrying my horn. The band all said I was damn lucky, but that wasn't the reason. I knew somehow it was my Papa watching over me as he said he would. Only I couldn't tell that to the guys. They'd never understand.

But I *knew*.

When we got back to New York, I gave Ralph Cooper twenty-five dollars for his "booking," even though the job came to me without him. The last time I gave another booker a lead, he gave it to some other band.

Word started getting around about me falling into top jobs and how I treated my guys special and all that. Musicians began calling me up all hours of the day and night, worrying me for some work. Every living soul wanted in.

After picking up more local one-nighters plus a weekend at the Savoy, another good break came along. Foch Allen, a black booker, got us a audition for the famous Smalls Paradise up on Seventh near 135th, owned by Ed Smalls, who opened it back in the mid-twenties. Had just about the best in black entertainment in Harlem, rated on the level of the old Connie's Inn. It was also one of the highest-paying band jobs in

New York—more then the Savoy, the Renaissance, or any of those big places.

We came to audition, but Mr. Smalls wasn't there. Only three or four black waiters sitting around. "Let's hear what these cats wanna bring in here," they kept saying as we warmed up. I knew a lot of guys that called themselves good musicians couldn't get a audition here—bands had to have something going to get this club date.

So we played our hottest numbers, and when we finished, nobody said nothing. One of the waiters told us to come back tomorrow as he got up and walked away.

The next day, there was two black bartenders sitting down front of the bandstand. The place was empty. "Go ahead, man," one of them said. So we auditioned again. "Yeah," the guy mumbled, "come back tomorrow."

So we kept coming back, and back again. We auditioned for every black ass in that place, from the manager down to the busboys, the hat check girl, and even the janitor. I knew they were trying me because I didn't have a name as a band leader. If I was going in, it was the hard way. Had to prove myself to everybody. And maybe to myself.

After coming back about nine times, one day we finally found Mr. Smalls sitting there with all the help crowded around him. We played our best four or five numbers and waited.

Some black flunky in the back tried to look good in front of the boss. "I bet yawl can't play no cal-ip-see-o," he drawled.

I didn't answer him, but Mr. Smalls nodded, and we hit off on a hot Calypso number.

"Been hearing good things about your band," he said in his high voice as we finished, "but seven pieces are not enough. Not in my place."

I told him how good we went over at the Greymore, how we broadcast and people all thought we was a big band, and how all my arrangements was only for seven men.

He thought a while. "Tell you what. Business is slow. Just dropped my chorus line and let Earle Warren out, and he had nine pieces. I'll give you four weeks, no option, and we'll see what happens." As he walked away he turned his head. "And later if you want to add two or three pieces, let me know."

We opened upstairs in Smalls early in May. This was a popular Harlem spot and had been for years. Wasn't unusual to look out in the audience and see comedians Olsen and Johnson sitting there, or Lena Horne, Lennie Hayton, Ethel Waters, or Joe Louis. One night, Sugar Ray Robinson came and sat in on drums.

After about two weeks, Mr. Frank Gibbs, the manager, called me off to the side.

Joe Allston got nervous. "I hope we finish the four weeks. Hope we finish," he cried.

But Mr. Gibbs patted me on the shoulder. "Clyde, I like what you're putting down," he said. "I been managing the Paradise since 1924 and never had a band in here that pleased *everybody* like you do. I see these old people on the floor, some of them can barely walk, but they out there shaking butts."

Now, that was exactly what I was trying to do—give the people what they wanted and pack the floor with bodies, young and old. Play those standards like *Star Dust* and *Honeysuckle Rose*, then sneak in the heavy ones when they be feeling ready. One party had us play the same waltz over four times and tipped us a ten each time. When the jitterbugs come out, I knew just the right swing numbers they wanted. If we had to get down, growl and moan, my slow blues always went over big.

"You got 'em all under your thumb," Mr. Gibbs said. "I'm giving you another four weeks with an option of four more. Keep up the good work."

Advertisement for Smalls Paradise featuring Clyde Bernhardt and his Blue Blazers, New York City, May 31, 1947.

I told the guys the good news.

"Goddamn," said Pazuza, "this old Heartburn is one lucky cat. Comes up here to the hardest black place in New York and has every damn nigger in the world liking him. Goddamn!"

After nine weeks at Smalls, business got better, and almost every night there was a full house. Nipsey Russell was M.C. At different times Dinah Washington, Billy Daniels, the Hillman Brothers, Baby Hines, and other class acts worked the floor show. Baby Hines was Earl Hines' real wife and one hell of a singer. I watched her do *Happiness Is a Thing Called Joe*, and women in the club had tears falling down their faces.

George and Chris was the Hillman Brothers—a great dance act. Black top hat and tails, white tie, white boutonniere, white gloves, black patent leather shoes, white spats, walking cane. When they did their soft shoe dance so easy and light, audiences went wild. George had a finale where he strutted off with high kicks, higher then his head and got shouting ovations. The Hillmans was class all the way.

The acts liked us because we could read their music, play in their correct tempo, do just what they expected. Nobody had problems with the Blue Blazers. Ever.

One day, Mr. Gibbs told me business was so good that Smalls was putting back the eight chorus girls and adding a soubrette. I thought that was good. Then he said I had to drop a man to help pay for the extras. Now, that didn't make sense to me. First my band wasn't big enough and now that business got better, it was too big.

Didn't think that was fair and told Mr. Gibbs so—we were a team, working together, compact, and we got along. I just wasn't going to do it, said I rather walk the streets and play jobs here and there, before I cut the band.

Mr. Gibbs gave me a week. Cut or leave.

One night during that "cut or leave" week, I saw Kitty Murray sitting down front. She been on tour with Edgar Hayes in 1941. Said she was working at Murphy's Cafe over in Newark and was scouting for a small band. After a couple sets she offered me the job. Paid scale and the offer came at the right time.

Gibbs got my notice that very night.

We started at Murphy's, 40 Park Place, on September 22, 1947, with a four-week contract. Murphy's was a nice place, in fact it was one of the best all-white places in Newark. Even the guy that cleaned the restroom was white.

Kitty was in charge of the program and the mistress of ceremonies. She sang, danced, and did comedy, working in front of six black chorus girls. It had been all-white entertainment too, but Kitty was making it darker.

I sang my blues, backed the acts, and played for dancing. They got in a radio line so we could broadcast three times a week over WAAT, Tuesday, Thursday, and Sunday nights from 11:30 to midnight.

Just like in Maine, mail started coming in from all over, again. Somebody from Canada wrote to say we sounded just as good as a colored band. I guess they hadn't heard Murphy's music policy had changed.

I showed the card to Mr. Murphy. "You passing now, Clyde?" he joked.

"Passing for what?" I answered. We both had a good laugh.

The band kept getting renewed. Sometime in December, Foch Allen brought over the popular blues singer, Wynonie Harris, to check out the Blue Blazers for a record date. There was a new recording ban coming up the first of 1948, and everybody was rushing to studios before the deadline. Wynonie asked me to back him for his new King record session. I agreed only if he didn't use my name, as I was still signed with Sonora.

We went in the National Studios in New York on Friday, December 12. Because I was working nights at Murphy's, I had them set the time in the afternoon from 2 to 5. Willie Moore was with Sy Oliver for a couple weeks, so I brought in another trumpet, Jesse Drakes. Don't recall the numbers we did, but there was four sides.

It would of been a good session, but that Harris guy was as rough as everybody said he was. Shouting and hollering all the time at Syd Nathan, who owned King. Not asking, but *telling* him he wanted a brand new Cadillac and Nathan should go right out during the session and buy him one. The Cadillac dealer was downstairs on the corner of Broadway and 57th. Then Harris got drunk, cussed, talked nasty to everybody and all that notoriety stuff. It was a hellish session.

During our break, Foch Allen came over and asked us to back a young singer right then for a audition. I always liked to give somebody a break. This fat gal was standing back in the corner. She called a B-flat song and began shouting the strongest blues I heard in years—she was rocking hard. Right in the middle, Syd Nathan and Wynonie Harris got up and went out to lunch. Man, I felt so sorry for her.

"Don't feel bad," I said as I stopped the band. "You got a great voice gal. What's your name?"

"They call me Big Maybelle," she said softly.

I heard later she did some records for Nathan and made herself a name but always thought she got treated badly that day.

So many talented people been treated like that by the big shots of this business. I saw how bad they did Ella in the thirties, when she first sang at the Savoy. Billie Holiday always talked of her turndowns when first starting out, how she went home and cried. People can be so mean-hearted, especially to their own.

Harris wanted us for his next session on Monday, but I turned him down, and the boys all backed me. I tell you, the man got on everybody's nerves, had no respect for anybody. Foch later told me Harris got Bob Merrill for the date and they had one hell of a argument in the studio—so bad that Merrill pulled a knife on Harris. No sir, I didn't care for that hell-raiser.

The records came out without a band credit like I wanted, and nobody every did know I was on it. But that was my Blue Blazers behind Wynonie Harris on his first King session.

We worked at Murphy's Cafe for a full six months, long after Kitty left and they put back some white acts. Business was so good, the local union in Newark started noticing. One of their delegates began pressuring me to let three of my men go so he could put in his white boys. Even brought them down so they could sit in and "get the feel." Said he would manage me and get the band other jobs. Had plenty of places "sewed up" he said.

I knew trouble when I saw it, and smelled it too—the racketeers were closing in on a good thing. I knew if I went along, Murphy's soon have a all-white Blue Blazers. Including me.

On March 22, 1948, I pulled the band out.

A very good club job outside Philadelphia came up next. They heard my broadcasts from Murphy's and offered each man a hundred and a quarter a week. Remember, that was when you could get room and board for fifteen dollars a week. The deal was all set, but then my guys started crying that their wives didn't want them going out of town and their kids would miss them—all that kind of stuff. I still didn't want to break the band up so we lost the job.

Then Syd Nathan wanted us to go on tour with Wynonie Harris, but we sure didn't want that either. I heard Hot Lips Page took the job but split with Harris over something in the middle of the tour and had to come back.

When I finally did get something lined up, three of my guys left for another band job and decided not to come back. It burned me because they were the very three the Newark union wanted to replace with white boys.

I felt disappointed and discouraged. Almost two years with the Blue Blazers, uphill all the way. Fighting for what I believed. Turning down single jobs and struggling to keep the guys together. Buying new arrangements. Building a good rep and trying to prove myself. Had a damn good little band here, and even other musicians told me that. Luis Russell said he liked us better then Louis Jordan.

But it was slipping away. Running a band did not seem to be in the cards for me. I disbanded the Blue Blazers.

27. Luis Russell's Orchestra, 1948–1951

Man, I felt bad for a long time after I broke up my Blazers. Packed my trombone away and started going out just as a singer. People always told me to go out and shout my blues as a feature single act. To tell the truth, I never rated myself as a top singer—it was always other people that liked my blues better then I liked them myself.

But it was a challenge, to see if I could do it. When I went in these nightclubs, I found those backup house bands were all young, most had no names, some couldn't even read music. And when I asked them to play a blues, what blues they knew, they played in the key of F. Everything they did was in F. The club bosses didn't know a hell of a lot of difference, so no use complaining.

Foch Allen booked me in the Paradise over in Linden, New Jersey. Then I picked up some one-nighters around the Metropolitan area. I quickly found out I was now just one more singer on the bill.

Times sure was tough. Many bands and musicians all working below scale, but I wouldn't do that. Not yet, at least.

Late in April of 1948 I got a call from Mort Browne, who said Bill Campbell, a good pianist, wanted me to record some of his numbers for a subsidiary company of Sonora. I knew the recording ban was still on but most companies and musicians was paying it no mind. Some high official in the union told me privately it was all right to take the session.

"Just don't talk your business in the street," he cautioned.

So I took the date with Bill and some young guitar player that Browne picked up. I sang *Roberta* and *That's Lulu* over in the United Studios on 51st Street. It was the first issue for Tru Blue. Browne thought up that label name and was handling all this for Sonora.

Bill and me did another Tru Blue session on May 19 with four extra pieces. We recorded four numbers and I just sang vocals. They wanted me to play some trombone also. I refused, afraid the union might make a example of somebody during the ban and catch me. I heard they

could fine leaders up to a thousand dollars, but singers were OK because they are not part of the musicians' union.

The records sounded pretty good and they started getting noticed.
Bill Cook of WAAT in Newark had me on, and we did some radio pub-
licity. Also booked me in his own place, the Club Caravan, singing blues
and playing trombone at a hundred a week. Of course, I sang *Let's
Have a Ball This Morning* and *Crazy 'bout the Boogie*, two of my Tru
Blue hits.

After about a month or so I went back working with Luis Russell as
sideman and singer. He was paying me more then I was getting at the
Club Caravan and I felt better working in a band. Like coming home.

Some of the guys from 1944 was still there. I remember Clarence
Grimes on alto, and Charlie Holmes filled in sometimes; Howard
Callender and Chester Boone in there too. George Scott been added on
trumpet. Nathaniel "Bones" Allen, Luther Brown, and myself were the
trombones.

Roy Haynes was on drums and John Motley came in once in a while
on piano. Lee Richardson was the vocalist, and Milton Buggs from
Cleveland, Ohio, came back often to fill for him. Altogether, six brass,
five reeds, and five rhythm.

Luis Russell featured my singing, and I did more blues in a set then
the regular vocalist did ballads.

Russell worked mostly in the Metropolitan area of New York—down
in the Village, up in Harlem, club dances all over. Many times we worked
at the Hotel St. George that had the biggest ballrooms in Brooklyn.
Really fine. Also the Terrace Ballroom in Newark for a while. Then two
or three nights a week up at the Savoy where things were slow because
working people just not coming out as often. Didn't have the folding
money.

Mort Browne got me another recording date. August 20, 1948, on a
Friday, to be exact. Mort was lining up talent for Decca and got me
together with Sam Price, the house pianist. Browne didn't exactly call
me direct. He was nobody's dummy. Suppose to be talent man for
Sonora and Tru Blue, and here he was working on the side for Decca.
Had Sam call me and left himself clear—that way he could always
blame Price for taking me.

When I got to the studio, Milt Gabler, the producer for Decca, was up
in the control booth, and Sam Price's group was just finishing a Ella
session. They wanted me as sideman, but I again refused because the
ban was still on. So I sang *Pretty Mama Blues* and *My Heart Belongs to
You*, two popular numbers they wanted.

After the session, I told Gabler about my exclusive Sonora and Tru

Blue contracts and how I was afraid to use my name for this date. Sure didn't want any trouble and neither did he. When the record came out it read "Clyde Bernard" on the label, but everybody knew it was me. Also got a five-year contract from Decca.

I ran into Hal Singer a few months later. I worked with him in the old McShann band. Started laughing when he saw me.

"Damn, if this isn't a coincidence," he said.

"Why's that, Hal?"

"I recorded an instrumental yesterday and named it after you."

"After me?"

"Yeah, I called it *Cornbread*." He laughed again. Everybody in the McShann band called me that and it used to tickle the hell out of him. *Cornbread* turned out to be a smash for Hal Singer. They even started calling *him* Cornbread after that. Then I had the laugh.

Luis Russell worked the Royal Theater in Baltimore, Maryland, on February 18, 1949. A big show with Dinah Washington, the famous Ravens, and a gang of other good acts.

Decca had me down sometime later to discuss more record dates, and I brought along two of my new songs to show Gabler: *Cracklin' Bread* and *Daisy Mae*. He looked them over and then handed me some numbers laying around his desk. I knew I couldn't do anything with them—they looked so amateurish and would of sure killed me quick. I was just climbing the ladder as a singer so I turned his songs down. Didn't get any record session that day.

I kept taking dates with Luis Russell all around the New York area through 1949. When I didn't hear no more from Decca, I got some of my Kansas City buddies together—Sam "The Man" Taylor, Dave Small, Earl Knight, René Hall, Gene Ramey, and Gus Johnson. Paid all the guys out of my own pocket and went down to the United Studios again where I made another of my demo records. I sang and this time played my horn because the recording ban was long over.

We did *Cracklin' Bread* and three of my other numbers and just on a hunch I took the disc over to Blue Note Records. Didn't know nobody there—walked right in the front door. They liked the songs and on October 6, 1949, took my group into Carnegie Hall to re-record in their own way. Said they wanted that special echo sound that was popular then.

The session was one big boresome date. Blue Note kept fussing with the mikes, running up and down the stage, moving us here, moving us there. Then coming back to move the mikes again. When they play back a number, someone holler: "Too loud." Then somebody else came running out to fix the balance again. Kept doing that over and over. Don't think those guys knew how to record a little band. I couldn't say anything, but when the sides were released, they were not as good as some of the rejects they threw out. Not even as good as my demo.

I showed Blue Note my Decca contract, and they said I couldn't be held to a exclusive clause because it didn't guarantee me a certain number of sides each year. But it sure worked my mind a long time after the Blue Note sides came out under my name.

Clyde Bernhardt appearing with Luis Russell's orchestra at the Royal Theater, Baltimore, Md., Feb. 18, 1949.

I wrote *Cracklin' Bread* early in 1949 after going to a party up on Sugar Hill. It was all about bad times and was one hell of a number. Mama once told me colored people used cracklin' way back in slavery times when all they had to eat was animal parts the old master threw away. Cracklin' is fat that comes from pork—you fry the grease out of it and all the crispy pieces left are called cracklin'. Then you bake that in cornbread in place of lard. It's more popular now in the North then the South.

As I remember, the song went like this:

Goin' to give a party
  Up on Sugar Hill,
Just a birthday party
  Uptown where I live.

Goin' to cut down on our eatin'
  So we can get along,
Goin' to serve some beans and neckbones
  So we can carry on.

Goin' down to my butcher
  And beg him for some fat,
Goin' to bake it till it's crispy
  It sure is good like that.

Yes, we gonna have some cracklin' bread
  Did you hear what I said?
We gonna have some cracklin' bread
  To go with the beans and bones.

There'll be no cake and chicken
  We won't be serving that,
It cost so much to live now
  We all must pay our tax.

Yes, we gonna have some cracklin' bread
  Cracklin' bread, good cracklin' bread,
We gonna serve some cracklin' bread
  With red beans and rice.

Can't afford no sweet potatoes
  Can't have no candied yams,
It cost so much to live now
  Can't serve no Virginia hams.

So, we got to live on cracklin' bread
  Beans and bones, rice and beans,
We gonna have some cracklin' bread
  Till the cost of living comes down.*

I sang that song many times since the record came out, and even today people tell me the words are still true. I guess some folks never do see good times.

Cracklin' got good air play, and Willie Bryant and a gang of others had it on their radio programs. Every day I heard it played over WAAT out of Newark.

Some time in January of 1950 Luis Russell went on a three-week tour working TOBA theaters in Ohio. We backed comedian Pigmeat Markham.

When Russell was off in 1950, I put another five-piece band together with Earl Knight, Joe Garland, Ted Sturgis, and Slick Jones working the Kinney Club and the Club Caravan in Newark. Then Garland took over while I went with Russell to the Riviera in St. Louis to back singer Ruth Brown for three weeks. When I got back in July, Garland and the boys were long gone.

So I kept working here and there with Luis Russell and sometimes with Johnny Jackson in Newark (no kin to the Jackson from McShann's band) and with Noble Sissle's pickup band. And when Garland came back and formed a large society orchestra with his brother, I gigged with him, too.

I had plenty free time to watch all those great shows at the Apollo. I remember Annisteen Allen with Lucky Millinder. She was damn good— sure could wail. Beulah Bryant was there too—always did like her work—sang heavy blues and had a feeling for comedy. When Kay Starr played the Apollo with Charlie Barnet's orchestra, I heard guys say they didn't believe she was white—had to be a high-yella chick they said. Man, was she *singing* them low-down blues.

On September 12, 1951, I went in the United Studios again for another demo session. Had six top jazzmen. All name musicians. Paid the men myself and booked three hours of studio time. We did *Cracklin'* over and *Daisy Mae*. Did those blues the way I liked: hot and shouting. When we tried to do other numbers, the producer kept interrupting our takes because his phone kept ringing. He say "cut" and be on the phone for five or ten minutes—all on my time, of course. As soon as the guys started bitching, I had to cool them down.

We start over and then something technical go wrong, and while it

* *Cracklin' Bread*, by Clyde Bernhardt. Copyright 1949 by Clyde Bernhardt.

was getting fixed, another call came in. Suddenly, my three hours up. I took my two good sides and left. Didn't make a fuss, but I was damn angry.

There was a little record company called Derby that wanted to put out my demo. I was still worried about that Decca contract—didn't know what could happen if they jumped on a small company that couldn't protect me. Especially if the record was a big seller, and when big companies smell money, you know that's trouble. So I thought of using another name again.

I knew I was going through a bad-luck cycle—hard times, scuffling for work, losing my bands. It was time to make a change, make a fresh start as another singer. I settled on my two middle names: Edric Barron. I cut that down to Ed Barron, as two and six are my lucky numbers, and that is the name I used.

The Ed Barron single came out on June 9, 1952, and it was a bigger hit then any of my Blue Notes. And if it had come out on Decca with their good distribution, it would of been a sensational smash. I knew that.

Cracklin' started getting jukebox play, first in the New York area, then out in Pennsylvania, then all through the South. It was in a gang of jukes everywhere and became my biggest hit. Musicians coming back from New Orleans told me they heard it in all the clubs down there. Publicity about me and my record started coming out everywhere— New York, Chicago, even Los Angeles.

On the success of the Derby record I went out as a single again. Got some work in white clubs in Pittsburgh and did pretty good spotted in the show as "Ed Barron, the Derby Blues Recording Star." I got three hundred dollars for a three-day weekend.

Mary Dee, the big-time DJ on station WHOD told me *Cracklin'* was the top record on Pittsburgh radio during the summer. The others on the charts at that time were *Lawdy Miss Clawdy* by Lloyd Price and *Have Mercy Baby* by Clyde McPhatter with the Dominoes. They weren't calling my record blues or jazz, they were calling it rhythm and blues. But as long as it swung, it was jazz to me. Mary Dee also told me *Cracklin'* was on every night as a regular lead-in for the Quaker Oats commercials.

Most of the clubs liked the name Ed Barron. Was short and fit good on those little signs outside. It was sort of fun being somebody else, especially when I could always go back to being Clyde Bernhardt for band work whenever I wanted. Don't know if Ed Barron helped me, but it damn sure didn't hurt me.

After I returned to New York, I called Derby to find out about my

royalty money on *Cracklin'*. I knew there be a bundle waiting behind
this hot record—I never had a hit as big as this.

The first time I called they had to "check it out." The next time, there
was "expenses" to account for, then some "distribution" problems came
up and all that kind of stuff. But I waited and kept calling.

When I finally got my check, I could barely buy a few loafs of
cracklin' bread with it. Later, a white friend that worked in the office
told me five thousand dollars credited to me in the books had gone
with the wind.

I trusted Derby all the way, and this shocked me terribly. It hurt
deeply for months and months, and my confidence fell to pieces. Can't
begin to say how ashamed I was of being beat out of that money.
Wouldn't dare tell anyone—friends, musicians, especially my family.
Knew just what they say and I was too depressed as it was.

For a long while I kept to myself. Didn't care if I ever made any more
records, or any more appearances. Or even stayed in the music business. Whatever I touched I was sure to come out with the short end.

So many good people trying to open doors for me while at the same
time others kept shutting them just as fast. I been hurt before, but never
so bad as this.

My bad-luck cycle was getting worse. That was very clear to me.

28. Joe Garland's Society Orchestra, 1952–1970

I been gigging around New York with Garland's new society orchestra
whenever Luis Russell laid off. By 1950, Garland was doing pretty good
on his own and really got rolling by 1951. Three, four, maybe five jobs
a week. At times he have as many as three bands working at the same
time under the one Garland name.

Although I was depressed over my failures, he kept calling me for
jobs. Always paid over union scale, and that was considered good. But
not as good as a single.

In 1952 I came back steady with Garland and he often let me shout
my blues. That made me feel better. Much better.

Joe Garland was lead tenor and band leader. Moses, his brother, was
the business man, booking agent, and sometime trumpet player. They

billed either of their names and sometimes both, but I noticed Moses had "M.G." on all the music stands.

Charlie Holmes was in there on alto and Leslie Carr filled in when he was out. Gene Mikell, who used to be with the Mills Blue Rhythm Band, came in sometimes and so did the highly rated Hilton Jefferson.

Sleepy Grider was on trumpet and when he died, Clarence Wheeler replaced him. Clarence told me he was from Philadelphia, Pennsylvania, but he sounded more like Philadelphia, Mississippi. Bernard Flood was on trumpet; Fred Robinson came in when they needed a second trombone; Freddie Gibbs, pianist, and James "Rip" Harewood, drums. Joe had others in there and bring in more when needed. Guys kept coming in and going out.

Garland furnished us with four different kinds of jackets for all occasions—one was tan with bright blue velvet lapels, another was brown with green lapels. We always wore black pants, white shirt, and a black bow tie and looked damn good.

The band worked mostly big-time black social clubs, society dances, formal parties, things like that in top ballrooms around the New York area. The Hotel New Yorker and the Diplomat. The Park Terrace Ballroom in the Bronx and the Masonic Temple over in Newark. People came in from New York City just to hold their private parties at those places. Also worked the Potentate's Ball at the Convention Hall in Asbury Park, New Jersey. Garland was almost a regular at all those hotels and halls.

When the band hit it, we played the latest popular songs, ballads, standards, swing, and hit parade numbers. I used to sing *Ko Ko Mo*, the big Perry Como and Gene & Eunice hits. Also had a jumping arrangement by Skippa Hall on my *Cracklin' Bread*.

But people kept asking what happened to Ed Barron. They liked the records and seemed to like the name, it was so short and catchy. So I got some good musician friends together again and along with Joe Garland went in the Fulton Recording Studio in New York and did *Blowin' My Top*, *Hey Miss Bertha*, and two other vocal numbers of mine. The date was January 12, 1953.

The owner of the Belmont Record Shop in Newark had a little label called Ruby, and he been after me for a time to put my songs out. So I gave him the masters and told him to go ahead. I figured it couldn't of been as bad a deal as Derby—nothing could.

When the two 78-rpm records came out in mid-1954, Ed Barron was alive again.

The records did pretty good. Bill Young of radio station WABZ in

Albemarle, North Carolina, had me down there, kept playing *Hey Miss Bertha* at least three times a day. But there was no promotion behind Ruby or they have bigger sales. Didn't bother going out as a single, either. Wasn't worth it.

As the 1950s wore on, I kept working regular with Joe Garland all around New York—steady, local hotel work all the way. No more long road trips. Home every night.

I settled into Garland's band very comfortably. The few times he let the clubs bill me as Ed Barron, Moses didn't take to that. I got paid extra, then.

One time, Garland took the band in the Renaissance Ballroom under bassist Ellsworth Reynolds, one of the officers in the Boys of Yesteryear Club and a veteran musician. He augmented Garland's group with a few more pieces to make it sound big. Reynolds didn't play nothing that night, but I noticed he had this big old tape machine sitting there. Told me later he recorded two of my blues and sent them on to Bertrand Demeusy, a French jazz writer and university professor. I got a little 45-rpm disc for myself, but nothing ever happened with the tape. Not as far as I know.

I was now about fifty-three years of age and been a professional musician for almost thirty-five. My work with Garland was down to mostly weekend dances. But by the late 1950s, the whole bottom fell out of the music business, my kind of music business. Rock and roll was taking over, and experienced bandsmen just not needed. Started hearing over and over how bad things got for a whole lot of musicians, how so many guys over sixty-five had little or no Social Security retirement checks coming in.

Kept seeing old-timers working day jobs around town—the great Paul Webster, who used to be with Jimmie Lunceford, was working in a change booth down in the subway. Told me he was doing good.

That frightened me. Like the first time I applied for unemployment checks, I found some of my best gigs never got credited to me. Of course, my money been ducted by clubs and bands, so I guess somebody got his sticky fingers on it. I smelled trouble coming for me a mile away. Worked my mind. Yes it did.

So, in 1958 I took my first full-time day job since I swept the streets of Harrisburg back in 1926. It was keeping records of textbooks in a local Newark school. Checked them in and out and all that.

It always bothered me I didn't go past the eighth grade in school, so I also enrolled in some adult evening courses at Newark's Central High

School. A couple nights a week I studied history, geography, math, and English—even took a touch typing course so I wouldn't have to pay people to prepare my business letters.

Kept playing whatever few jobs came along with Garland and on March 30, 1962, when some civil service tests came up, I took them. I remember I took the tests at 6 P.M. and had to run over to a job at the Terrace Ballroom where Garland was playing a dance.

Left my studies in 1963 with a high school equivalency and on June 3, at the age of fifty-seven, started work as a custodian at the Peshine Avenue School in Newark. My job was washing windows and walls, mopping floors, sweeping the halls. And keeping toilets and teachers' lounges supplied.

Many people told me not to take that job.

"That's not for you, Clyde," they sneer, "sometimes it get dirty."

Hell, when I was cleaning Harrisburg streets, I swept up dirtier then that. They had a whole gang of horses in that town, you know.

"You don't have to do that kind of work," they kept telling me.

"I know that, but I choose to do it," I say. If my friends thought I was falling low, they didn't know how low the band business was. This was honest and good-paying work. Had security, time off, sick days, and all that. And every damn payday I knew for sure the ducts were going toward my Social Security.

Yes sir, I chose that job.

Never told anyone in the school I was a musician—didn't think it was anybody's business.

When the dance season started in September, Garland called me for a big party down at the Terrace. Very formal with gowns, tuxedos, flowers. And it happened to be for the Newark teachers' fraternity.

We all had on our dark, neat uniforms. I sang *Don't Leave Me Baby* during the first set and broke up the house. Everybody whooping and hollering.

After taking my bow, I sat down to see this white teacher from my school walking up sort of slow-like. Stood looking at me for a while.

"Excuse me," she finally said, "I notice that you look so much like someone who works at my school. I know you couldn't be that man, because he's not a musician. But you could be his brother—or double."

"What's his name?" I asked innocently.

"His name is Mr. Clyde." That's what the teachers and students all called me. "I don't know his full name," she said, "but he's an excellent worker and a very nice man."

"It's me, Mrs. Cranford," I said. "Clyde Bernhardt is my name."

"What? What in the world are you doing working at Peshine with a talent like yours? Mr. Clyde, please come over and meet my friends."

I sat at their table telling them all about the music business. About those long weeks without work. Nowhere to play and knowing damn well I was still capable. A man had to eat and pay his rent, I said.

After that, word got around the school. The personnel man for all of Newark's school system called and wanted to put me in Peshine's music department.

"Never had a practicing musician in your school," he told me. "Those kids need someone like you." When I told him I never went to college, he said he'd pull some strings.

But I didn't want any part of it. Hell, I was tutoring two young kids at the time and they were mad they couldn't play like me after a couple lessons. They didn't want to practice. Or play scales. No routine—just start right out to play, that's what they wanted. Damn sure weren't made out of the same material as the kids when I went to school.

No. I was going to keep doing just what I was hired to do. Didn't need more problems being a teacher.

Late in 1963, bassist Hayes Alvis, who sometimes worked in the Garland orchestra, wanted me to go with him on a European tour he was setting up. But I had as much work as I wanted now, with my new day job and all.

Garland lost almost all his jobs by 1965—they just faded away. I think many of the older people that kept those private-club dances going were dying off. Things were different—people were different. The music was different. This was all new times.

I was glad I had my day job.

Sammy Scott, who I knew in Harrisburg in 1919 when he was a young kid playing drums in the high school band, kept giving me encouragement. He was living out in Queens, New York.

"Clyde, you a good musician. There's always another job comin' along."

He sent some material on me over to the British writer, Derrick Stewart-Baxter. We started up a long correspondence, and after a while the Englishman began publishing a series of articles in the popular *Jazz Journal* magazine about me and my career.

Never before in my life had that much been written about me. When he came over to the States in June of 1968, I got together a few guys and rented a rehearsal hall so he could hear me play and sing. I think the hall cost six dollars a hour. It was on Broadway and 52d, and

Derrick brought along his tape machine. It was damn difficult to get anything, so he didn't take back much.

In September, I got other musicians together for a studio session and sent him off tapes of eight songs—instrumental and vocals. Said he try to interest some British record company.

I kept working with Joe Garland off and on until November 1970. One night, traveling home by subway after a job up at the Fountainhead Inn in New Rochelle, I saw a man get mugged. Two big, ugly black men got beside this guy that was sleeping and took every damn thing out of his pockets. Grabbed his watch, tore his ring off, roughed him up. When the doors opened, they both took off. I was so nervous and scared, I could hardly speak.

The minute I got home I called Joe Garland and told him what happened. I said from then on he was to drive me direct to my house after each job and pick me up for the next. I been riding trains all around New York and in and out of Newark since 1928, but sure didn't feel safe in them no more. But Joe gave me the run around, said it be too far out of his way, didn't have the time, and couldn't be bothered.

The choice was mine and I made it. I would not take any more pickup work that came my way. From anybody. I was finished. Things have to end sometime, and I knew my playing days was over. And I was left with just memories. Damn good memories. The Midnite Ramblers. King Oliver. The Alabamians. Andrade. Hayes and going to Europe. McShann and Parker. The Whitman Sisters and all the others. Even the Blue Blazers.

All just memories now.

And the places I played—the Arcadia with its mirrored walls. The exciting Savoy and those wild Lindy Hoppers. The Renaissance. Roseland. The Roosevelt, Statler, Commodore, Hotel Pennsylvania. The fine old Astor. Most of them gone, too.

So, it was time to retire from my musical life. Time to reflect. Stick to my custodian job—that was my life now.

But I kept practicing my trombone every night for two or three hours. Just to keep my lip up, of course.

29. Hayes Alvis and His Pioneers of Jazz, 1972

When I finally retired from my custodian job on February 1, 1972, at the age of sixty-six, I hadn't worked a music gig for about fourteen months. The longest I been out of music in my entire career.

I was now on Social Security and also getting a little extra pension. At that time, civil service workers at the Board of Education had to pay into the Teachers' Pension Fund, so I got that coming in also.

Yes sir. Taking a full-time day job people said "wasn't for me," was the smartest thing I ever done in my life.

In 1971, a album called "Blowing My Top" came out in England on the Matchbox label. It was my 1968 session all put together with my Derby and Ruby sides. Even two of my '48 Tru Blues. After years of hard work, Derrick Stewart-Baxter finally came through, and I had my first LP record album.

People started sending me magazine reviews. Said my album was "tasteful," "richtoned," "delicate," and "sensitive." Had they only said it was good to hear old Clyde again, that be good enough for me. Started getting fan letters from England, France, and Germany. White people writing, wanting to know more about me and the bands I worked in. Europeans remembering me from the '38 Hayes tour. Said they also saw me during the war years at the Ubangi and up at the Savoy.

All nice letters. So friendly. And every letter that came in, I answered. Some wrote more then once. I figured if they take the time to write, I do the same for them.

I began to realize how much my music meant to me. How much I missed it. Performing. Singing. I got so encouraged by all the publicity off Derrick's articles and my new record that when Hayes Alvis called me for some work in March, I didn't turn him down. Hayes been playing string bass with Garland and before that with Louis Armstrong and Duke Ellington. He was now working a day job down at local 802 and gigging some at night.

"Clyde," he said, "I like to use you on some white concerts I'm doin'. Nothing steady, but it pays good."

I wasn't sure I was up to doing those loose jam-session type concerts. Did all that stuff back in '25 and with Tillie Vennie and Odie Cromwell. Take those trombone solos by ear—long, loud swoops like in *Tiger Rag* and get everybody excited.

But that old ad-lib stuff kind of died out in the Big Band era. Orga-

nized bands had all those special arrangements and heavy manuscript
sheets with not much space for improvised solos.

"Songs from the twenties just what bands are playing these days,"
he added. "And it's all new music to a whole lot of young people
out there."

So he wrote out the titles and key signatures of the numbers he was
playing. Classics like *Yes Sir, That's My Baby; Five Foot Two, Eyes of
Blue*; and *Hard-To-Get Gertie*. Still had a stack of them on the bottom of
my trunk and since I kept my lip up, wasn't much to get back in it.

It was like being young again.

We did a concert in Worcester, Massachusetts, on March seventeenth
and the next day in Meriden for the Connecticut Traditional Jazz Club.
Hayes called his band the Pioneers of Jazz—Doc Cheatham was on
trumpet; Herb Hall, the brother of Edmond, played clarinet; Wilbert
Kirk, drums; Jimmy Evans on piano; Hayes, string bass; and me on
trombone.

Played those good old songs and it went over real big, just as Alvis
said. Lots of applauding and loud whistling. I realized he was right:

*My good friend Hayes Alvis relaxing at the home of Dr. Albert
Vollmer, Larchmont, N.Y., 1972. (Photo courtesy of Dr. Albert Vollmer.)*

Those people liked the old music played by the old-timers. And the young kids thought they discovered something.

After that, I took other jobs with Hayes and also with Mel Morris, a white drummer that worked clubs and restaurants up and down New Jersey with his Marauders group. I was the only black in his band, and I'm not bragging, but those white people just ate up my blues—never sat on their hands like some black audiences do. And after every job, Mel drove me right back to my door.

Around that time, Moses Garland offered me another job.

"When you gonna pick me up?" I asked.

"Now, Clyde, you know I rather not come in your neighborhood." He lived up in Montclair, some ten miles north. Hell, I been living in Newark since 1950 and nobody ever bothered me, day or night. Never lived in a slum, but damn, I guess he rated everything south of Montclair as bad territory.

"Some of your audience," I said, "live right in my building. If you can't do this, forget it."

Never heard from Moses or Joe Garland again.

It was mid-1972 that I went to England for a few weeks' vacation. Never been there and so many people still writing me. People I never met.

Left Kennedy Airport on TWA airlines, Monday night, June the twelfth. It was the first time I been in a airplane since I went up in that old crate with Marion Hardy in '32. Couldn't believe this plane was so big, long, and wide. Hundreds of people sitting inside. And when that damn 747 took off: SHHH . . . WOOSH. We were gone.

People was so nice to me in England—fussing, treating me like someone special. Taking loads of pictures. I stayed at Stewart-Baxter's house and everybody all came in, musicians and fans, keeping me up until four in the morning talking about the old days, about bands, musicians, America. Felt like visiting royalty. Derrick got me some guest appearances in clubs and colleges and a interview on the BBC. Some jazz concerts too. One in a old castle, looked like maybe six hundred years old.

I guess I been rediscovered. Or discovered. Whatever.

30. The Harlem Blues and Jazz Band, 1972–1979

When I returned home from England, I got some solid New York guys together again for another session and went in the Sanders Recording Studio over on 48th. Derrick and me talked about recording with a bigger band, with old-timers that had the feeling for older songs and could provide me with strong blues backing like Joe Turner and Jimmy Rushing always had.

This time I called my group the Harlem Blues and Jazz Band because I always wanted to give Harlem credit for all the greats that played there in the 1920s and thirties. Everybody reads about bands working Chicago, Kansas City, and New Orleans, but I knew Harlem was the melting pot and wanted everybody else to know, too.

I had Jack Butler on trumpet; Charlie Holmes, alto; Happy Caldwell, tenor; Earl Knight, piano; Snags Allen, guitar; Jimmy Shirley, bass; Rip Harewood on drums; and I took the singing and trombone parts. These were the good guys. Could play hell out of the blues and kept a firm, steady beat all the way.

At the recording session I let the boys stretch out, play as they felt, really dig in and push. Everybody had plenty of solo space. I taped twelve numbers, all vocals, on July 17, 1972, after one rehearsal.

I remember there was this white fellow in the studio at the time that old man Sanders called in. Didn't know who the hell he was but right away he wanted to buy my tape, pay all expenses, and sign us up for club work. Was fast talking, trying to tie me up—a real slicker. As soon as I could, I sent the tape over to England.

Some weeks later, Dr. Albert A. Vollmer, a orthodontist that lives up in Larchmont, New York, called me. He's a big jazz fan and friend to all musicians. Heard me playing with Alvis, and I agreed to come up to a little houseparty he was having on August 14.

His house looked just like a mansion sitting up on a hill. Lots of trees. Tall roof way up. Ducks swimming in a back lake. There was at least a hundred people at this "little" party, some walking outside on the lawn or sitting around the pool, eating and drinking. Some were just standing and talking, while others were listening to Barry Martyn and his six-piece British dixieland band playing right in the middle of the living room.

Hayes Alvis was there too, and so was Wild Bill Davison and J. C. Higginbotham. People from England and Europe. Fans. Writers. Friends. And a gang of other musicians.

As the party went on, all the guys sat in and sounded so loose, so
relaxed. I sang a lot of blues and took some hot solos. Doc even put me
up overnight, and the next day I rode back to town with Barry Martyn.

I finished the rest of the year playing more pickup jobs with Mel
Morris, and I even brought pianist Jay Cole in his band.

"Don't get me any colored guy with a big Afro," he told me. "They're
too militant."

Jay was the younger brother of drummer Cozy Cole and a wonderful,
quiet man. He fit in good.

Right after Christmas, Alvis called to tell me he had a list of jobs lined
up for his Pioneers of Jazz and was going to feature me with top billing.
We were both excited about the work that was coming our way.

Two days later, Doc Vollmer called that Hayes Alvis died in his sleep.
I was very shocked—he was just about a year younger then me and
seemed in pretty good health. Had a pacemaker, but never bothered
him. All of Hayes' jobs was cancelled behind that.

My second LP album, "Blues and Jazz from Harlem" with eight numbers came out on December 22 in England and Doc had copies. This
was the July session I did on my own in New York. The reviews talked
of the great oldtimers coming back, of musicians that should of got
their jazz notice long ago but didn't.

My guitarist, Snags Allen, for example, been working for years with
the Supremes when I got him for the session.

The album became a smash all over England and Europe. Got a good
advance and royalty check every three months from the record company, Saydisc, a part of the Matchbox Company. That didn't happen
often in America—foreign business people are good to deal with
that way.

In the spring of 1973, Doc called again and we talked long about the
possibilities of working the Harlem Blues and Jazz Band. Getting paying
jobs. Went up to his March 4 party to talk details. Jay drove and Cozy
came along too.

As we rode quietly along the New Jersey Turnpike toward the George
Washington Bridge, Jay turned to me.

"Tell me Clyde," he said, "how come you known so many important
white people in your life?"

That was a question I long thought about. Harold Oxley. Leonard
Feather. Mort Browne. Derrick Stewart-Baxter. All very important to me
in opening up doors.

As we crossed the old Bronx and headed up to Larchmont on the
New England Thruway, I kept looking out the window. I didn't know

the answer to Jay's question. But I knew for certain my bad-luck cycle was over.

It was another of those sensational parties at Dot and Doc Vollmer's house. Musicians coming out of the walls. New York guys. Chicago guys. The house was full. A whole lot of wives and friends packed in there, too.

The Chicago boys came in from a concert in Connecticut the night before and were playing hot when we arrived. When they finished, Doc had the New York guys hit some numbers. Then he asked me to sit in and take charge.

I remember we stomped off *Sweet Georgia Brown*. I let the guys take their solos and when they did, I set a steady riff behind them—made it sound real heavy, and even the Chicago boys started listening and applauding. When someone asked for a blues, I did Rudy Toombs' *5–10–15 Hours*, and it went over so good that Doc Vollmer jumped in on his soprano sax and took some choruses himself.

Later, Doc called me aside. "The Harlem Blues and Jazz Band should be out working jobs," he said. "About six tight pieces. And I think you ought to be leader with your name out front."

It was a interesting offer, but I kept thinking about all the trouble I had with my other bands. And troubles other leaders always had—especially when they started doing good.

"Leading a band is just too much heartache for me," I said. "Don't know if I can handle it."

"I'll try to get you some bookings," he insisted. "Maybe a record date, too."

"Tell you what, Doc," I said. "I'll front the band. Be the M.C., call numbers, stomp off and do things like that. But you gotta take over the business end and manage it. Handle the money part. Hire and fire. See the guys get to the job and all that."

"I guess I can do that, Clyde."

So we had a agreement. While Doc was getting the details worked out, I kept gigging with Mel Morris and Jay Cole in and around Newark.

At Doc's next party in June of 1973, I introduced him to the veteran singer from Newark, Miss Rhapsody, and suggested he feature her as a added attraction. Her real name was Viola Wells and had picked up that stage name back in the thirties. Had a big career on TOBA, and I remember my brother in '35 being crazy about her singing. When I heard her in 1942 she was working in front of Count Basie's orchestra at the Apollo.

At this June party we just about had a band put together. George

James was on alto—worked with Fats Waller, Louis Armstrong, and others; Franc Williams, a top trumpet man, been with Art Tatum and Duke Ellington; Tommy Benford drummed with Jelly Roll Morton (and more then 107 other bands as he so often said).

Barbara Dreiwitz, a young white girl, played tuba in Woody Allen's group around New York; Jay Cole—his real name was June Reubin Cole—worked with bassist Doles Dickens at the Zanzibar and small black groups all around Newark.

Jay was a damn good arranger and knew how to make his ideas work, so I made him a partner. Called the band: the Clyde Bernhardt/Jay Cole Harlem Blues and Jazz Band. And Doc agreed to make Miss Rhapsody our lady singer.

This was one hell of a band. High-spirited, everybody into it and drove a beat that made people just jump up. Nobody listening could keep still. And every damn player knew how to take care of a blues. Every one.

Man, we rocked the house all day at that June party, and people kept saying how good we worked together.

That's the way most experienced veterans are—doesn't take much to fit in with one another.

Had a rehearsal up at the Vollmer's a few months later and selected our favorite jazz and blues numbers. Set up the solos, set up the order. Adolphus "Doc" Cheatham filled in on trumpet and Charlie Holmes on alto, but everybody else was there. Including Miss Rhap.

During our rehearsal break everybody got to talking about the old days and the many great blues singers we all saw or worked with. Heavy names flying around: Bessie Smith, Ma Rainey, Mamie and Clara Smith, Ethel Waters, Sarah Martin, and on and on—all the best.

"But," I finally said, "that old Princess White didn't back up from none of them. She was about the very best stomp-down blues singer I ever saw, and I heard her at her prime in 1918."

"Yeah," added Cheatham. "I played many times behind her at the Bijou in Nashville. That woman could lay down some blues, man." He shook his head thinking about it. "When Princess did her thing, that house was in her hands."

"I wonder where Princess is at?" I asked.

"Last I heard she was living in Winston-Salem," Cheatham said, "and that was more then thirty years ago."

"If she *is* living," I said, "she be way up in her nineties by now."

I knew most of the other singers we were talking about were long gone, and Princess was a grown woman when I was a kid.

Jay Cole left *and Dr. Albert Vollmer* right *discussing our recording session at Warp Studios, New York City, Nov. 10, 1973. (Photo courtesy of Dr. Albert Vollmer.)*

I don't know, I had this mysterious feeling about her—she kept coming to my mind. The following day I went down to the Negro Actors Guild to see if they had any record of her death or knew her whereabouts. Asked a lot of old-timers also. Nobody knew.

The Harlem Blues and Jazz Band recorded its first record at the Warp Studios in New York on November 10, 1973. *Stagolee, Frankie and Johnny,* and *You Don't Know My Mind* was some of my vocals and Rhap did *Sweet Man* among others. Ten days later we went back in the studio and put down mostly straight instrumentals to balance out our first session.

The album was called "More Blues and Jazz from Harlem," and Doc put out the record under his own 400 W. 150 label, which was actually Charlie Holmes' address. Eight songs was released and Doc added a ninth, my *5–10–15 Hours* taped at the March party. It was a terrific album, and he had to repress it a couple times because it sold out.

I was getting on to seventy years of age by now. This was also about the time I was being bothered by someone I thought to be my friend— won't call the name because I still respect this individual—but the pressure got very strong. Objected to my involvement with the band, said I was "stupid" not going on my own, play my own dates, make my own records. Said bad things about Doc Vollmer and stuff like that.

Hell, my luck cycle was going good now and here I was suppose to change it. I knew what I was doing, but the pressure kept getting nastier. Insulting. Couldn't figure it out. Started losing sleep, started to worrying, getting indigestion pains every day.

By June 3, 1974, I was feeling bad. *Very bad*. It was so terrible, I called my brother to take me right over to the Beth Israel Medical Center emergency room. The doctor took some tests and told me I was having a heart attack—said if I waited one more day, it would of been too late.

Maybe it was caused by the pressure I was getting. Perhaps my long, hard years of working on the road was the cause—things like that do build up. But when the hammer falls, that's it.

I was in the hospital three weeks and two days and didn't play for months after that. Not even to practice, and I always practiced every day except Sunday from the time I started trombone lessons in 1922.

Doc Vollmer held up all bookings until I recovered. It wasn't until September 22 that my doctor gave me permission to play—if I promised to take it easy. No heavy stuff, he said.

Some weeks after I got back on my feet, October twenty-seventh to be exact, Rhap invited me and some of the boys to her church for a special gospel program. This was at the New Eden Baptist Church over on South 12th in Newark. Not too far from where I lived.

We all sat toward the back of the church, and during the program Rhap gave me a poke in the ribs with her elbow. I leaned over.

"See that lady sitting down there at the end of the third row?" she whispered. "That's Mother Durrah and she's ninety-three years old." I had to look again because the woman seemed only in her sixties.

She was sitting tall and erect, had a pretty hat on and a fox-fur cape spread nicely around her shoulders. "She's the mother of our church," Rhap added.

Later, as we walked out in the dining area where they was serving hot fried chicken, chitlin's, and sweet-potato pies, the lady in the third row came strolling over briskly.

"Mother Durrah," said Rhap, "I'd like you to meet Clyde Bernhardt." I looked in her eyes and damn if I didn't get a mysterious feeling. I knew those eyes.

Rhap continued: "When Mother Durrah used to be a headliner in show business she went by the name of Princess White."

I was speechless. It *was* Princess White! She put on some pounds, but it was her. Tall. Angular. Indian complexion. I grabbed both her hands in mine.

"Princess White, Princess White," I kept saying over and over. She smiled and memories of all her beautiful music came flooding back to me.

As we sat eating sweet-potato pies, I told her about the first time I saw her at the Community Theater in Badin, North Carolina. It was April of 1918. She was singing the *Hesitating Blues* and broke up the house.

She laughed. "Oh Lord, I done forgot all those times."

"And you sang *Darktown Strutter's Ball* and *Ja-Da, Ja-Da, Jing Jing Jing*, two great numbers. Nobody around there had ever heard those new songs before." She laughed again. "And in 1920 I delivered you a telegram at the Brooks Dreamland Theater and you give me a dollar tip because the message was from Charles P. Bailey of the 81 Theater in Atlanta that offered you a open-ended booking at top dollar of seventy-five a week."

She let out a howl. "Honey, I didn't think nobody remembered this old lady like that. Talk on, boy, talk on."

I reminded her about the time I backed her at the Lafayette in 1933 with the Whitmans. And me seeing Ethel Waters up in the box every night watching her closely as she sang *Stormy Weather*. I thought she was one of the greatest jazz and blues singers that ever lived and told her that, too. We talked on and on. It was a sweet reunion.

I couldn't resist asking the big question. "Are you still singing, Princess?"

"Yes, I'm still singing, but I'm working for the Lord now." When I explained that I had my own band and wanted her to come on as a special walk-on guest, she looked surprised. "Oh Clyde, I retired in 1948 and I was old then. Nobody knows me now—my singing in public is over."

Her pastor, the Reverend J. H. Shorter, happened to walk by and she introduced us. "Reverend, this old boy here is trying to talk me back into show business."

"Nothing wrong with that," Reverend Shorter said, sitting down beside her. "God gives some of us the talent to express ourselves better then others. If a person doesn't use it, no matter how old she is, then that is a sin."

She thought a while. "I was a name long before they had microphones, before radio, before television," she said. "Who wants to hear a old lady like me sing?"

I thought the pastor's words gave her a little encouragement, but she kept laughing it off. We exchanged numbers and had many long phone conversations after that. But she wouldn't come back.

On November 8, the Harlem Blues and Jazz Band went on its first job, the Mamaroneck High School auditorium up in Larchmont, New York. The audience ate up everything we did. They didn't have a microphone there and I got to really shouting the blues. Had to control myself—not good to take chances behind a heart attack.

In the months to follow we worked many other concerts and private parties. I never realized how much music meant to me since I was working with the Harlem Blues and Jazz Band—enjoyed it more then anything else I could think of doing. Playing and singing the good numbers, hearing people all whooping and hollering, coming over, asking questions, wanting to know more about the band. Shaking Jay's hand. My hand. Treating us so respectful.

It was February 4, 1975, that Jay's wife, Ada, called. "Pray for Jay," she said. "He's in the hospital in critical condition."

I was shocked when Jay Cole died that night. Felt like a bad dream. Never did find out the cause—he just left suddenly and was gone. And so was a good friend.

Earl Knight took his place in the band for a while, and then I brought in Jimmy Evans.

It was sometime in April that Princess White called again. "I hate to move," she told me, "but my doctor said it be better not to climb all these stairs. I was hoping you could loan me two hundred dollars to get out. Pay it back when I can."

"Can't do that Princess," I told her, "but know who might. Doc Vollmer got us booked in a few months, and I'll ask him to put you on the show. If you play that job you could earn the two hundred on your own."

"Two hundred dollars for one job? In my best days I never made that in a week."

"Well, that's what you get now."

"Honey, who in hell wants to hear a old lady like me sing?"

"You might be older then me," I said firmly, "but I know later things then you. There's a damn big audience out there that wasn't even born when you *retired*. They don't know the rep you had and all the shows you been on. They wanna hear good old-timers like you perform. That's who wants to hear you sing."

"I wouldn't know what to sing, no how. I'm not up on the current songs."

"No, no, Princess," I interrupted, "you gotta use the songs that made you famous. Like *Peepin' in the Wrong Keyhole*."

"I remember that one. I also did *Every Woman's Blues*."

"That's it!"

"And *Sittin' on Top of the World*."

"Yeah, that be good, too."

It was quiet for a while. "Well," she finally sighed, "hard times make a monkey eat red pepper."

And so she agreed. I told Doc Vollmer the next day: "If this woman can still sing, we gonna have a sensation."

While Princess was getting herself ready, I went on a tour to Europe as a sideman with Barry Martyn and his "Night in New Orleans" show for the month of May.

It was a damn good show with some musicians playing solo spots with their trio or mixing together in Martyn's three bands: the Legends of Jazz, the New Orleans Marching Band, and the New Orleans Society Orchestra. The last was led by trumpet man Leo Dejan, who played old A. J. Piron arrangements. We dressed in different uniforms depending on what band we played in. Barney Bigard was on the show, so was Ralph Sutton, Art Hodes, Cozy Cole, Alton Purnell, Louis Nelson, Wingy Manone, and a whole gang of other musicians.

The people all liked the show. It had so much to offer. We played all over England, Germany, Austria, Holland, and Belgium.

I remember we once worked in a giant circus tent for the Gent Festival in Belgium. It was one of the biggest jazz events in all Europe. Just before the finale, Barry Martyn came over and asked me to fill in with a blues vocal to stretch the program. Got some of the guys together, told them the vamp I wanted, the key, the chords, the changes, and did my

5–10–15 Hours number and almost stopped the show. Man, those Europeans about went crazy.

I saw Barry back there holding up two fingers so I went right into *You Don't Know My Mind.* The guys riffed and just followed along— stop-breaks and all. The people thought it was a special arrangement, and I had to bow off or there be no time for the grand finale.

As I walked off stage, I saw Wingy Manone running about. Came right over.

"What in living hell you doing singin' *my* goddamn blues?" he shouted as his face all twisted around. Wingy had the reputation as a Southern white that could be loud when he wanted.

Maybe some of those New Orleans boys be scared of him, but not me. "*Your* blues?" I asked, looking him straight in the eye.

"That's right, *my* blues. I invented the blues!"

Now, I don't know who invented the blues, but I damn well knew it wasn't him.

"You a damn liar," I shouted back. Those other New Orleans boys all started coming around, not used to hearing anybody talk to whites like that. Manone didn't know I had Indian and a few other colors in me, and that's a mighty combination. I continued hollering: "I was born in the South too, been hearing the blues long before you ever born. Don't hand me that bullshit."

For the moment I forgot he was about a year older then me, but he didn't know that. And I sure didn't care.

"You understand what I say?" I continued. "And if you don't like me singing blues, go tell Mr. Barry Martyn. He standing right over there. That man hired me, not you."

Never had any more trouble on the show. That's the way you got to treat guys that want to discredit people.

And Barry had me do a vocal number in every show after that for the rest of the tour.

After I returned to the States I went up to Doc Vollmer for band rehearsal along with Miss Rhap and Princess White. That was early in June. When Princess got up to do her number, I thought she sounded just about like I remembered her some forty-two years before—she belted those blues like she never left the business.

We played the Connecticut Traditional Jazz Club concert June twenty-first at the Holiday Inn in Meridan, Connecticut. Princess had on this pretty new purple and black gown she made. Rhap wore her long white silk dress, and I had my white suit with the two pleats in the back and dark brown alligator shoes. Feature performers, all of us, only Princess White wasn't on the billing. She was to be a surprise walk-on guest.

I sang *Tishomingo Blues* and *Yellow Dog Blues*. Rhap did her theme, *Brown Gal*, and then *Bye Bye Baby*. The audience showed their appreciation with long, loud applause. The band played a set of jazz, pop, and blues standards, and before each song I mentioned the famous singers I saw that sang them: Ma Rainey, Mamie. Bessie. And I included Princess among the list of names.

When it come time to close the show, I came forward and made this announcement: "Ladies and Gentlemen," I said, "I have a big surprise for you. In the house tonight is one of the greatest of all blues singers. I been knowing her since I was a boy and she's still singing today. May I present the legendary, PRINCESS WHITE!"

And up she stood to a round of applause, walked briskly down the aisle and up to the mike.

"Thank you very much," she said. "This old band leader here thinks you might wanna hear this ninety-four-year-old gal sing some songs." The audience gasped on hearing her age and gave her a loud cheer of approval. "I been doing this for a living more years then I can call and these boys wanna get me back into it—now I gotta learn it all over again."

She sang her *Peepin' in the Wrong Keyhole*, and man, that woman knew how to work a audience—moving around, shouting, smiling, making them laugh. Pointing with authority. Frowning. Singing lines like she just wrote them the day before. Was like the old days again at the Community Theater in Badin.

When she finished, those people just about went out of their minds. I tell you, she *upset* that house. Everybody stood up, whistled, stomped, applauded.

Princess couldn't believe the reaction she was getting. "Wait just a minute," she hollered over the shouts, "wait a minute. I got one more for you."

Then she went into *Every Woman's Blues*, and that was such a sensation it even woke up the few Negroes sitting there. Her power was everywhere. After another number she closed with *Sittin' on Top of the World* to another standing ovation and had to beg off, flashing a big smile across her face.

She got so excited that Rhap had to get her a drink of water as she returned to her table, and Barbara Kukla, Rhap's friend, kept patting her head with a damp paper napkin. Somebody else was fanning her.

We all came home that night knowing in our hearts the show was a

*The Harlem Blues and Jazz Band in rehearsal at the home of
Dr. Albert Vollmer, Larchmont, N.Y., 1975.* Left to right: *Clyde
Bernhardt (tb), Doc Cheatham (t), Barbara Dreiwitz (tu), Tommy
Benford (d), George James (as), Jimmy Evans (p). (Photo by Andrew
Wittenborn; courtesy of Dr. Albert Vollmer.)*

success. The girls took a hotel room up there and came back the next
day, just as a precaution for Princess. They tell me a few numbers we
did that night came out on the Connecticut Traditional Jazz Club label,
including one by Princess. It was her first recording in almost ninety
years of show business.

After that, she called me almost every day asking about when the
next job was coming up. Said she was making more gowns, even taking
a new publicity picture of herself. "Honey," she said, "you gonna be
blessed as long as you live for helping out this old person."

On August 26, we all played before the New York Council for the
Performing Arts and then out in Harbor Island in Mamaroneck, New
York. Princess got so excited at that show she danced and strutted a
whole chorus number up on stage. In November when we did the
Overseas Jazz Club in New York's Hotel Biltmore, she broke out laughing at those old, saucy lyrics she was singing. And she wrote some of
them herself some sixty years before. I had to stop the band a few times
while she had a good belly laugh.

Everybody went in the studio again for three more record sessions:

September 11, 16, and October 9, 1975. Dill Jones came in on piano for the last session.

I've heard a lot of critics say there's no way a white man can play the blues. Or sing the blues. See, I know they're wrong—guys like Dill Jones, Art Hodes, Jack Teagarden, and many others play more blues then many black guys can. A few years ago I heard a great blues singer down in St. Petersburg, Florida. When the other guys found out he was white, they were damn surprised. I wasn't. Feelings don't know no color.

We recorded a gang of songs at those three sessions. Instrumentals and vocals by Princess, Rhap, and myself. All heavy on blues and jump numbers.

I told Doc to change the name of his label to Barron, the name I used on my early singles which went over so big. And I had him print the album in green, my lucky color. He took my advice and the album was a smash. A big seller.

It was nearly Christmas of 1975 when Princess had her heart attack. When I visited her, she was sitting up in a hospital bed in a flowered jacket, hair all made up in a bun, reading glasses hanging around her neck, and was telling off her nurse.

Finally she turned to me. "Honey, pay no mind to all this. It's not my

Unretouched studio portrait of the legendary Princess White at the age of ninety-four when she joined the Harlem Blues and Jazz Band, New York City, 1975. (Photo courtesy of Sheldon Harris.)

first heart problem and won't be my last. This old gal be out of here soon and you can count on me for more jobs."

She was in the hospital about a month and stayed at home for a few more.

The Emelin Theater job in Mamaroneck was scheduled for March 21, 1976. I got a call from her about a week before the date.

"What time you gonna pick me up?"

"Now Princess," I begged, "take it easy. You still weak. Rest up and maybe later I have something for you."

She didn't take kindly to that. "No damn snot-nosed rascal," she shouted, "is gonna tell this woman what she suppose to do and what she not suppose to do."

I thought I was a little old at seventy to be called a snot-nosed rascal, but I always respected my elders. I let it pass.

She continued: "I want that job, and you or nobody else is gonna tell me no. If the Man upstairs wants me, He take me if I'm working or sitting in a damn old rocker by the window." And she hung up.

When Doc picked me up for the Emelin date, Princess was in the car. She didn't say a single word, so I didn't either.

It was at least a half hour before Doc broke the ice. "Pretty quiet back there," he said. "Nobody talkin' to anybody today?"

"Nobody spoke to *me* when he got in back here," she said coldly.

"Nobody said hello to me either," I answered, "and I sure ain't done nothin' to nobody for it."

She laughed. "You sure ain't, honey. You been good to me all the time I knowed you." She took my hand. "Hello, Clyde," she said.

We put on a fine show that night. Rhap was in good form and I did my best blues. Dill Jones was suppose to be on piano, but he got hung up someplace, and Jay McShann, who Doc brought along, filled for him.

When Princess came out to do her numbers, I played her get-on music. Doc put a chair on stage but she stood next to it, erect as always, looking beautiful in her long, fancy gown she made.

"Thank you folks," she said slowly. "My doc told me to take it easy tonight because I just turned ninety-five." The audience was shocked because nobody known her true age.

She sang her song firmly, but I thought a little on the weak side. After another song, she looked out over the audience with a faint smile as they kept applauding wildly.

"You have to excuse me," she said, "but I got these old butterflies in my stomach tonight. I'll take a short rest and come back and do more for you later."

As the audience continued to shout and stomp, I played her get-off music, and she slowly walked off stage. Cheers still ringing throughout the theater as I glanced around and noticed she collapsed in Rhap's arms. In another moment she was flat on her back and Doc Vollmer was giving her mouth-to-mouth resuscitation. People all running about. A ambulance was called. Firemen ran in from across the street with oxygen.

They tell me I kept playing her get-off music all the while, but I don't remember that. I knew she was gone.

Many people spoke nice things about her at her funeral, but they hadn't known her more then a year. I read her obituary in the *New York Times* and in British papers too. They knew her now. Heard people talking about her everywhere—how great a singer she was and how famous she been in her day. And how she almost started a new career. Got standing ovations wherever she went. Made records in her nineties.

I brought her back, just trying to do good. Now she was gone.

Her death took something out of me. All I could think of over and over were her words: "Who wants to hear a old lady like me sing?"

After Princess died I did other jobs with the band. Also went out again with Barry Martyn and his show with tours in England, Belgium, Holland, and Germany.

When I returned, I worked the Philadelphia Folk Festival in August with the Harlem Blues and Jazz Band that was later shown on national television.

It was on September 16, 1976, that the band left from Kennedy Airport for its first European tour. Franc Williams, George James, Tommy Benford, Dill Jones, Barbara Dreiwitz, and myself made up the group. Rhap was our extra added attraction. We were ready for the big test.

We arrived in Hamburg to see a German band waiting for us at the airport playing hot jazz numbers. Flowers for Miss Rhapsody. Newspaper reporters all over the place, asking questions, taking photographs. The next day we were headlines in all three of Hamburg's leading newspapers. Pictures on the front page and all.

When we played a local jazz club in Hamburg, they had to stop selling tickets it was so packed and jammed. People fighting to get in. From there we went to Copenhagen and worked in and out of town for about ten days. Also did a television show in Copenhagen on September 19 with Wild Bill Davison.

In Stockholm we played about six different concerts at the Atlantic Musikcafe, which was bigger then the Zanzibar or Cotton Club in New York, and it was sold out every night. Bosse Stenhammar, the owner of the place, seemed to like my singing and kept after me and Doc to add more blues to the program. On the way back, we worked some London dates.

Everyone we met over there was so wonderful and appreciative. One man in Sweden showed me a program of Edgar Hayes he saved when I played there in '38. Was so crazy about that torn paper, wouldn't let it out of his hands so I could make a copy—scared it might fall apart.

Some of those people seemed to get hysterical during our shows, acted like they were overtaken by our music. Loud jumping up and down, screaming. Some run up while I was singing and start to hugging and kissing me—a few guys on this side and two or three old gals on the other. Could hardly finish my blues. I knew they didn't mean no harm, but I never been grabbed like that before, and I must say, sometimes I got afraid. But I didn't let them know that, they were really nice people. Just carried away.

In my whole career I never dreamed someday I would get so much attention from fans wanting to shake my hand, asking for autographs. Invite me to their homes. Knowing about me—even have books with my name in it. They knew me better then anyone in my own country, that's for certain.

Doc Vollmer was my strength during that first tour. And to the band, also. If he didn't speak the language, make accommodations, keep guys moving, adjust everything to make it all fit—I couldn't of gone through the tour. He made it possible for all of us to be the sensation we were—without big problems or even little hassles.

I respect him for that.

From then on, the Harlem Blues and Jazz Band was in demand. Johnny Williams came in on string bass to replace Barbara Dreiwitz, and for the next few years we worked mostly jazz concerts, festivals, college dates, clubs, and dances all over. Played the Glen Island Casino in New Rochelle. Came into New York's West End Club for a time. Often worked over in New Jersey. Played a lot up in Westchester for private parties and outdoor events.

And every year the band returned to Europe for another long tour, working in and out of England, Germany, Holland, Switzerland, Sweden, all through the continent. With some studio recordings, radio, and TV appearances, too.

Whenever the band be laying off back home, I returned to Europe as a soloist, gigging in Belgium and Holland with some of the leading European musicians. Also took some work in Wales that my friend David Griffiths booked for me. And I toured again with Barry Martyn whenever I was available.

The Harlem Blues and Jazz Band appearing at the Pizza Express Jazz Club, London, England, May 16, 1977. Left to right: *George James (as), Franc Williams (t), Clyde Bernhardt (ldr/tb/v), Tommy Benford (d), Dill Jones (p), Johnny Williams (sb). (Photo by Sylvia Pitcher, courtesy of Dr. Albert Vollmer.)*

By the end of the seventies, Bob Williams had taken Franc Williams' place in the band and Ram Ramirez came in for Dill Jones. It was a hell of a good band.

As I told Doc up front, I never wanted the problems of running a band—had enough in my time of disagreeable people, arguing people. But from the beginning, one or two guys in the band acted arrogant. Didn't agree with the music selections. Kept trying me. But I paid it no mind—or seemed not to.

Once one of the guys came on the bandstand forty minutes late and didn't even say "excuse me"—didn't even say "hello," either. That wasn't too friendly. But Doc was lenient and didn't notice that kind of business. But I did.

Musicians like that are their own worst enemy and don't show their behinds until the band starts progressing—that's when you find out who is who. Stuff like that makes a lot of unhappiness. For everyone.

My doctor warned me to keep away from worrisome problems, but it kept on building with many other little, upsetting things over the nearly seven years I was with the band. Finally, on May 21, 1979, in Lausanne, Switzerland, I gave Doc my notice. My health was more important to me then anything else. Or anybody.

JAZZ SOCIETY STUTTGART E.V.

Verein zur Förderung und Pflege des Jazz – 7000 Stuttgart 1, Vogelsangstraße 32

DIXIELAND HALL
JUNI PROGRAMM
7000 Stuttgart 1, Marienstraße 3 (KETTERER)
Öffnungszeiten: An Spieltagen von 19.45 –1 Uhr

Freitag, 2.Juni 1978
Clyde Bernhardt & his Harlem
Blues- and Jazz Band
Clyde Bernhardt spielt eine
wichtige Rolle in der Jazz-
musik und sein Einfluß auf
die heutige Szene nimmt stän-
dig zu. In den frühen 30er
Jahren begann er als Blues-
Sänger mit dem legendären
King Oliver.
Er war Posaunist bei Fats
Waller, Lil Armstrong, Luis
Russel, Claude Hopkins und
Edgar Hayes.
Die Tourneen von Clyde Bern-
hardt & his Harlem Blues- und
Jazz Band nach Europa (1976
und 1977) brachten spontane
Erfolge.Ein wirklicher Triumpf
war sein Auftritt in der "New
Orleans Nacht" des 1977er
"Oude Stijl Festivals" in
Breda (Holland), wo die Band
von über 3.000 jazzbegeister-
ten Zuhörern gefeiert wurde
und erst nach mehreren Zugaben
die Bühne räumen konnte.
Die Harlem Blues- und Jazz-
Band tritt in folgender Be-
setzung auf:
Miss Rhapsody (Viola Wells)
gehört schon lange Zeit zur
Fortsetzung Seite 3

Program cover for the Stuttgart Jazz Society, June 1978, Dixieland Hall, Stuttgart, West Germany.

To me, the Harlem Blues and Jazz Band was like family. I was proud to work with them, be out front and in the spotlight, hear applause, and get all that notice. Doc had put me higher then I ever been before. But even families break up. I had to leave.

31. The Legends of Jazz, 1979–1986

Barry Martyn had his Legends of Jazz since 1972 and started up a second group out in Los Angeles. Asked me to join that group permanently and work a record date with them. But I was still finishing up with my other band and couldn't take the date. So he left room for me on the records, and in July of 1979, I went in a New York studio and over-dubbed some trombone parts on a couple numbers and a vocal on my *Red River Blues.*

His regular Legends had Andrew Blakeney who played trumpet with Kid Ory back in the forties; New Orleans pianist Alton Purnell; clarinet and tenor man Sammy Lee; Adolphus Morris, string bassist; and trombonist Louis Nelson.

Barry Martyn, the leader and drummer, was the only white in the group, and the youngest member. Everyone else was in his seventies or eighties.

The original Legends recorded on January 2, 1980, and both band sessions came out together on the Blue Boy label.

Barry's second group didn't get off the ground, so I took Louis Nelson's place with the originals, and later Floyd Turnham came in for Sammy Lee on tenor and clarinet regularly.

There were many gal singers in there, too, one at a time of course. Carol Cass and I did a number together, *Oh Mr. Clyde, Play That Trombone,* and it went over big. Deborah Woodson, who appeared in New York shows, took over later with her big voice—that gal knows how to upset a audience even though she's very young. And we still do that duo act together.

When I joined, the guys all thought I was a Kansas City musician. Or maybe New Orleans. Said I played more Southern style then some born down there.

See, they didn't know I grew up listening to New Orleans brass men and a lot of that rubbed off on me. A little riff here, a little phrase there. Mix it up just like gumbo soup in my own way.

I think I'm blessed at my late age because I now blow certain lip trills

and vibratos that I couldn't do at top speed in my big band days. I admit
I played higher then, but with my denture plates I'm glad I still hit a
high C when I have to.

The Legends of Jazz work on a show called "1,000 Years of Jazz" and
includes the Original Hoofers, four hot specialty dancers. The show
is booked by Mel Howard of the International Ballet and Festival
Corporation.

Lon Chaney, the leader of the Original Hoofers, does his flash specialty, a paddle-and-roll step. Ralph Brown is the same dancer I worked
with in 1944 at the Club Plantation in St. Louis. He brings back a hell of
a lot of memories when he demonstrates Bill Robinson's famous style.
Jimmy Slyde glides around the stage as if he is ice skating—a sensation.
George Hillman still does this terrific head-high kicking stuff he did
when I backed him and his brother at Smalls, and he's the oldest of
the dancers.

Everything the boys do—spins, flips, bent-knee steps, spread-eagle
jumps, taps, soft shoe, acrobatic—makes one hell of a act. Many of them
worked top places like the Cotton Club in the old days.

The Legends make a damn nice appearance on the show—maroon
jackets with a fancy patch on the pocket. We played those good old
jazz, blues, and popular numbers like *Darktown Strutters' Ball*; *St.
Louis Blues*; *Bill Bailey*; and *Bugle Call Rag*. Barry spots me for a vocal
solo—*Red River Blues* or one of my other originals. A terrific two-
hour show.

The day I joined, July 23, 1979, I put in a long band rehearsal, over-
dubbed that Blue Boy record, and by suppertime was rushing out to
Kennedy Airport to leave on a heavy tour of Italy and Yugoslavia with
the show.

I can't begin to call all the places we worked ever since. England,
France, Germany, Austria, Belgium, and Holland. Switzerland, Denmark,
Norway, and Finland. And Monaco. The West Indies. The Virgin Islands.
Central America. Down through South America. Up to Canada. At least
twenty-five countries and hundreds of cities around the world and
about every state in the U.S.

We once appeared in Las Vegas at the Theater for Performing Arts at
the Aladdin Hotel—the biggest damn auditorium I ever saw in my life.
We made a TV show out in Los Angeles on August 26, 1981. Played the
Lincoln Center in New York City; the Ohio Theater in Columbus, the
largest in the state; the Teatro De La Ciudad in Mexico City; appeared
on a live TV show in Greece, and was interviewed over the BBC in
London. Also played a private performance for Prince Rainier, his family
and friends, at the Princess Grace Theater in Monte Carlo.

The audiences are beautiful everywhere we go. When I hear Europeans and South Americans cheering, I know they probably don't understand all the lyrics but still want more. I always said that jazz is a international language and people all over the world sure understand it.

I can't be more pleased with the Legends. How could a man think of retirement when he is still needed? Doing what he enjoys. Being appreciated.

When I take a riff, do something I didn't do before, the musicians around me all smile. "That sound nice, man," they say. What more can I ask for?

God has certainly been good to me. Yes sir.

I often think how Papa told me he would watch over me my whole life. And I know he is doing just that. I know.

One of the best bookings we ever got was at Ford's Theater in Washington, D.C. We opened the ninth of September 1982 and stayed five weeks. The show was flashed on the TV news, articles in newspapers, radio interviews. Reviews everywhere.

I never heard as much applause as I did in that theater. I always known Washington to be like Baltimore—mighty tough to please. That

Barry Martyn and his Legends of Jazz, Helsinki, Finland, Nov. 6, 1983. Front row, left to right: *Floyd Turnham (ts/cl), Herbert Permillion (tp/voc), Deborah Woodson (voc), Clyde Bernhardt (tb/voc);* back row, left to right: *Walter Lewis (p/v), Barry Martyn (ldr/d/v), Adolphus Morris (sb). (Photo by and courtesy of Bjorn Barnheim.)*

town had the rep of not applauding even if Jesus Christ himself came on stage. I played there before with some of the top names—Bill Robinson, the Nicholas Brothers, the Ink Spots, and plenty others—all went over good, but I never saw any of them get standing ovations like we got in that town. I thought there was nothing that could top the excitement we were creating at Ford's Theater. Nothing.

But I was wrong.

During our run, they said we were all invited to the White House for lunch with President Ronald Reagan, and at night there would be a command performance for the President at the theater.

September 25, 1982, was the date. We arrived outside 1600 Pennsylvania Avenue in our black tuxedos, and the security was heavy. We got

The greatest thrill of my life was to greet President Ronald Reagan at the White House, Washington, D.C., Sept. 25, 1982. (Photo courtesy of the White House.)

checked out, patted down, and they took their time looking long at my identification—worse then going through a airport.

Stepping into the White House, I could not believe how elegant it was. The fancy panelled walls, even the ceiling was decorated. Heavy window drapes folded just right. Tremendous chandeliers hanging low with sparkling cut-glass and gold. Fine porcelain, antique furniture. I was overwhelmed.

This little old trombone player from North Carolina coming to meet the President. I'm not political, but to me he represents all of America. I see him for who he is: the Number One Man. Can't get no higher.

While I was standing in the reception room waiting, I thought of the other great moments in my life. The time I brought money home from shining shoes for my sick Papa. My first job with Tillie Vennie in 1925. The time my family cried seeing me with the Whitmans. Breaking up the Apollo with Russell. Leading my own bands. Finding Princess White. All precious memories I will never forget.

But this, this was the *finale* of them all. A dream. My hands were trembling. I felt Papa was near.

I looked up. Press photographers and TV news cameras all about. I never seen so many before. Flashbulbs going off everywhere, important government people coming in.

Suddenly, this friendly, smiling man walked towards me with his hand extended. I took it with both my hands and shook it vigorously.

"So glad to have you with us," he said to me. It was the President of the United States.

I couldn't answer, for I choked up. But one voice was far down within me.

Papa. Papa. Your little shoeshine boy has been accepted.

Coda

So, as I now pass my eightieth year, I have a lot to reflect on.

I've lived long. Seen much. And learned a hell of a lot. Most of my family is gone, but I still visit good friends and relatives almost every year down in North Carolina and Pennsylvania and enjoy talking over the old days.

Just recently, I visited the place in New London where I was living in 1915. About everything is gone now, with one exception—the old oak tree that Papa was sitting under when he died. I walked up to that tree and stood in the exact spot, thinking about my life for maybe a hour. Even touched the tree once or twice. I felt comforted.

I never wanted to be more then I thought I was. I knew where I came from and saw what I accomplished. Of course, I done a whole lot of dumb things in my life, but not intentionally—just didn't know no better. I think I'm smarter now and realized we all must take bad luck along with the good. I have much to thank God for letting things come my way and having important people help me find my way. I always put Him first in my life.

But for reasons too deep to understand, I met so many that want to hold me back. Even as a kid, people criticized me. When I became a musician they laughed at my efforts, tried to discredit me. When I got to working top jobs, they seemed jealous of my success. Talked nasty. Snubbed me.

I heard it said I'm too sensitive, but it's a damn hard pill to swallow. I work hard, try to do my best to make something of myself and people, instead of encouraging me, try to pull me down. Never did understand that.

There are also some high-minded blacks I meet that come down hard on jazz and blues.

"Oh, jazz," they sneer, "that's Uncle Tom music."

Let me tell them that somebody's been pumping a line of jive in their heads. This is American heritage music. It's all we can claim, and when I say we, I'm talking about all Americans. Any color American. We all have something to be proud of.

When I hear my *own* running down what our forefathers made famous, I get angry—it's a disgrace. Some black kids think they too damn good to play jazz. Or sing the blues. Well, they going to find out the hard way if they don't change their attitude, the white kids will take it and go. There's a hell of a lot of whites out there playing and singing this music that are very good. They're not imitating it, they are *playing* it. And making money. They put a claim on something we threw down.

I tell colored people that jazz, blues, and even rock all comes from the church and they get mad. Don't want to hear that. Mae Whitman often said, if you turn jazz around, ain't nothing but gospel music. And that's the truth. All music is God's music. He gives us ideas so we can express ourselves any way we want.

The whole world loves American music. China. Russia. In Japan they have a group going under the name of the New Orleans Jazz Band, and I

*Clyde Bernhardt and book collaborator Sheldon Harris, Jan. 1982.
(Photo courtesy of Sheldon Harris.)*

know damn well some of them never even been here. That's how much they love our music.

I hope this book encourages people to try hard to accomplish what they want to do. Study. Even sacrifice. If they got good common sense, they will find it pays off.

I know there are family and friends that may or may not respect me for what I've done in my life. But I don't care anymore. I respect myself and that's what it's all about.

I'm having a ball now. Bought myself a piano and taking lessons again. Maybe when I retire, I'll have a good hobby.

In the meantime I'm still playing my horn, singing my blues, still traveling the world. And having a damn good time doing it.

At my age, nothing surprises me anymore. Except when one of them big-eyed young gals come up to me on the job and starts in to flirting.

"Hi big daddy," she smiles big. Never looks more then eighteen, of course. "Sure like if you took me out tonight," she purrs.

"What?"

"You just my type, honey. Older men turn me on!"

"Gal, I'm old enough to be your grandpappy. What in hell you think I can do?"

"Just what the other men do."

"Fool. That's just what I *can't* do."

Man, that young gal just takes off fast and is long gone. Squealing and laughing.

Yes sir. I'm having a ball now.

Discography

I thank the following for helping me put together my recording details:
David Griffiths; Sheldon Harris; the Institute of Jazz Studies at Rutgers
University, Newark, New Jersey; Phil Schaap; Derrick Stewart-Baxter;
Dr. Albert Vollmer.

Abbreviations

a	alto sax	ldr	leader
arr	arranger	mgr	manager
bs	baritone sax	p	piano
bj	banjo	Pol.	Polydor
Br.	Brunswick	sb	string bass
c	cornet	ss	soprano sax
ch	chorus	t	trumpet
cl	clarinet	tb	trombone
CTJC	Connecticut Traditional Jazz Club	ts	tenor sax
		tu	tuba
d	drums	v	vocalist
Dec.	Decca	vib	vibraphone
el-g	electric guitar	vio	violin
fb	fender bass	Voc.	Vocalion
fh	flugelhorn	Vri.	Variety
g	guitar		

Clyde Bernhardt

Clyde Bernhardt (v); Walter Bennett (p).
New York City, Spring 1932

Some of These Days (vCB)   (Rejected test)

Waitin' for the Evenin' Mail
(vCB)   (Rejected test)

Alex Hill and His Hollywood Sepians

Joe Thomas (t); Dick Green (t); Clyde Bernhardt (tb); Fonley Jordan
(tb); Albert Nicholas (cl/as); George James (as); Eugene Sedric (ts);
Alex Hill (ldr/p); Eddie Gibbs (g); Billy Taylor (sb); Harry Dial (d).
   New York City, Sept. 10, 1934

15879-1	*Ain't It Nice?*	Voc. 2826, Br. A500495, Jazz Doc. 7999
15880-1	*Functionizin'*	Voc. 2826, Br. A500495, Jazz Doc. 7999
	Harlem Living Room Suite	(Rejected)
	(untitled)	(Rejected)

Edgar Hayes and His Orchestra

Bernard Flood (t/v); Henry Goodwin (t); Shelton Hemphill (t); Robert
Horton (tb); Clyde Bernhardt (tb); John Haughton (tb); Stanley Palmer
(as); Crawford Wethington (ts); Joe Garland (ts); Edgar Hayes (ldr/p);
Andy Jackson (g); Elmer James (sb); Kenny Clarke (d); Orlando
Robeson (v).
   New York City, Mar. 9, 1937

M-198-1-2	*Sweet Is the Word for You* (vOR)	Vri 513
M-199-2	*Sylvia* (vOR)	(Rejected)
M-200-1	*Just a Quiet Evening* (vOR)	Vri 513
M-201-1-2-3	*Manhattan Jam*	Vri 586, Voc. 3773

NOTE: Variety 513 as Orlando Robeson.

Personnel same as for Mar. 9, 1937, except Leonard Davis (t) replaces
Hemphill; Joe Britton (tb) replaces Haughton; Rudy Powell (cl/as) re-
places Palmer; Roger Boyd (as) replaces Skerritt.
   New York City, May 25, 1937

62217-A	*Caravan*	Dec. 1338, M-30082, X-1484, Br. 80139, 02448, A-81417, A-505101, Coral 6.22419, Swing Fan 1003
62217-B	*Caravan*	Br. 02448
62218-A	*Edgar Steps Out*	Dec. 1338, M-30082, X-1456, Br. 80139, 02448, A-81417, A-505101, Coral 6.22419, Swing Fan 1003
62450-A	*Laughing at Life* (vBF/ch)	Dec. 1416, Br. A-81420, Swing Fan 1003, Coral 6.22419
62220-A	*Stompin' at the Renny*	Dec. 1416, Br. 02520, A-81420, A-82682

NOTE: Clyde Bernhardt states that matrix 62450-A by Bernard Flood was recorded at this session and 62219-A was by James Anderson from a 1938 date (see below, at "Early 1938").

Personnel same as for May 25, 1937, except David James (tb) replaces Britton. Add Ruth Ellington (v).
New York City, July 27, 1937

62451-A	*High, Wide, and Handsome* (vRE)	Dec. 1382, M-30081, Br. 02482, A-81418
62452-A	*Satan Takes a Holiday*	Dec. 1382, BM-1007, M-30081, Br. 02482, A-81418, Swing Fan 1003, Coral 6.22419

NOTE: Brunswick 02482 of title *Satan Takes a Holiday* is retitled *Spooky Takes a Holiday*.

Clyde Bernhardt

Clyde Bernhardt (v); Edgar Hayes (p).
New York City, July 1937

	Without You (vCB)	(Rejected test)
	Gate You Swing Me Down (vCB)	(Rejected test)

Edgar Hayes and His Orchestra

Personnel same as for July 27, 1937, except Bill Darnell (v) replaces Ellington.

New York City, Oct. 11, 1937

62675-A	*Queen Isabella*	Dec. 1527, X-1460, Br. 02540, A-81421, Swing Fan 1003, Coral 6.22419
62676-A	*Old King Cole* (vBD)	Dec. 1527, BM-1177, Br. 02540, M-30116, Br. 02574, A-81418, Swing Fan 1003, Coral 6.22419
62677-A	*Shindig* (vBD)	Dec. 2048, Br. 02540, A-81421, Swing Fan 1003
62678-A	*Let's Love* (vBD)	Dec. 1665

Bernhard Flood (t); Henry Goodwin (t); Leonard Davis (t); Robert Horton (tb); David James (tb); Clyde Bernhardt (tb/v); Rudy Powell (cl/as); Roger Boyd (as); William Mitchner (ts); Joe Garland (ts/bs); Edgar Hayes (ldr/p); Eddie Gibbs (g); Frank Darling (sb); Kenny Clarke (d/vib); Earlene Howell (v); James Clay Anderson (v).

New York City, Jan. 14, 1938

63157-A	*Meet the Band*	Dec. 1940, Swing Fan 1003, Coral 6.22419
63158-A	*Fugitive from a Harem*	Dec. 1748, M-30130, Br. 02596, Coral 6.22419
63159-A	*Swingin' in the Promised Land*	Dec. 1665, Br. (G) 87095
63160-A	*Barbary Coast Blues* (vEH)	Dec. 1940, BM-1177, M-30116, Br. 02574, A-81472, Swing Fan 1003, Coral 6.22419

Personnel similar to above.

Early 1938

62219-A	*Laughing at Life* (vJCA/ch)	Br. 02520, A-81420, Swing Fan 1003

NOTE: Clyde Bernhardt states that this was not a studio recording but probably an air-check from this period and not from the May 25, 1937, session as the matrix number indicates. Anderson is listed as Ralph Sawyer on the label.

Personnel same as for Jan. 14, 1938.
New York City, Feb. 17, 1938

63294-A	*Help Me*	Dec. 2193, Y-5416, Swing Fan 1003, Coral 6.22419
63295-A	*Without You* (vCB)	Dec. 2193, Y-5416, Swing Fan 1003, Coral 6.22419
63296-A	*You're My First Thought Every Morning* (vJCA)	Dec. 2048
63297-A	*In the Mood*	Dec. 1882, BM-1053, M-30145, MU-60027, Br. 80139, 02620, A-81714, Pol. A-61171, Coral 6.22419
63298-A	*Star Dust*	Dec. 1882, 25106, M-30145, MU-60027, Br. 02620, A-81714, Coral 6.22419
63299-A	*Sophisticated Swing*	Dec. 1748, M-30130, Br. 02596, Swing Fan 1003, Coral 6.22419

The Luckey Roberts Orchestra and Choir

Bernard Flood (t); Leonard Davis (t); Clyde Bernhardt (tb); Nelson Kincaid (cl); Luckey Roberts (ldr/p); Mrs. Roberts (v); unknown choir and others from the Edgar Hayes band according to Clyde Bernhardt.
New York City, June 1938

| | *Massachusetts* | (Unknown transcription) |

NOTE: Clyde Bernhardt recalls at least eight numbers recorded at this session.

Clyde Bernhardt

Clyde Bernhardt (v); Cliff Jackson (p).
New York City, Mar. 1942

> *Lay Your Habits Down*
> (vCB)   (Rejected test)
>
> *So Long Blues* (vCB)   (Rejected test)

The Dave Nelson Orchestra

Dave Nelson (ldr/t); Tommy Stevenson (t); pos. Jack Butler (t); Clyde
Bernhardt (tb); and others.
   New York City, mid-1942

> *I Have Plans for You*   —
>
> *Throwing it in the Creek*

NOTE: Clyde Bernhardt recalls at least twelve numbers recorded at this
session.

Clyde Bernhardt and His Kansas City Buddies

Clyde Bernhardt (ldr/tb/v); Charlie Parker (as); Jay McShann (p); Eugene Ramey (sb); Gus Johnson (d).
   New York City, Jan. 1945

> *Triflin' Woman Blues* (vCB)   (Rejected test)
>
> *Would You Do Me a Favor?*   (Rejected test)
> (vCB)
>
> *Lay Your Habits Down*   (Rejected test)
> (vCB)
>
> *So Good This Morning*   (Rejected test)
> (vCB)

Dud Bascomb and His Orchestra

Dud Bascomb (ldr/t); Clyde Bernhardt (tb/v); James Whitney (tb);
Steve Pulliam (tb); Bill Swindell (as); Joe Evans (as); Paul Bascomb (ts);
John Hartzfield (ts); Dave McRae (bs/mgr); pos. Robert Harley (p); pos-
sibly Nick Fenton (sb); possibly Charles Simon (d); Kenny Preston (v).
Plus unidentified 2 t; 1 as; 1 g.
   New York City, May 1945

133   *Time and Again* (vKP)   DeLuxe 2004, 3004

134	*Let's Jump*	DeLuxe 2005, 3005
135	*Somebody's Knockin'* (vCB)	DeLuxe 2005, 3005
136	*Victory Bells*	DeLuxe 2004, 3004

Leonard Feather's Blue Six

Joe Guy (t); Clyde Bernhardt (tb/v); Tab Smith (as); Leonard Feather (ldr/p); Jimmy Shirley (g); Al Hall (sb); Walter Johnson (d).
New York City, Nov. 26, 1945

5341	*Lost Weekend Blues* (*Juice on the Loose*) (vCB)	Musicraft 345, Sutton SU-276
5342	*Blues in the Red* (vCB)	Musicraft 348
5343	*The Lady in Debt* (vCB)	Musicraft 345
5344	*Scandal-Monger Mama* (vCB)	Musicraft 348

Pete Johnson and His All Stars

Hot Lips Page (t); Clyde Bernhardt (tb); Don Stovall (as); Budd Johnson (ts); Pete Johnson (ldr/p); Jimmy Shirley (g); Abe Bolar (sb); Jack Parker (d); Etta Jones (v).
New York City, Jan. 2, 1946

NSC97	*I May Be Wonderful* (vEJ)	National 4001, Savoy MG-14018
NSC98	*Man Wanted* (vEJ)	Savoy MG-14018
NSC99	*1946 Stomp*	National 4001, Savoy MG-14018
NSC101	*Atomic Boogie*	National 4003, Savoy MG-14018
NSC102	*Back Room Blues*	National 4003, Savoy MG-14018

NOTE: Savoy MG-14018 of title *1946 Stomp* is retitled *1280 Stomp*.

Clyde Bernhardt

Clyde Bernhardt (tb/v); Pete Brown (t/as); Leonard Feather (ldr/p);
Sam Allen (g); Al McKibbon (sb); Eddie Dougherty (d).
New York City, Feb. 21, 1946

5404	*Blues Behind Bars* (vCB)	Musicraft 506
5405	*Blues Without Booze* (vCB)	Musicraft 506
5406	*Living in a World of Gloom*	(Rejected)
5407	*Blues to End All Blues*	(Rejected)

Clyde Bernhardt and His Blue Blazers

Clyde Bernhardt (ldr/tb/v); George Scott (t); Joe Allston (as); Freddie
Williams (ts); Jimmy Phipps (p); Joe Scott (sb); Clay Burt (d).
New York City, Sept. 16, 1946

SR 1849-2	*Sweet Jam Jam* (vCB)	Sonora 100
SR 1850-1	*Triflin' Woman Blues* (vCB)	Sonora 100
SR 1851-1	*Lay Your Habits Down* (vCB)	Sonora 101
SR 1852-2	*Would You Do Me a Favor?* (vCB)	Sonora 101

Personnel same as for Sept. 16, 1946, except Willie Moore (t) replaces
George Scott; Stafford Simon (ts) replaces Williams; Skippa Hall (p) re-
places Phipps.
New York City, Jan. 21, 1947

	I'm Henpecked (vCB)	Sonora 106
	My Little Dog Got Kittens (vCB)	Sonora 106
SR 1979-1	*Good Woman Blues* (vCB)	Sonora 109

SR 1981-1	*If It's Any News to You* (vCB)	Sonora 109

Wynonie Harris

Wynonie Harris (v); Jesse Drakes (t); Clyde Bernhardt (ldr/tb); Joe Allston (as); Stafford Simon (ts); Skippa Hall (p); Joe Scott (sb); Clay Burt (d).
New York City, Dec. 12, 1947

5314	*Love Is Like Rain* (vWH)	King 4217
5315-1	*Rose Get Your Clothes* (vWH)	King 4202, Gusto GD-5040X
5316	(Unknown title)	(Rejected)
5317-1	*Wynonies Boogie* (vWH)	King 4202, Route 66 KIX-3, Gusto GD-5040X

NOTE: Unknown title may in fact be *Crazy Love*, which appeared on Polydor 623.273.

Clyde Bernhardt

Clyde Bernhardt (v); Bill Campbell (ldr/p); unknown (g).
New York City, Apr. 1948

	Roberta Get out of Bed (vCB)	Tru Blue—
	That's Lulu (vCB)	Tru Blue—

Clyde Bernhardt (v); Cecil Scott (ts/cl); Bill Campbell (ldr/p); Nathaniel Cross (el-g); Joe Scott (sb); Slick Jones (d).
New York City, May 19, 1948

	Baby Tell Me (vCB)	Tru Blue—, Matchbox SDR-216
	Jail House Blues (vCB)	Tru Blue—, Matchbox SDR-216
119-A	*Let's Have a Ball This Morning* (vCB)	Tru Blue 119
119-B	*I'm Crazy 'bout the Boogie* (vCB)	Tru Blue 119

Clyde Bernard

Clyde Bernard (Clyde Bernhardt) (v); George James (as); John Hardee (ts); Albert Nicholas (cl); Sam Price (ldr/p); ———— Williams (g); Walter Williams (sb).

New York City, Aug. 20, 1948

| 74592 | *Pretty Mama Blues* (vCB) | Decca 48087 |
| 74593 | *My Heart Belongs to You* (vCB) | Decca 48087 |

Clyde Bernhardt and His Kansas City Buddies

Clyde Bernhardt (ldr/tb/v); Sam "The Man" Taylor (ts); Dave Small (bs); Earl Knight (p); René Hall (g); Eugene Ramey (sb); Gus Johnson (d).

New York City, Sept. 1949

	Cracklin' Bread (vCB)	(Rejected test)
	Meet Me on the Corner (vCB)	(Rejected test)
	Don't Tell It (vCB)	(Rejected test)
	Chattanooga Woman (vCB)	(Rejected test)

Personnel same as for Sept. 1949.

New York City, Oct. 6, 1949

BN 366	*Cracklin' Bread* (vCB/ch)	Blue Note 1202
BN367	*Meet Me on the Corner* (vCB)	Blue Note 1202
BN368	*Don't Tell It* (vCB)	Blue Note 1203
BN369	*Chattanooga* (vCB)	Blue Note 1203

Ed Barron

Ed Barron (Clyde Bernhardt) (ldr/tb/v); Buddy Tate (ts); George James (bs); Joe Black (p); Everett Barksdale (g); Walter Page (sb); Jimmy Crawford (d).

New York City, Sept. 12, 1951

| D-777 | *Daisy Mae* (vCB) | Derby 780, Matchbox SDR-216 |
| D-778 | *Cracklin' Bread* (vCB/ch) | Derby 780, Matchbox SDR-216 |

Ed Barron and His Orchestra

Ed Barron (Clyde Bernhardt) (ldr/tb/v); Sam "The Man" Taylor (ts); Joe Garland (ts); Charlie Fowlkes (bs); Kenny Kersey (p); Everett Barksdale (g); Joe Benjamin (sb); Clay Burt (d).
New York City, Jan. 12, 1953

S-605-M	*Hey Miss Bertha* (vCB)	Ruby 104, Matchbox SDR-216
S-606-M	*Barron Boogie* (vCB)	Ruby 104, Matchbox SDR-216
S-800	*It's Been a Long Time Baby* (vCB)	Ruby 106, Matchbox SDR-216
S-801	*Blowin' My Top* (vCB)	Ruby 106, Matchbox SDR-216

NOTE: Ruby 106 identified only as Ed Barron on label.

Ellsworth Reynolds' Orchestra

Ellsworth Reynolds (ldr); Moses Garland (t); Louis Metcalf (t); Clarence Wheeler (t); Clyde Bernhardt (tb/v); Charlie Holmes (as); Joe Garland (ldr/ts); Norman Thornton (bs); Garvin Bushell (cl); Freddie Gibbs (p); Freddie White (g); June Coles (sb); Rip Harewood (d); Howard Johnson (arr).
New York City, May 15, 1959

| *Don't Leave Me Baby* (vCB) | (Unissued) |
| *Rockin' and Rolling All Night Long* (vCB) | (Unissued) |

NOTE: This is a demo-tape made during a live performance at the Renaissance Ballroom.

Clyde Bernhardt and His Band

Clyde Bernhardt (ldr/tb/v); Earl Knight (p); Charles Jackson (g);
Thomas Barney (fb); Frankie Dunlop (d).
New York City, June 22, 1968

Perdido	Matchbox SDR-216
You Excite Me Baby (vCB)	(Unissued)
Trees	(Unissued)
How Sweet It Is	(Unissued)
St. Louis Blues (vCB)	(Unissued)

Personnel same as for June 22, 1968, except Napoleon Allen (g) replaces Jackson; Sammy Scott (d) replaces Dunlop.
New York City, Sept. 14, 1968

Indiana	Matchbox SDR-216
After Hours Blues (vCB)	Matchbox SDR-216
Don't You Think I Ought to Know (vCB)	Matchbox SDR-216
Sweet, Sweet Mama Blues (vCB)	Matchbox SDR-216
Don't Leave Me Baby (vCB)	Matchbox SDR-216
You Excite Me (vCB)	Matchbox SDR-216
Ode to Billie Joe (vCB)	Matchbox SDR-216
The Saints (vCB)	Matchbox SDR-216

Hayes Alvis and His Pioneers of Jazz

Doc Cheatham (t); Clyde Bernhardt (tb/v); Herb Hall (cl); Jimmy Evans
(p); Hayes Alvis (ldr/sb); Wilbert Kirk (d).
Meriden, Conn., Mar. 18, 1972

St. Louis Blues (vCB)	CTJC SLP-8
Old Fashioned Love	CTJC SLP-8
Royal Garden Blues	CTJC SLP-8

NOTE: Recorded in concert for the Connecticut Traditional Jazz Club.

Clyde Bernhardt and His Harlem Blues and Jazz Band

Clyde Bernhardt (ldr/tb/v); Jack Butler (t); Charlies Holmes (as); Happy Caldwell (ts); Earl Knight (p); Napoleon Allen (g); Jimmy Shirley (fb); James Harewood (d).

New York City, July 17, 1972

I Got Rhythm (vCB)	(Unissued)
Lazy River (vCB)	Saydisc SDL-228
Nobody's Sweetheart (vCB)	Saydisc SDL-228
Triflin' Woman Blues (vCB)	Saydisc SDL-228
Who's Sorry Now (vCB)	(Unissued)
Sugar Blues (vCB)	Saydisc SDL-228
After You've Gone (vCB)	Saydisc SDL-228
Good Rolling Blues (vCB)	Saydisc SDL-228
Meet Me on the Corner (vCB)	(Unissued)
Georgia on My Mind (vCB)	Saydisc SDL-228
There'll Be Some Changes Made (vCB)	Saydisc SDL-228
Royal Garden Blues (vCB)	(Unissued)

Clyde Bernhardt/Jay Cole and the Harlem Blues and Jazz Band

Clyde Bernhardt (ldr/tb/v); Albert Vollmer (ss); Happy Caldwell (ts); Gene Mikell (ts); Barbara Dreiwitz (tu); Reuben Jay Cole (ldr/p); Cozy Cole (d).

Larchmont, N.Y., Mar. 4, 1973

Fifteen Hours (5−10−15 Hours) (vCB)	400 W. 150 VLP-400

NOTE: Recorded during a private party at the home of Dr. Albert Vollmer.

Clyde Bernhardt (ldr/tb/v); Doc Cheatham (t); Charlie Holmes (as); Barbara Dreiwitz (tu); Reuben Jay Cole (ldr/p); Tommy Benford (d); Miss Rhapsody (v).

New York City, Nov. 10, 1973

Frankie and Johnny (vCB)	400 W. 150 VLP-400
Squeeze Me (vCB)	400 W. 150 VLP-400
Stagolee (vCB)	400 W. 150 VLP-400
You Don't Know My Mind Blues (vCB)	400 W. 150 VLP-400
My Lucky Day (vMR)	(Unissued)
After You've Gone (vMR)	(Unissued)
I'm Satisfied (vMR)	(Unissued)
Sweet Man (vMR)	400 W. 150 VLP-400
Bye Bye Baby (vMR)	(Unissued)

NOTE: Spoken asides by Cheatham and Bernhardt on *Squeeze Me.*

Personnel same as for Nov. 10, 1973.
New York City, Nov. 20, 1973

Washington and Lee Swing	Barron VLP-403
Mahoghany Hall Stomp	Barron VLP-403
Ballin' the Jack (vCB)	Barron VLP-403
Please Don't Talk About Me When I'm Gone	400 W. 150 VLP-400
Tishomingo Blues	400 W. 150 VLP-400
She's Got What I Need	400 W. 150 VLP-400

Clyde Bernhardt and the Harlem Blues and Jazz Band

Clyde Bernhardt (ldr/tb/v); John Bucher (c); George James (as); Barbara Dreiwitz (tu); Jimmy Evans (p); Tommy Benford (d); Princess White (v).
Meriden, Conn., June 21, 1975

Please Don't Talk About Me When I'm Gone	CTJC SLP-11
I Would Do Most Anything for You	CTJC SLP-11

> *Sittin' on Top of the World*
> (vPW) CTJC SLP-11

NOTE: Recorded in concert for the Connecticut Traditional Jazz Club.

Personnel same as for June 21, 1975, except Franc Williams (t/fh) replaces Bucher; Miss Rhapsody (v) replaces White.
New York City, Sept. 11, 1975

> *C. C. Rider* (vMR) Barron VLP-401, WAM
> 780.061

> *Brown Gal* (vMR) Barron VLP-403

> *Bye Bye Baby* (vMR) Barron VLP-401, WAM
> 780.061

> *Red River Blues* (vCB) Barron VLP-401, WAM
> 780.061

> *Royal Garden Blues* (vCB) (Unissued)

> *How Come You Do Me Like*
> *You Do?* Barron VLP-401, WAM
> 780.061

Personnel same as for Sept. 11, 1975, except Doc Cheatham (t) replaces Williams and Princess White (v) replaces Miss Rhapsody.
New York City, Sept. 16, 1975

> *Sittin' on Top of the World*
> (vPW) Barron VLP-401, WAM
> 780.061

> *Every Woman's Blues* (vPW) Barron VLP-401, WAM
> 780.061

> *Old Fashioned Love* (vPW) (Unissued)

Franc Williams (t) replaces Cheatham.

> *Exactly Like You* (vPW) (Unissued)

Collective personnel: Clyde Bernhardt (ldr/tb); Doc Cheatham (t); Franc Williams (t/fh); Charlie Holmes (as); George James (as/ss); Barbara Dreiwitz (tu); Jimmy Evans (p); Dill Jones (p); Tommy Benford (d); Princess White (v).
New York City, Oct. 9, 1975

Peepin' in the Wrong Keyhole (vPW)	Barron VLP-401, WAM 780.061
Marie (vPW)	(Unissued)
My Mother's Eyes (vPW)	(Unissued)
Red Wing	Barron VLP-401, WAM 780.061
You've Gotta See Mama Every Night	Barron VLP-401, WAM 780.061
One Hour	(Unissued)
Careless Love	Barron VLP-401, WAM 780.061
Bugle Call Rag	Barron VLP-401, WAM 780.061
Somebody Stole My Gal	Barron VLP-401, WAM 780.061

Clyde Bernhardt (ldr/tb/v); Franc Williams (t/fh); George James (as); Dill Jones (p); Johnny Williams (sb); Tommy Benford (d); Miss Rhapsody (v).
   London, England, May 16, 1977

Indiana	Barron VLP-7.402
Shake That Thing (vCB)	Barron VLP-7.402
Please Don't Talk About Me When I'm Gone	Barron VLP-7.402
After You've Gone (vMR)	Barron VLP-7.402

NOTE: Recorded in concert at the Pizza Express.

Personnel same as for May 16, 1977, except Peter Meyer (g/bj) added and Miss Rhapsody omitted.
   Hamburg, Germany, May 18, 1977

Shake That Thing (vCB)	WAM 781.067
Honeysuckle Rose	Barron VLP-403

Prelude to a Kiss	(Unissued)
Yellow Dog Blues (vCB)	(Unissued)
Peter Meyer's Blues	(Unissued)
Misty	(Unissued)

Personnel same as for May 18, 1977, except Peter Meyer omitted, although his guitar may be dubbed in first title. Add Miss Rhapsody (v).
  Hamburg, Germany, May 20, 1977

How Can I Believe You?	(Unissued)
Route 66 (vMR)	Barron VLP-403
Music Maestro Please (vMR)	(Unissued)
That Ain't Right (vMR)	(Unissued)
A Hundred Years from Today (vMR)	(Unissued)
Bye and Bye	Barron VLP-403
C Jam Blues	(Unissued)

Personnel same as for May 20, 1977.
  Breda, Holland, May 21, 1977

Please Don't Talk About Me When I'm Gone	Jazz Crooner 215772
Route 66 (vMR)	Jazz Crooner 215772

NOTE: These two titles appear as part of album "International Traditional Jazz Festival, Breda 1977 Concerthall Live," vol. 8.

Clyde Bernhardt (ldr/tb); Bobby Williams (t); George James (as); Ram Ramirez (p); Johnny Williams (sb); Tommy Benford (d).
  Breda, Holland, c. May 25, 1979

Misty	Jazz Crooner 242526579

NOTE: This title appears as part of album "Ninth International Traditional Jazz Festival, Breda 1979 Concerthall Live," vol. 12.

The Legends of Jazz

Leo Dejan (ldr/t); Clyde Bernhardt (tb/v); Floyd Turnham (ts/cl); Jon Marks (p); Benny Booker (sb); Teddy Edwards (d/v).
Los Angeles, June 25, 1979

Boogie Woogie	Blue Boy 1001
Red River Blues (vCB)	Blue Boy 1001
Sheik of Araby (vTE)	Blue Boy 1001
When You're Smiling (vTE)	Blue Boy 1001
You Rascal, You (vTE)	Blue Boy 1001

NOTE: Clyde Bernhardt's trombone and vocal parts were overdubbed in a New York studio on July 23, 1979.

Clyde Bernhardt and the Harlem Blues and Jazz Band

Personnel same as for c. May 25, 1979, except Shelton Gary (d) replaces Benford and Lawrence Lucie (g) added.
New York City, July 12–13, 1979

Sweet Georgia Brown	—
Please Don't Talk About Me When I'm Gone	—
5–10–15 Hours (vCB)	—
St. Louis Blues (vCB)	—
You Don't Know My Mind (vCB)	—

NOTE: This is a live broadcast over WKCR-FM remote from the West End Club. There may be other numbers from this date.

Selected Bibliography

A listing of major articles and references about or by Clyde Bernhardt.

Books

Bruyninckx, Walter. *Sixty Years of Recorded Jazz, 1917–1977*. Belgium: Privately published, 1977–83.

Chilton, John. *Who's Who of Jazz: Storyville to Swing Street*. London: The Bloomsbury Book Shop, 1970; Philadelphia: Chilton Book Co., 1972; New York: Time-Life Special Edition, 1978.

Claghorn, Charles E. *Biographical Dictionary of Jazz*. Englewood Cliffs, N.J.: Prentice-Hall, 1982.

Harris, Sheldon. *Blues Who's Who: A Biographical Dictionary of Blues Singers*. New Rochelle, N.Y.: Arlington House, 1979; New York: Da Capo Press, 1981.

Jepsen, Jorgen Grunnet. *Jazz Records (1942–1965)*. Vol 1. Denmark: Privately published, 1966.

Magazines

Annual Review of Jazz Studies, I, 1982. "Talking About King Oliver: An Oral History Excerpt."

Jazz Journal (U.K.), Sept. 1967, Oct. 1967, Jan. 1968, Feb. 1968. "The Clyde Bernhardt Story." 4 parts.

Jazz Journal International (U.K.), Sept. 1977. "Jazz in the 70s."

———, Aug. 1978. "The Bernhardt Band in Belgium."

———, July 1979. "The Clyde Bernhardt Harlem Blues and Jazz Band."

Mississippi Rag, Dec. 1976. "Harlem Goes to Europe."

Record Research, June 1980, Sept. 1980, Nov. 1980, Feb. 1981, Apr. 1981, July 1981, Oct. 1981, Dec. 1981, Mar.–Apr. 1982, July 1982, Jan. 1983, Mar.–Apr. 1983, Sept. 1983. "A Nostalgic Tribute to Musical Americana: Reminiscences of Musical Artist Clyde Bernhardt." 13 parts.

Rhythm, Mar. 1947. "Introducing: Clyde, His Trombone and the Blues."
Storyville (U.K.), Dec. 1972–Jan. 1973. "Clyde Bernhardt."
Swingtime (Belgium), Sept. 1976. "Clyde Bernhardt."

Newspapers

The Brighton and Hove Gazette (U.K.), June 24, 1972. "Clyde Praises the Local Jazzmen."
The Charlotte News (N.C.), Sept. 3, 1974. "His Teacher Told Him He'd Be Good."
The Harrisburg Patriot News (Pa.), June 8, 1980. "Nearly 60 Years a Jazzman."
The Hartford Courant (Conn.), Apr. 16, 1979. "Bernhardt Band Burns Hot, Saucy."
Lokalnachrichten (Germany), Sept. 20, 1979. "Uralt-Jazzer brachten Haus jum Kochen."
The Mamaroneck Daily Times (N.Y.), Aug. 26, 1975. "Jazz Warmed Hearts at Harbor Island."
———, Aug. 14, 1976. "Jazz Returns to Area Sunday."
———, Aug. 18, 1976. "Bernhardt and Company Jazz up Harbor Island."
The New Jersey Afro-American (Newark, N.J.), May 17, 1980. "Bob Queen's Review."
The Newark Star-Ledger (N.J.), July 14, 1980. "Oldtime Jazzman Sings Blues over a Lifetime of Fame."
———, Aug. 23, 1982. "Trombonist to Play at Lincoln Center."
The Pittsburgh Post-Gazette (Pa.), Sept. 19, 1981. "Age Has Not Wearied These Stars of Jazz and Tap."
The Salisbury Evening Post (N.C.), Sept. 4, 1974. "Bernhardt Has Played with the Greats."
The Stanly News and Press (Albemarle, N.C.), c. Sept. 1966. "Stanly Man Was Top Trombonist."
———, Apr. 3, 1979. "Clyde Bernhardt."
———, June 10, 1980. "Clyde Bernhardt."
———, Mar. 27, 1981. "Clyde Bernhardt in New Blues Book."
———, Apr. 14, 1981. "Name Change."
———, Dec. 18, 1981. "Fan Letter from Clyde Received by ye Scribe."
———, Apr. 13, 1982. "1,000 Years."
———, June 18, 1982. "Clyde Bernhardt Thanks Everyone for Hospitality."
———, Dec. 21, 1982. "Surprise of a Lifetime."

————, Nov. 27, 1984. "Interesting Letter."

————, Dec. 11, 1984. "Clyde Bernhardt."

————, June 4, 1985. "Fred Morgan's Musings."

————, Aug. 27, 1985. "Clyde Bernhardt."

————, Sept. 3, 1985. "Still Playing at 80."

The Washington Post (D.C.), Aug. 4, 1981, "1,000 Years of Jazz."

Index

Most entries have been identified by instrument, profession, location, relationship or otherwise, for easy reference. Instrument abbreviations are as listed on page 231. All italicized entries are song titles unless otherwise noted. Italicized page numbers indicate photograph.